BOLTON WANDERERS
FOOTBALL CLUB
THE OFFICIAL YEARBOOK 2006/07

Editorial
Daniel Reuben, Paul Holliday and Keeley Temple

Sidan Press Team
Simon Rosen, Julian Hill-Wood, Marc Fiszman, Mark Peters, Karim Biria, Rob Cubbon,
Anette Lundebye, Marina Kravchenko, Gareth Peters, Janet Calcott, Trevor Scimes, John Fitzroy,
Jenny Middlemarch, Anders Rasmussen, Lim Wai-Lee, Emma Turner, Charles Grove, Tim Ryman

Photography
Action Images

Sidan Press, 63-64 Margaret St, London W1W 8SW
Tel: 020 7580 0200
Email: info@sidanpress.com

sidanpress.com

Club Directory

Bolton Wanderers Football Club
Reebok Stadium
Burnden Way
Bolton BL6 6JW

Tel: 01204 673 673
Fax: 01204 673 773
Email: reception@bwfc.co.uk

Ticket and Membership Office
Tel: 0871 871 2932
Fax: 0871 871 8183
Email: ticketsales@bwfc.co.uk

Promotions Department
Tel: 01204 673 663
Fax: 01204 673 776
Email: promotions@bwfc.co.uk

Corporate Sales Department
Tel: 01204 673 761
Fax: 01204 673 677
Email: sales@bwfc.co.uk

Club Superstore
Tel: 01204 673 650
Fax: 01204 673 649
Email: shop@bwfc.co.uk
www.bwfcsuperstore.co.uk

Communications Department
Tel: 01204 673 675
Fax: 01204 469 047
Email: publicity@bwfc.co.uk

Football in the Community
Tel: 01204 480 601
Fax: 01204 480 603
Email: fitc@bwfc.co.uk

Visitor & Tour Centre
Tel: 01204 673 670

Board Members

Chairman
Phil Gartside

Vice Chairman
WB Warburton

Directors
E Davies OBE, A Duckworth, G Seymour,
G Warburton, D McBain, P Mulligan

Vice Presidents
GE Ashworth, T Edge, J Lightbown, HD Warburton

Honorary Vice Presidents
Dr D Dennard, D Singleton, F Smith JP

President/Honorary Director
Nat Lofthouse OBE

Behind the Team

Manager
Sam Allardyce

Assistant Manager
Sammy Lee

First Team Coach
Ricky Sbragia

Head of Sports Science and Medicine
Mark Taylor

Strength and Conditioning Coach
Mark Howard

Academy Manager
Chris Sulley

Football Secretary
Simon Marland

Contents

Chairman's message

Welcome to the start of our sixth consecutive season as a Premier League football club.

Although we didn't quite manage to qualify for the UEFA Cup for a second successive term, we can still think of last season as being very successful.

Sam, his staff and players achieved quite a lot during what turned out to be a long and tough season.

The extra games in the UEFA Cup ensured the playing schedule was hectic, but the players did themselves justice as they only narrowly missed out on a place in the quarter-finals.

Every year the Premier League gets tougher, but we are looking to continually improve. This is down to all the hard work Sam, his staff and players put in throughout the year.

We are certain that this year will be no different and you can rest assured that everybody will be working flat-out to ensure that your club will be reaching new heights, both on and off the field.

We hope you find this yearbook a good read once again.

It will prove to be an invaluable source of reference as the months of the season get underway.

Before I finish these notes I would like to express my heartfelt thanks to you all for your continued support and I hope that this forthcoming season will be very enjoyable for you all.

Phil Gartside
Chairman

Manager's message

The start of what promises to be another tough yet exciting campaign is now upon us and I'd like to welcome you all as we aim to write another chapter in the history of Bolton Wanderers Football Club.

Last season was, perhaps, the most memorable campaign in the history of the club as we embarked on our debut campaign in Europe.

We also advanced quite far in both domestic cup competitions and managed to claim a fantastic eighth-placed finish in the Barclays Premiership.

Year upon year we set very high standards for ourselves and this coming season will be no exception.

Sadly there will not be UEFA Cup football for us this term, but we will be doing our utmost to put that right for next season. We also want to succeed in both cup competitions and try to win some silverware that this football club deserves.

This season will be challenging as we continually strive to raise the bar, but I have every confidence in my squad of players.

Also, we hope you find this yearbook very useful. It's packed with information relating to the Club and is a great read.

Finally, I'd like to thank you for your fantastic support last season and I hope to see you all cheering on the lads this season.

**Big Sam
Manager**

Junior Whites Membership now over 10,000

The 2005/2006 season was not only a fantastic season on the pitch but it was also a great season for our hugely successful Junior Whites club which now has over 10,000 members – a fantastic achievement since our re-launch in 2003 and membership is growing fast!

Wanderers were amongst the first in the Premier League to offer free membership to young supporters under the age of 16 and the scheme is now widely regarded as one of the most successful.

The club initiative, involves a six figure annual investment aiming to capture the imagination of young supporters throughout the region.

The aim of the Junior Whites is to be completely inclusive to encourage children from all backgrounds to become active members and to enable them to experience top flight football at the Reebok Stadium.

Not only is the Junior Whites one of the most successful, it is also one of the most active supporters clubs in the country in terms of the regularity of our meetings and the scope of our activities. Activities available to members range from monthly parties where they are able to meet BWFC players to football coaching and school holiday activities plus much, much more!

Thanks to the Junior Whites Sponsors Coca-Cola, Reebok and the Bolton Evening News we are able to offer an exciting package of benefits to all members which include:

- The opportunity to become the official team mascot at a Premier League match.
- Exclusive Junior Whites TeamCard enabling members to participate in the revolutionary BWFC loyalty scheme allowing members to collect TeamCard points at Junior Whites events and over 40 partners nationwide.
- Membership Certificate.
- Voucher for half price replica shirt on 7th Birthday.
- Exclusive free gift.
- Voucher for a FREE tour of the Reebok Stadium
- Birthday card
- Christmas card
- Two free match tickets every season to watch the Wanderers in the Premier League
- Four newsletters per year
- Meet the players' events throughout the year
- Special away trips to events and matches around the UK
- Exclusive access to weekly football training sessions

With the number of Junior Whites members set to rise significantly and more new and unique events planned for over the 2006/2007 season it really is an exciting time to be part of the Junior Whites. With members not only in Bolton, but up and down the country and across the world, the clubs commitment to the Bolton Wanderers fans of the future is certainly paying off!

For further information on the Junior Whites Membership Programme, please contact: 01204 673770

Study@BWFC

What is Study@BWFC?

Study@BWFC is an out-of-hours study centre, which young people from schools all over Bolton attend on a voluntary basis. The centre aims to provide a programme of activities that complement the work of schools in raising achievement in Literacy, Numeracy and ICT, but aims to be distinctly different.

What is Playing for Success?

BWFC were one of the first football clubs to provide a Study Centre for their local community.

The current Study Centre was opened in March 1999 as part of the initiative, 'Playing for Success' and a further extension was opened in September 2003 by Sam Allardyce.

The Government, in partnership with Premiership and First Division football clubs, Local Education Authorities and businesses has been establishing out of hours learning centres at football clubs all over the country.

Due to the success of the initiative, the programme has been 'rolled out' to include other sports such as cricket and rugby.

Who can attend Study@BWFC?

Students between the ages of 10 and 14 attend the centre each evening between 3.30pm and 7.30pm. Any school in Bolton can send students, who they feel will benefit and commit themselves to attending the centre.

Attendance at Study@BWFC is a reward for students who are already doing well in school but are prepared to put in 'extra time' to improve their levels of achievement further. In addition to the PFS initiative

the centre offers additional sessions for all ages and abilities.

What happens at Study@BWFC?

The learning programme and facilities offered are distinctively different to 'school'; amongst the benefits to students are the opportunities to learn from BWFC players and to use the Reebok Stadium itself to improve their skills in many subject areas.

Sessions are fun, relaxed and informal and have proven to build self-confidence and self-esteem.

National evaluations have shown that football-based Study Centres have helped to raise mental arithmetic scores by 21 months and reading scores by 15 months!

It is clear that something remarkable happens to learners at Study@BWFC, which defies measurement or explanation.

In addition to this Study@BWFC also provides numerous other activities which reach thousands of children each year this includes daytime activities, outreach sessions, Robosoccer courses, Video Animation, holiday sessions, PFS Academy, Family Learning and much, much more.

Study@BWFC
The Reebok Stadium
Burnden Way
Bolton BL6 6JW
Tel: 01204 669911
email: info@studybwfc.co.uk
Website: www.bwfcstudy.co.uk

Football in the Community

Bolton Wanderers was one of the first clubs in the country to pioneer the Football in the Community scheme.

Over 16 years later, we are still very proud to boast one of the best schemes of its kind anywhere in the county, which is down in no small measure to our Community Manager Geoff Lomax, the former Manchester City midfielder, who has been in charge since 1989.

The Community Programme, as it is officially known, was established in 1986 as a pilot scheme involving six clubs in the North West of England. Bolton was one of them.

With support from The Professional Footballers' Association, The Football League, The FA Premier League and The Football Association, the scheme now supports every league club in England and Wales.

The aims of Football in the Community are to encourage more people to watch and play the game, to support their local club and improve the image of the game.

The range of activities that we offer includes; in-term coaching, after school courses, holiday courses, lunchtime sessions, sponsored events. We also offer coaching for specific groups such as people with special needs, the disabled and girls only courses.

We try to reach as many people as possible. Last year almost 45,000 children and adults experienced some part of what Bolton Wanderers Football in the Community can offer.

In-term coaching takes place during PE lessons. We work with schools throughout Bolton, Chorley and the surrounding areas. We can work with any class regardless of age or ability. All sessions are fun based, run in a safe environment and conducted by qualified PFA Coaches.

After School courses are run for one and a half hours each day after school for one week. The courses are open to boys and girls of all abilities. Children will be taught a range of skills and techniques used in the game of football. Including passing, turning, dribbling, shooting and more. Lots of fun games will

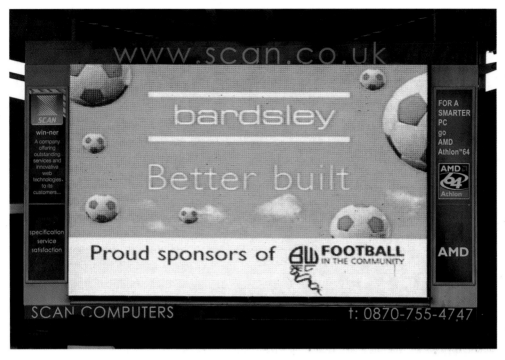

also be played and all sessions will end in matches. All children who attend the course will receive a certificate of achievement, a trophy and other gifts at a presentation. We currently visit two schools during lunch times taking one class at a time for coaching sessions and matches.

The sessions still continue in wet weather. We come prepared with Football and Bolton Wanderers puzzles, quizzes and colouring sheets.

These courses are held during every school holiday. Most courses are open to boys and girls aged 5-12.

We hold a variety of different holiday courses. The General Coaching courses cover a range of skills and techniques used by today's footballers. Specialised strikers and goalkeepers courses concentrate on specific aspects of the game. Just Football days are very popular. Children play football all day in teams with and against their friends. You score points to win prizes. Little Wanderers are short, very basic courses for boys and girls aged 3 and 4. As with all our courses we try to provide youngsters with a good start to what could be their future.

All our courses end with a presentation, where children are presented with a selection of gifts and prizes. Often on hand to help us is Bolton Wanderers Mascot Lofty the Lion who is a massive hit with the children.

Bolton Wanderers Football in the Community now offer a wide variety of girl's only coaching options including After School and Holiday courses as well as a girls Development Group. This is possible thanks to funding from both Coca Cola and Sportsmatch.

Since last year the disability programme has come on leaps and bounds. We now have leagues at open age, Under 16s and Under 14s playing in the first competitive leagues of their kind. Also our Under 16 girls team represented Bolton Wanderers at the Greater Manchester Youth Games.

Please telephone 01204 480601 if you would like any further information about Bolton Wanderers Football in the Community.

Promotions

LIFELIN£

Now in its 23rd year, Lifeline has continued to go from strength to strength. For just £2.00 a week you could be part of Lifeline. There's a chance of winning up to £2,500 every week, 52 weeks of the year plus the added bonus of winning one of our two remaining bonus prizes of £10,000. Application forms are available from the Club Superstore, Ticket Office, Town Centre outlet (Market Place) or at the Promotions Department.

As a Lifeline member, you also have a number of benefits, which include 5% off the price of a season ticket, priority on match tickets plus exclusive party nights. Call now on 01204 673774.

GOLDLIN£

Just £1 will guarantee your membership of the Goldline Daily Draw. £500 can be won each weekday, Monday to Friday, and we also give away hundreds of pounds in consolation prizes every week. Can you afford not to be a member?

As a Goldline member you will also receive free entry into the National Lottery Draw for both Saturday and Wednesday, as part of a syndicate of no more than 100 members. There are various methods of payment, from door to door collections, to standing order direct from your bank. The choice is yours! For full details please contact 01204 673772.

LOTT£RY SCRATCH TICKETS

Our brand new "Striker" instant win scratchcard is in the shops now!!

Our new ticket is proving to be a great success, with cash prizes up to £1000.

With six games to play for just £1 it's great value and great fun.

Tickets are on sale at local shops and pubs in Bolton and surrounding districts but for those of you who have one of our agents to collect either Goldline or Lifeline subscriptions from your home, then why not ask for an instant win ticket on his next visit – you might be our next big winner!!!

GOLD£N GAMBL£

Our Golden Gamble Matchday 50/50 draw ticket is as popular as ever. For just £1.00 you have the chance of walking away from the game with a cheque up to £2000 (dependent on sales) and there are lots of other exciting prizes on offer too !. Sellers are located at all turnstiles around the Reebok - make sure you don't miss out on your chance of winning.

Walkway of Fame & Book of Remembrance

Supporters of Bolton can become part of the history of our great club. Wanderers are offering fans the opportunity to purchase their own place of history along the Wanderers Walkway of Fame.

For just £39.99, a single brick can be inscribed with two rows of up to 16 characters each. Alternatively, a double brick inscribed with up to four rows of 16 characters each can be purchased for £74.99. For £99 a black memorial brick can be inscribed in gold for a loved one or alternatively for £25 you can have your message entered into our Book of Remembrance, which is situated outside the Promotions Department. For more details contact 01204 673663.

Travel Club

For just £5 you can join then Official Travel Club and save £££'s. Save at least £3 per booking, travel in comfort and forget about parking.

Telephone 01204 673663 for further details.

Corporate Hospitality

The Bolton Wanderers Corporate Sales Department organises the matchday hospitality of up to 2,500 guests. From 8 or 10 seat boxes to the 700-strong Premier Suite there is a variety of availability for all requirements. The range of hospitality packages available includes the ever popular Platinum Suite and, the luxurious surroundings of the Chairman's Suite to name but two.

The department also co-ordinates all in-stadia advertising including perimeter boards, matchday programme and videoscreen advertising.

In addition, the department also organises large-scale events such as the Player of the Year Dinner, Chairman's Ball and Wanderers for the Day.

Player of the Year Dinner 2007

Following the huge success of last year's event, preparations are now beginning in earnest for the sixth annual dinner. This season's event will be bigger and better with attendance by the full first team squad, directors and management of the Club.

Wanderers For The Day 2007

Have you ever dreamed of playing for a Premiership side? Have you ever wanted to score the winning goal at the Reebok Stadium? Well, now's your chance!

In May and June 2007, Bolton Wanderers are hiring out the Reebok Stadium pitch for full 11-a-side games for teams wishing to play on the Reebok turf and follow in the footsteps of Jay Jay Okocha and Stelios.

All requests should be directed through the sales team on 01204 673761 or email **sales@bwfc.co.uk**

Publications

Matchday Programme

The Bolton Wanderers matchday programme has been acknowledged as the most improved programme in the Barclays Premiership by Programme Monthly – the 'bible' for programme enthusiasts.

The Wanderers programme is excellent value at £3.00 for a bumper 84 pages, making it one of the biggest programmes in the top-flight.

Packed with exclusive interviews and features, the programme is certainly a great read for Wanderers supporters.

The matchday programme is a fundamental aspect of following your football club, and is as much a part of the match ritual as a pint and a pie.

The Club's aim is to give our supporters the best matchday experience possible and by producing a quality programme we believe we are helping in this regard.

Extra Time Magazine

Extra Time is Bolton Wanderers official magazine. The 48 page full colour glossy publication is sent quarterly to season ticket holders and corporate members. Every issue features exclusive interviews with players and coaching staff and is regarded as an excellent read by the Bolton faithful.

"I love Extra Time - it keeps me informed of what's going on at the Reebok"
John Gillingham, Horwich.

"Extra Time gets underneath the skin of what the players are thinking and gives you an insight into our superstars at the Wanderers."
David Milligan, Bolton.

Official Website – bwfc.co.uk

The official Bolton Wanderers website is continuing to go from strength to strength. **BWFC.co.uk** provides Wanderers fans with a complete service; bringing exclusive and official news as it breaks, publishing exclusive interviews with Wanderers stars and much, much more.

The website is a two-way service. Supporters can help the Club's fortunes by regularly logging onto the site and taking advantage of the many services it provides. From SMS subscriptions to betting on-line through **bwfcBET.co.uk**, Wanderers fans can play a part in earning the Club vital and valuable revenue.

Make sure **bwfc.co.uk** is your first port of call. It's the only website which provides you with exclusive, official and up-to-the-minute news,

Wanderers World

Wanderers World is the only place where you can get behind the scenes at The Reebok Stadium and find out the latest news and views from Bolton Wanderers FC.
Daily News Bulletin • Latest Injury News • Exclusive Features • Reserve News • Academy Updates • Great Features

Never miss the action. Exclusive online highlights of all this season's League and Carling Cup matches plus a few great games from the past.
Broadband Video • Downloads • Match Stats • Manager Quote • Match Summary

The true matchday experience for every League and Cup match, both home and away.
Live Commentary • Starting Line-Ups • Real-time Stats •Text Commentary • Divisional Scores • Goal Flashes

It's your choice, search for specific match incidents you remember, or even your favourite goals. This state-of-the-art technology empowers fans like never before. Plus coming soon there's official video voting.
Searchable archive • Goal of the month • Save of the month

Log onto **http://world.bwfc.co.uk/**

Ticket Information

How to buy a match ticket?

Tickets for matches at the Reebok Stadium are available from the following sources:

By Phone – 0871 871 2932

For ticket related enquiries, please telephone the above number. Credit card bookings using Visa, Mastercard, Switch and Delta can be made on this number.

Please note, that a £1.50 booking fee is charged on all orders. If you are booking tickets in advance, you must bring your credit card with you when collecting your tickets.

Selling restrictions will apply for certain matches and during this time orders by telephone won't be permitted.

On Line

We are now able to process orders online. Please visit **www.bwfc.co.uk** for further details.

Selling restrictions will apply for certain matches and during this time orders online won't be permitted.

Book your tickets online and you won't have to pay a booking fee.

By Post

Postal applications are available from the Ticket & Membership Office and in downloadable format. Please visit **www.bwfc.co.uk** for further details.

Please note, that a £1.50 booking fee is charged on all orders.

Please send your application to: Ticket & Membership Office, BWFC, Reebok Stadium, Burnden Way, Bolton BL6 6JW

For the most up to date information on ticket availability, visit the official website at **www.bwfc.co.uk**

We would remind all supporters to retain the ticket stubs for all home and away games that they attend this season, in case they are used for priority ticket allocation later this season.

Matchday Ticket Prices 2006-07				
Stand	Category A+	Category A	Category B	Category C
East/West Upper				
Adult	£39	£36	£32	£29
Senior Citizen	£28	£25	£22	£20
Junior	£21	£19	£16	£14
East/West Lower				
Adult	£36	£33	£28	£25
Senior Citizen	£26	£23	£20	£17
Junior	£16	£14	£12	£10
North/South Upper				
Adult	£39	£36	£32	£29
Senior Citizen	£28	£25	£22	£20
Junior	£21	£19	£16	£14
North/South Lower				
Adult	£31	£28	£24	£21
Senior Citizen	£24	£22	£18	£16
Junior	£16	£14	£12	£10
Family				
1 adult +1 junior	£44	£39	£32	£26
2 adults +2 juniors	£88	£78	£64	£52

In Person

We sell tickets by personal application at the ticket office. The Ticket and Membership Office is open from 9.30am to 5.00pm Monday to Friday.   On the weekday prior to a home game the ticket office remains open until 7.00pm.

On a Saturday (non-matchday) the ticket office is open from 9.30am to 3.00pm.

On a Saturday (matchday) the ticket office is open from 9.30am until 20 minutes after the final whistle.

By Fax – 0871 871 8183

Please state clearly the game(s) you wish to buy tickets for, the number of tickets you want, which stand you want to sit if applicable, the ticket price and your credit card details including name, address, contact telephone number, credit card number and expiry date.

Please note, that a £1.50 booking fee is charged on all orders. If you are booking tickets in advance, you must bring your credit card with you when collecting your tickets.

Ticket Information For People With Disabilities

Tickets for people with disabilities are available in the following areas:

West Stand Lower Tier
Wheelchair and Ambulant (uncovered)
North Stand Lower
Wheelchair and Ambulant (uncovered)
South Stand Lower
Wheelchair and Ambulant (uncovered)
BT Suite
Wheelchair (behind glass)

Prices range from £21.00 to £35.00 depending on match category and all prices include a free carer's ticket.

Contact 0871 871 2932 for more information

How to Read the Stats

This year's review is better than ever, packed with the sort of in-depth stats which really get you close to the action. If you'd like to know why a particular match turned out the way it did, how a player's form varied over the course of the season, or how Wanderers have fared against their biggest rivals, you'll find all the info inside.

To make sure you're getting the most out of the stats, we're including this section to highlight the information presented by some of the charts and tables.

Colours

Wanderers vs Opposition
There are lots of comparisons between Wanderers and our opponents throughout the book. Wanderers stats are shown in blue; opponents are shown in grey:

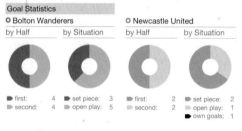

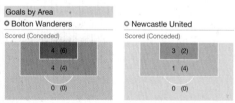

Figure 1: Wanderers stats are in blue; opposition stats are grey.

WDL, Scored, Conceded
When reviewing match results, wins, draws and losses are indicated by green, grey and orange blocks, respectively. For goals, green blocks indicate goals scored; orange blocks show goals conceded:

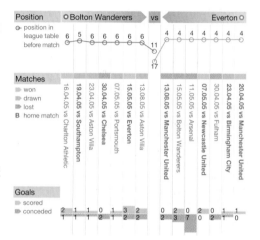

Figure 2: Wins, draws, losses and goals are clearly colour-coded.

Match Reports

The Match Report section contains reports, quotes, facts and stats from every Wanderers match of the 2005/06 season.

Stats Order (Home and Away)
The order of the stats varies depending on whether a match was home or away: for home matches, Wanderers stats are shown on the left, for away matches they're on the right:

Premiership Totals	Bolton	Everton
Premiership Appearances	1,630	1,810
Team Appearances	1,033	995
Goals Scored	201	145
Assists	160	108
Clean Sheets (goalkeepers)	35	130
Yellow Cards	231	194
Red Cards	9	15
Full Internationals	10	8

Figure 3: For home matches, Wanderers stats appear on the left.

Premiership Totals	○ Aston Villa	Bolton ○
Premiership Appearances	1,649	1,545
Team Appearances	827	948
Goals Scored	195	190
Assists	157	148
Clean Sheets (goalkeepers)	59	35
Yellow Cards	169	219
Red Cards	6	9
Full Internationals	10	9

Figure 4: For away matches, Wanderers stats appear on the right.

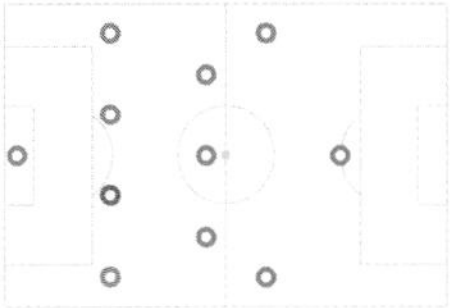

Form Coming into Fixture

Stats are from the previous seven league games. For the first few matches, these stats include games from the end of the previous season.

Team Statistics

Stats are for starters and playing subs. The "Premiership Totals" chart measures performance within the Premiership (with the exception of "Full Internationals").

Premiership Totals	○ Bolton	Newcastle ○
Premiership Appearances	1,515	2,011
Team Appearances	918	1,018
Goals Scored	196	358
Assists	147	216
Clean Sheets (goalkeepers)	35	69
Yellow Cards	215	248
Red Cards	7	13
Full Internationals	11	9

Age/Height

Bolton Wanderers Age | Newcastle United Age

▶ **28 yrs, 9 mo** ▶ 26 yrs, 8 mo

Bolton Wanderers Height | Newcastle United Height

▶ **6'** ▶ 5'11"

Figure 5: Team statistics are for starters and playing subs.

Player Profiles

The Player Profile section provides season reviews and comprehensive stats for Wanderers' players. The section is organised by position, starting with goalkeepers.

Pitch Diagram

The diagram shows all positions the player played during 2005/06. The main position is denoted by a dark blue circle; alternative positions are denoted by light blue circles:

Figure 6: Major positions are shown in dark blue; minor positions are shown in light blue.

Player Performance

All stats show league performance, with the exception of the "Cup Games" table. The "League Performance" chart provides an excellent overview of the player's performance over the course of the season. At a glance, you can see when and how much he played, and how he contributed to the team's overall performance at different stages of the season. Note that outfield players receive a "clean sheet" when they play 75 or more minutes in a game where Wanderers didn't concede a goal.

Career History

Due to the difficulties involved in obtaining reliable stats for international clubs, the "Clubs" table is incomplete for players who have played for non-English clubs. The names of all clubs have been included for the reader's interest, but international stats have been left blank.

The Opposition

The Opposition section shows how Wanderers sizes up against the other 19 teams in the Premiership.

Points / Position

The points / position chart is a snapshot of the last 10 years' league performance of Wanderers and the opponent. For any season when the two teams met in the league, the results of their clashes are shown at the bottom of the chart.

Premiership Head-to-Head

Stats are only for the two teams' meetings in the Premiership.

2-2

Aston Villa ○
Bolton Wanderers ○

► Radhi Jaidi climbs highest

Event Line

4 ○ ⊕ Phillips / H / OP / 6Y	
Assist: Hughes	
6 ○ ⊕ Davies / RF / OP / 6Y	
Assist: Jaidi	
8 ○ ⊕ Campo / H / C / IA	
Assist: Speed	
9 ○ ⊕ Davis / RF / OP / 6Y	
Assist: Phillips	
26 ○ ▨ Diouf	

Half time 2-2

54 ○ ⇄ Okocha > Campo	
88 ○ ▨ Ben Haim	

Full time 2-2

Bolton Wanderers and Aston Villa shared the spoils during an entertaining Barclays Premiership opener in which both sides netted twice inside the first nine minutes.

A blistering opening period saw David O'Leary's side snatch the lead after four minutes through new signing Kevin Phillips before Wanderers hit back through Kevin Davies and Ivan Campo to lead 2-1.

Villa midfielder Steven Davis equalised almost immediately to level the scores at 2-2 after just nine remarkably high-tempo minutes.

Neither side proved capable of sustaining their early momentum, but it was Bolton who came closest to finding a winner after largely dominating the second period.

Wanderers midfielder Kevin Nolan, preferred to Jay-Jay Okocha in the starting line-up, looked to have a struck a late winner only to see the effort disallowed for offside.

And while it may have been the opening day of the season, there was little sign of any ring-rustiness from either set of players.

Quote

 Sam Allardyce

The decision to disallow Kevin Nolan's goal is a major one that has gone against us.

Venue:	Villa Park	Referee:	M.A.Riley - 05/06	**Aston Villa**
Attendance:	33,263	Matches:	0	**Bolton Wanderers**
Capacity:	42,573	Yellow Cards:	0	
Occupancy:	78%	Red Cards:	0	

Form Coming into Fixture

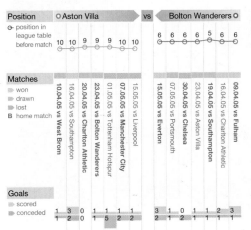

Position

Aston Villa vs Bolton Wanderers

Aston Villa: 10 10 9 9 9 10 10
Bolton Wanderers: 6 6 6 6 5 6 6

position in league table before match

Matches

- won
- drawn
- lost
- B home match

Aston Villa:
- 10.04.05 vs West Brom
- 16.04.05 vs Southampton
- 20.04.05 vs Charlton Athletic
- 23.04.05 vs Bolton Wanderers
- 01.05.05 vs Tottenham Hotspur
- 07.05.05 vs Manchester City
- 15.05.05 vs Liverpool

Bolton Wanderers:
- 15.05.05 vs Everton
- 07.05.05 vs Portsmouth
- 30.04.05 vs Chelsea
- 23.04.05 vs Aston Villa
- 19.04.05 vs Southampton
- 16.04.05 vs Charlton Athletic
- 09.04.05 vs Fulham

Goals

	scored	conceded

Aston Villa: scored 1 3 0 1 1 1 1 / conceded 1 2 0 1 5 2 2
Bolton Wanderers: scored 3 1 0 1 1 2 3 / conceded 2 1 2 1 1 1 1

Goal Statistics

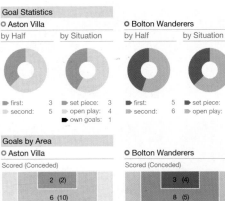

Aston Villa

by Half / by Situation

- first: 3
- second: 5
- set piece: 3
- open play: 4
- own goals: 1

Bolton Wanderers

by Half / by Situation

- first: 5
- second: 6
- set piece: 4
- open play: 7

Goals by Area

Aston Villa

Scored (Conceded)

| 2 (2) |
| 6 (10) |
| 0 (1) |

Bolton Wanderers

Scored (Conceded)

| 3 (4) |
| 8 (5) |
| 0 (0) |

Team Statistics

Starting Line-Ups

Aston Villa:
Sorensen, Samuel, Barry, Laursen, Davis, Mellberg, McCann, Phillips, Angel, Hughes, Solano

Bolton Wanderers:
Jaaskelainen, Pedersen, Hunt, Nolan, Ben Haim, Davies, Campo Okocha, Jaidi, Speed, Diouf, Gardner

Aston Villa: 4/4/2
Bolton Wanderers: 4/5/1

Unused Sub: Ridgewell, Taylor, Djemba-Djemba, Hendrie, Moore

Unused Sub: Walker, Faye, Stelios, Vaz Te

Premiership Totals	Aston Villa	Bolton
Premiership Appearances	1,649	1,545
Team Appearances	827	948
Goals Scored	195	190
Assists	157	148
Clean Sheets (goalkeepers)	59	35
Yellow Cards	169	219
Red Cards	6	9
Full Internationals	10	9

Age/Height

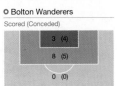

	Aston Villa	Bolton Wanderers
Age	27 yrs, 4 mo	28 yrs, 2 mo
Height	5'11"	6'

Match Statistics

League Table after Fixture

		Played	Won	Drawn	Lost	For	Against	Pts
5	Aston Villa	1	0	1	0	2	2	1
6	Bolton	1	0	1	0	2	2	1
7	Birmingham	1	0	1	0	0	0	1
8	Fulham	1	0	1	0	0	0	1
9	Liverpool	1	0	1	0	0	0	1
10	Man City	1	0	1	0	0	0	1
11	Middlesbrough	1	0	1	0	0	0	1
12	West Brom	1	0	1	0	0	0	1
13	Arsenal	0	0	0	0	0	0	0

Statistics	Aston Villa	Bolton
Goals	2	2
Shots on Target	2	6
Shots off Target	1	7
Hit Woodwork	0	0
Possession %	50	50
Corners	7	8
Offsides	4	2
Fouls	14	16
Disciplinary Points	0	8

0-1

Bolton Wanderers ○
Everton ○

▶ El-Hadji Diouf keeps Tony Hibbert at bay

Event Line

33 ○ ⇄ Osman > Pistone	
Half time 0-0	
52 ○ ⊕ Bent M / RF / OP / 6Y	
Assist: Cahill	
60 ○ ⇄ McFadden > Bent M	
67 ○ ⇄ Giannakopoulos > Pedersen	
78 ○ ⇄ Campo > Hunt	
83 ○ ⇄ Vaz Te > Ben Haim	
89 ○ Kilbane	
Full time 0-1	

Marcus Bent completed a smash and grab win for Everton when he converted his side's only effort of the game just after the interval and in doing so consigned profligate Wanderers to a most unjust defeat.

The former Ipswich man had the simplest of opportunities eight minutes after the restart to give his side all three points when he tapped Tim Cahill's low cross into an unguarded net after Duncan Ferguson caused confusion in the Wanderers box.

But Wanderers will rue a glut of missed chances after they dominated the entire game.

Quote

❻ Sam Allardyce

We battered Everton from start to finish and dominated the game, but a lack of quality let us down.

Venue:	Reebok Stadium	Referee:	A.G.Wiley - 05/06		Bolton Wanderers
Attendance:	25,608	Matches:	2		Everton
Capacity:	28,101	Yellow Cards:	5		
Occupancy:	91%	Red Cards:	1		

Form Coming into Fixture

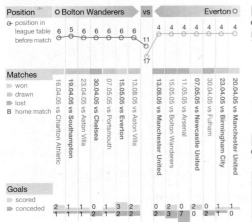

Position	○ Bolton Wanderers	vs	Everton ○

- position in league table before match
  - Bolton: 6 5 6 6 6 6 6 — 11, 17
  - Everton: 4 4 4 4 4 4 4

Matches
- won
- drawn
- lost
- B home match

16.04.05 vs Charlton Athletic
19.04.05 vs Southampton
23.04.05 vs Aston Villa
30.04.05 vs Chelsea
07.05.05 vs Portsmouth
15.05.05 vs Everton
13.08.05 vs Aston Villa
13.08.05 vs Manchester United
15.05.05 vs Bolton Wanderers
11.05.05 vs Arsenal
07.05.05 vs Newcastle United
30.04.05 vs Fulham
20.04.05 vs Birmingham City

Goals
- scored
- conceded

Bolton	2	1	1	0	1	3	2		Everton	0	2	0	2	0	1	1
	1	1	1	2	1	2	2			2	3	7	0	2	1	0

Goal Statistics

○ Bolton Wanderers

by Half
- first: 5
- second: 5

by Situation
- set piece: 4
- open play: 6

○ Everton

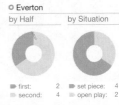

by Half
- first: 2
- second: 4

by Situation
- set piece: 4
- open play: 2

Goals by Area

○ Bolton Wanderers — Scored (Conceded)

- 4 (5)
- 6 (5)
- 0 (0)

○ Everton — Scored (Conceded)

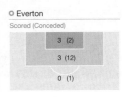

- 3 (2)
- 3 (12)
- 0 (1)

Team Statistics

Starting Line-Ups

Bolton Wanderers:
Jaaskelainen; Gardner, Jaidi, Ben Haim (Vaz Te), Hunt (Campo); Diouf, Okocha, Speed, Davies, Nolan (Pedersen/Stelios)

Everton:
Martyn; Hibbert, Yobo, Weir, Pistone (Osman); Bent M (McFadden), Arteta, Neville, Kilbane, Cahill; Ferguson

▶ 4/5/1

Unused Sub: Walker, Faye

▶ 4/5/1

Unused Sub: Wright, Davies, Vaughan

Premiership Totals

	○ Bolton	Everton ○
Premiership Appearances	1,630	1,810
Team Appearances	1,033	995
Goals Scored	201	145
Assists	160	108
Clean Sheets (goalkeepers)	35	130
Yellow Cards	231	194
Red Cards	9	15
Full Internationals	10	8

Age/Height

Bolton Wanderers Age	Everton Age
▶ 27 yrs, 9 mo	**▶ 28 yrs, 3 mo**
Bolton Wanderers Height	Everton Height
▶ 6'	**▶ 6'**

Match Statistics

League Table after Fixture

		Played	Won	Drawn	Lost	For	Against	Pts
↑	11 Everton	2	1	0	1	1	2	3
●	12 Aston Villa	2	0	1	1	2	3	1
↓	13 Bolton	2	0	1	1	2	3	1
↓	14 Birmingham	2	0	1	1	1	2	1
↓	15 Fulham	2	0	1	1	1	2	1
↓	16 Middlesbrough	2	0	1	1	0	2	1
↓	17 Newcastle	2	0	1	1	0	2	1
●	18 Wigan	2	0	0	2	0	2	0
●	19 Portsmouth	2	0	0	2	1	4	0

Statistics

	○ Bolton	Everton ○
Goals	0	1
Shots on Target	6	1
Shots off Target	10	2
Hit Woodwork	1	0
Possession %	51	49
Corners	8	3
Offsides	1	2
Fouls	10	13
Disciplinary Points	0	4

2-0

Bolton Wanderers ○
Newcastle United ○

➡ Ivan Campo keeps the ball moving

Event Line

23 ○ ⇄	Diagne-Faye > Jaidi	
34 ○ ▢	Taylor	
37 ○ ⊕	Diouf / H / OP / 6Y	
	Assist: Hunt	
Half time 1-0		
50 ○ ⊕	Giannakopoulos / RF / OP / 6Y	
	Assist: Speed	
60 ○ ⇄	Clark > Faye	
67 ○ ⇄	Milner > Bowyer	
70 ○ ⇄	Campo > Davies	
87 ○ ⇄	Borgetti > Diouf	
Full time 2-0		

El-Hadji Diouf and Stelios both grabbed their first goals of the campaign to give Wanderers a deserved victory against Newcastle United.

The Wanderers players responded to Sam Allardyce's pre-match request of greater concentration and clinical finishing to see off the Magpies in a one-sided affair.

Despite speculation linking him with a move to Liverpool earlier in the day, Stelios was named in the starting line-up at the expense of the injured Ricardo Gardner. Henrik Pedersen, normally a forward, proved to be an able deputy for the Jamaican with a fine performance at left-back.

Although Gary Speed was forced to clear Lee Bowyer's spinning volley off his line inside five minutes, Jussi Jaaskelainen was only required to make one save during the entire game thanks to the outstanding defence in front of him.

Quote

❝ Sam Allardyce

My praise goes to Henrik Pedersen first and foremost. He played at full-back and it's the first time he's played there in the Premiership.

Premiership Milestone

➡ **100**

Jay-Jay Okocha made his 100th Premiership appearance.

Venue:	Reebok Stadium	Referee:	R.Styles - 05/06	Bolton Wanderers
Attendance:	25,904	Matches:	3	Newcastle United
Capacity:	28,101	Yellow Cards:	7	
Occupancy:	92%	Red Cards:	0	

Form Coming into Fixture

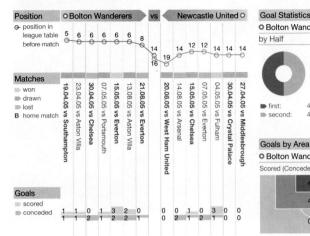

Position	O Bolton Wanderers	vs	Newcastle United O

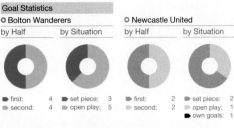

Goal Statistics

O Bolton Wanderers

by Half	by Situation

- first: 4
- second: 4
- set piece: 3
- open play: 5

O Newcastle United

by Half	by Situation

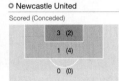

- first: 2
- second: 2
- set piece: 2
- open play: 1
- own goals: 1

Goals by Area

O Bolton Wanderers

Scored (Conceded)

4 (6)
4 (4)
0 (0)

O Newcastle United

Scored (Conceded)

3 (2)
1 (4)
0 (0)

Matches: won, drawn, lost, B home match

Goals: scored, conceded

Bolton Wanderers matches:
19.04.05 vs Southampton | 23.04.05 vs Aston Villa | 30.04.05 vs Portsmouth | 07.05.05 vs Everton | 15.05.05 vs Aston Villa | 13.08.05 vs Everton | 21.08.05 vs Everton

Goals scored: 1 1 0 1 3 2 0
Goals conceded: 1 1 2 2 2 2 1

Newcastle United matches:
20.08.05 vs West Ham United | 14.08.05 vs Arsenal | 15.05.05 vs Chelsea | 07.05.05 vs Everton | 04.04.05 vs Fulham | 30.04.05 vs Crystal Palace | 27.04.05 vs Middlesbrough

Goals scored: 0 0 1 0 3 0 0
Goals conceded: 2 1 2 1 0 0 0

Team Statistics

Starting Line-Ups

Bolton Wanderers (left)
Jaaskelainen; Pedersen, Stelios, Nolan, Jaidi/Faye, Speed, Davies/Campo, Ben Haim, Okocha, Hunt, Diouf/Borgetti

Newcastle United (right)
Given; Bowyer/Milner, Carr, Jenas, Boumsong, Shearer, Parker, Taylor, Faye/Clark, Ameobi, Babayaro

Bolton: 4/5/1
Newcastle: 4/5/1

Unused Sub: Walker, Vaz Te
Unused Sub: Harper, Elliott, N'Zogbia

Premiership Totals	O Bolton	Newcastle O
Premiership Appearances	1,515	2,011
Team Appearances	918	1,018
Goals Scored	196	358
Assists	147	216
Clean Sheets (goalkeepers)	35	69
Yellow Cards	215	248
Red Cards	7	13
Full Internationals	11	9

Age/Height

Bolton Wanderers Age: **28 yrs, 9 mo**

Newcastle United Age: **26 yrs, 8 mo**

Bolton Wanderers Height: **6'**

Newcastle United Height: **5'11"**

Match Statistics

League Table after Fixture

		Played	Won	Drawn	Lost	For	Against	Pts
●	2 Tottenham	3	2	1	0	4	0	7
↓	3 Man City	3	2	1	0	4	2	7
↑	4 Arsenal	3	2	0	1	6	2	6
↓	5 Charlton	2	2	0	0	4	1	6
↓	6 Man Utd	2	2	0	0	3	0	6
↓	7 West Ham	2	1	1	0	3	1	4
↑	8 Bolton	3	1	1	1	4	3	4
...	...	...	...	...	...	...	...	...
↓	18 Newcastle	3	0	1	2	0	4	1

Statistics	O Bolton	Newcastle O
Goals	2	0
Shots on Target	6	4
Shots off Target	8	3
Hit Woodwork	0	0
Possession %	53	47
Corners	4	3
Offsides	3	3
Fouls	12	17
Disciplinary Points	0	4

1-2

West Ham United ○
Bolton Wanderers ○

▶ Stelios congratulates goalscorer Ivan Campo

Event Line

Half time 0-0

51 ○ ▮	Diouf	
52 ○ ⇄	Campo > Diouf	
55 ○ ▮	Repka	
56 ○ ▮	Davies	
59 ○ ⊕	Nolan / RF / C / 6Y	
	Assist: Davies	
60 ○ ⇄	Aliadiere > Etherington	
62 ○ ▮	Giannakopoulos	
65 ○ ⇄	Zamora > Harewood	
76 ○ ▮	Speed	
83 ○ ⇄	Ward > Gabbidon	
83 ○ ⇄	Diagne-Faye > Davies	
85 ○ ⊕	Campo / RF / OP / IA	
	Assist: Okocha	
87 ○ ⇄	Borgetti > Okocha	
90 ○ ⊕	Sheringham / RF / P / IA	
	Assist: Mullins	

Full time 1-2

Wanderers recorded their second Barclays Premiership win on the trot thanks to smart goals from Kevin Nolan and Ivan Campo.

Although Teddy Sheringham's last-minute penalty beat Jussi Jaaskelainen, Wanderers hung on to claim a marvellous three points during a match of high drama.

Bruno N'Gotty's timely return from a three-match suspension allowed him to slot in the centre of defence alongside Tal Ben Haim at the expense of Radhi Jaidi who injured a hamstring during the midweek victory over Newcastle United.

The big Frenchman and his fellow defenders had their work cut out during the early exchanges against a dynamic Hammers outfit whose fluid passing and quick movement often had them on the back foot.

But the visitors finished the game strongly and proved to be more clinical than their opponents.

Quote

❝ **Sam Allardyce**

It was difficult for us out there, but our character and experience told through in the end.

Premiership Milestone

▶ **150**

Jussi Jaaskelainen made his 150th Premiership appearance.

Venue:	Upton Park	Referee:	P.Dowd - 05/06	**West Ham United**
Attendance:	31,629	Matches:	4	**Bolton Wanderers**
Capacity:	35,647	Yellow Cards:	12	
Occupancy:	89%	Red Cards:	0	

Form Coming into Fixture

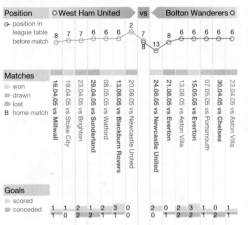

Position	West Ham United vs Bolton Wanderers
position in league table before match	8 7 7 6 6 6 2 7 8 6 6 6 6 6

Matches
- won
- drawn
- lost
- B home match

16.04.05 vs Millwall
19.04.05 vs Stoke City
23.04.05 vs Brighton
29.04.05 vs Sunderland
08.05.05 vs Watford
13.08.05 vs Blackburn Rovers
20.08.05 vs Newcastle United
24.08.05 vs Newcastle United
21.08.05 vs Everton
13.08.05 vs Aston Villa
15.05.05 vs Everton
07.05.05 vs Portsmouth
30.04.05 vs Chelsea
23.04.05 vs Aston Villa

Goals
- scored: 1 1 2 1 2 3 0 | 2 0 2 3 1 0 1
- conceded: 1 0 2 2 1 1 0 | 0 1 2 2 1 2 1

Goal Statistics

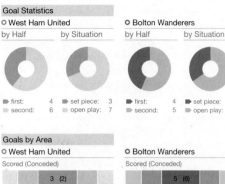

West Ham United

by Half | by Situation
- first: 4
- second: 6
- set piece: 3
- open play: 7

Bolton Wanderers

by Half | by Situation
- first: 4
- second: 5
- set piece: 3
- open play: 6

Goals by Area

West Ham United
Scored (Conceded)
- 3 (2)
- 6 (5)
- 1 (0)

Bolton Wanderers
Scored (Conceded)
- 5 (6)
- 4 (3)
- 0 (0)

Team Statistics

Starting Line-Ups

West Ham United:
Carroll; Konchesky, Etherington (Aliadiere), Stelios, Hunt; Nolan; Gabbidon (Ward), Mullins, Harewood (Zamora), Ben Haim, Jaaskelainen; Davies (Faye), Speed; Ferdinand, Reo-Coker, Sheringham, N'Gotty; Okocha (Borgetti); Repka, Benayoun, Diouf (Campo), Pedersen

4/4/2 | **4/5/1**

Unused Sub: Hislop, Dailly | Unused Sub: Walker, Nakata

Premiership Totals	West Ham	Bolton
Premiership Appearances	761	1,618
Team Appearances	85	1,021
Goals Scored	150	198
Assists	104	152
Clean Sheets (goalkeepers)	25	36
Yellow Cards	80	223
Red Cards	6	9
Full Internationals	6	11

Age/Height

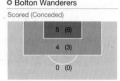

West Ham United Age: **25 yrs, 9 mo** | Bolton Wanderers Age: **29 yrs**

West Ham United Height: **6'** | Bolton Wanderers Height: **6'**

Match Statistics

League Table after Fixture

		Played	Won	Drawn	Lost	For	Against	Pts
• 1	Chelsea	4	4	0	0	8	0	12
↑ 2	Man City	4	3	1	0	6	3	10
↑ 3	Bolton	4	2	1	1	6	4	7
↓ 4	Tottenham	4	2	1	1	4	2	7
↓ 5	Arsenal	3	2	0	1	6	2	6
↓ 6	Charlton	2	2	0	0	4	1	6
↓ 7	Man Utd	2	2	0	0	3	0	6
↑ 8	Aston Villa	4	1	2	1	4	4	5
↓ 9	West Ham	3	1	1	1	4	3	4

Statistics	West Ham	Bolton
Goals	1	2
Shots on Target	7	6
Shots off Target	7	4
Hit Woodwork	1	1
Possession %	55	45
Corners	7	7
Offsides	2	5
Fouls	12	16
Disciplinary Points	4	16

0-0

Bolton Wanderers ○
Blackburn Rovers ○

➡ Jay-Jay Okocha shows off his skills

Event Line	
23 ○ ▢	Campo
41 ○ ▢	Matteo
43 ○ ▢	Savage
Half time 0-0	
56 ○ ⇄	Gardner > Giannakopoulos
58 ○ ⇄	Kuqi > Jansen
58 ○ ⇄	Bentley > Pedersen
70 ○ ⇄	Borgetti > Davies
78 ○ ⇄	Hunt > Okocha
Full time 0-0	

Wanderers had to settle for a point in this goalless Lancashire derby at the Reebok Stadium with both sides failing to find a killer instinct in front of goal.

Although both keepers were forced into making important saves during the occasion, the game was virtually bereft of much goalmouth action – despite Blackburn's late surge towards the end of the match.

Ivan Campo had been recalled to the starting line-up at the expense of Nicky Hunt, whose midweek action for the England under 21s resulted in him starting from the bench.

Wanderers went into the game hoping to grab a result that would put them in good spirits for the following Thursday night's UEFA Cup debut against Lokomotiv Plovdiv.

Quote

 Sam Allardyce

When we get closed down we find it incredibly difficult to break sides down.

Venue:	Reebok Stadium	Referee:	G.Poll - 05/06	**Bolton Wanderers**
Attendance:	24,405	Matches:	4	**Blackburn Rovers**
Capacity:	28,101	Yellow Cards:	17	
Occupancy:	87%	Red Cards:	1	

Form Coming into Fixture

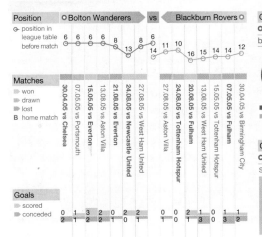

Position	O Bolton Wanderers	vs	Blackburn Rovers O

position in league table before match: 6 6 6 6 8 8 6 13 14 11 10 16 15 14 14 12

Matches	
won	
drawn	
lost	
B home match	

Bolton: 30.04.05 vs Chelsea, 07.05.05 vs Portsmouth, 15.05.05 vs Everton, 13.08.05 vs Aston Villa, 21.08.05 vs Everton, 24.08.05 vs Newcastle United, 27.08.05 vs West Ham United

Blackburn: 27.08.05 vs Aston Villa, 24.08.05 vs Tottenham Hotspur, 20.08.05 vs Fulham, 13.08.05 vs West Ham United, 15.05.05 vs Tottenham Hotspur, 07.05.05 vs Fulham, 30.04.05 vs Birmingham City

Goals															
scored	0	1	3	2	0	2	2		0	0	2	1	0	1	1
conceded	2	1	2	2	1	0	1		1	0	1	3	0	3	2

Goal Statistics

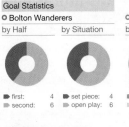

O Bolton Wanderers	
by Half	by Situation

first: 4, second: 6 — set piece: 4, open play: 6

O Blackburn Rovers	
by Half	by Situation

first: 4, second: 1 — set piece: 2, open play: 3

Goals by Area

O Bolton Wanderers
Scored (Conceded)

6 (5)
4 (4)
0 (0)

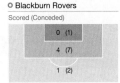

O Blackburn Rovers
Scored (Conceded)

0 (1)
4 (7)
1 (2)

Team Statistics

Starting Line-Ups

Bolton Wanderers: Jaaskelainen; Pedersen, Diouf, Emerton, Neill, Nolan, Savage, N'Gotty, Khizanishvili, Speed, Davies (Borgetti), Jansen (Kuqi), Mokoena, Friedel, Ben Haim, Nelson, Okocha (Hunt), Reid, Campo, Stelios (Gardner), Pedersen (Bentley), Matteo

4/5/1 — 4/5/1

Bolton Wanderers Height 5'11"
Blackburn Rovers Height 6'

Unused Sub: Walker, Nakata
Unused Sub: Enckelman, Tugay, Dickov

Premiership Totals	O Bolton	Blackburn O
Premiership Appearances	1,750	1,164
Team Appearances	1,153	601
Goals Scored	205	63
Assists	167	89
Clean Sheets (goalkeepers)	36	52
Yellow Cards	242	162
Red Cards	11	7
Full Internationals	11	11

Age/Height

Bolton Wanderers Age: **29 yrs**
Blackburn Rovers Age: **27 yrs, 2 mo**

Match Statistics

League Table after Fixture

		Played	Won	Drawn	Lost	For	Against	Pts
● 4	Man Utd	4	3	1	0	6	1	10
↑ 5	Bolton	5	2	2	1	6	4	8
↓ 6	Tottenham	5	2	2	1	4	2	8
● 7	Middlesbrough	5	2	1	2	5	6	7
● 8	Arsenal	4	2	0	2	7	4	6
● 9	Wigan	4	2	0	2	3	3	6
● 10	Liverpool	3	1	2	0	1	0	5
● 11	Aston Villa	4	1	2	1	4	4	5
↑ 12	Blackburn	5	1	2	2	3	5	5

Statistics	O Bolton	Blackburn O
Goals	0	0
Shots on Target	6	3
Shots off Target	6	4
Hit Woodwork	0	0
Possession %	52	48
Corners	4	4
Offsides	0	1
Fouls	18	17
Disciplinary Points	4	8

2-1

Bolton Wanderers ○
PFC Lokomotiv Plovdiv ○

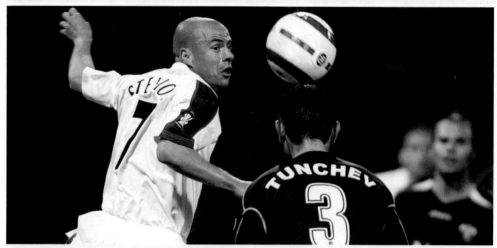

▶ Stelios climbs highest in the box

Event Line

8 ○ ▢ Djordani	
28 ○ ⊕ Jancevski / RF / OP / IA	
Assist: Ivanov	
31 ○ ▢ Nakata	
Half time 0-1	
46 ○ ⇄ Georgiev > Halimi	
57 ○ ⇄ Borgetti > Pedersen	
61 ○ ▢ Jancevski	
66 ○ ⇄ Fernandes > Giannakopoulos	
66 ○ ⇄ Nolan > Okocha	
68 ○ ▢ Iliev G	
72 ○ ⊕ Diouf / H / OP / IA	
Assist: Hunt	
80 ○ ⇄ Vandev > Iliev G	
87 ○ ▢ Gardner	
90 ○ ⊕ Borgetti / RF / OP / IA	
Assist: Nakata	
90 ○ ⇄ Stoynev > Jancevski	
Full time 2-1	

El-Hadji Diouf enjoyed the distinction of becoming Bolton Wanderers' first goal scorer in Europe as his side came from behind to take a slender advantage to Bulgaria for the second-leg of this tie.

The Wanderers frontman netted his second goal of the season deep into the second-half to cancel out Boban Janchevski's shock 28th minute opener.

Substitute Jared Borgetti then netted his first goal in a Wanderers shirt to secure an injury time victory in front of just under 20,000 Reebok Stadium spectators.

With an eye firmly focused on Saturday's Barclays Premiership trip to the City of Manchester Stadium, Sam Allardyce made four changes to his side for their European bow against Lokomotiv Plovdiv.

Loan signing Hidetoshi Nakata was handed his debut, while Nicky Hunt, Radhi Jaidi and Ricardo Gardner all came in for Gary Speed, Kevin Nolan, Kevin Davies and Tal Ben Haim.

Venue:	Reebok Stadium	Referee:	D.Ceferin (SLO)		**Bolton Wanderers**

Venue: Reebok Stadium   Referee: D.Ceferin (SLO)

Attendance: 19,723

Capacity: 28,101

Occupancy: 70%

Bolton Wanderers
PFC Lokomotiv Plovdiv

► El-Hadji Diouf celebrates opening Bolton's European account

Match Statistics

Starting Line-Ups

Pedersen   Gardner   Iliev G   Ivanov
Borgetti   Vandev

Nakata

N'Gotty   Krizmanic   Kotev

Halimi
Georgiev

Jaaskelainen Campo   Diouf   Kolev S

Jaidi   Jancevski   Djordani
              Stoynev Dimitrov

Okocha
Nolan

Hunt   Stelios   Petrov   Tunchev
       Fernandes

► **4/5/1**   ► **4/4/1/1**

Unused Sub: Walker, Faye, O'Brien, Davies

Unused Sub: Kamburov, Zlatinski, Mihaylov, Hristev

Statistics	○ Bolton	Loko Plovdiv ○
Goals	2	1
Shots on Target	4	3
Shots off Target	7	3
Hit Woodwork	0	0
Possession %	60	40
Corners	11	0
Offsides	1	5
Fouls	18	17
Disciplinary Points	8	12

Quote

❝ **Sam Allardyce**

We needed not to concede and it's going to be difficult in Bulgaria.

0-1

Manchester City ○
Bolton Wanderers ○

▶ Ivan Campo keeps a close eye on Darius Vassell

Event Line

26 ○ ⇄ Jihai > Sinclair	
Half time 0-0	
46 ○ ⇄ Campo > Diagne-Faye	
50 ○ ▪ Davies	
56 ○ ⇄ Nakata > Diouf	
66 ○ ⇄ Gardner > Giannakopoul‹	
81 ○ ⇄ Ireland > Barton	
90 ○ ▪ Dunne	
90 ○ ⊕ Speed / LF / P / IA	
Assist: Pedersen	
Full time 0-1	

Wanderers completed the ultimate smash and grab victory to claim three points against Manchester City.

Gary Speed hit a 90th minute penalty – completely against the run of play - to stun the City of Manchester Stadium after the hosts dominated proceedings, hitting the woodwork on no less than four occasions.

Sam Allardyce made five changes as Wanderers returned to the tough reality of the Barclays Premiership following Thursday night's historic UEFA Cup exploits.

Speed recovered from the hamstring injury that prevented his inclusion in the 2-1 victory against Lokomotiv Plovdiv, coming into the side at the expense of skipper Jay Jay Okocha, a victim of an ankle injury.

Abdoulaye Faye made his first start for the Club, and Kevin Nolan, Kevin Davies and Tal Ben Haim returned to the starting XI.

Radhi Jaidi retained his place in the side and partnered Bruno N'Gotty in the centre of defence with Ben Haim slotting in at right back.

Quote

⦅⦆ Sam Allardyce

It reminds me of our game with Everton earlier in the season. We got mugged then and we've mugged Man City today.

Premiership Milestone

▶ Debut

Hidetoshi Nakata made his Premiership debut.

Venue:	City of Manchester Stadium	Referee:	M.L.Dean - 05/06		**Manchester City**
Attendance:	43,137	Matches:	3		**Bolton Wanderers**
Capacity:	48,000	Yellow Cards:	6		
Occupancy:	90%	Red Cards:	0		

Form Coming into Fixture

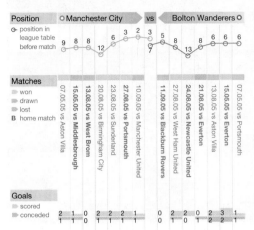

Position	○ Manchester City	vs	Bolton Wanderers ○
position in league table before match	9 8 8 3 2 3 6 12		5 8 13 8 6 6 6 7

Matches
- won
- drawn
- lost
- B home match

Manchester City matches: 07.05.05 vs Aston Villa, 15.05.05 vs Middlesbrough, 13.08.05 vs West Brom, 20.08.05 vs Sunderland, 23.08.05 vs Birmingham City, 27.08.05 vs Portsmouth, 10.09.05 vs Manchester United

Bolton Wanderers matches: 11.09.05 vs Blackburn Rovers, 27.08.05 vs West Ham United, 24.08.05 vs Newcastle United, 21.08.05 vs Everton, 13.08.05 vs Aston Villa, 15.05.05 vs Everton, 07.05.05 vs Portsmouth

Goals
- scored
- conceded

scored	2	1	0	2	2	2	1		0	2	0	2	3	1
conceded	1	1	0	1	1	1			0	1	0	1	2	2	1

Goal Statistics

○ Manchester City — by Half / by Situation

first:	5	set piece:	0
second:	5	open play:	10

○ Bolton Wanderers — by Half / by Situation

first:	4	set piece:	4
second:	6	open play:	6

Goals by Area

○ Manchester City — Scored (Conceded)

2 (2)
8 (3)
0 (1)

○ Bolton Wanderers — Scored (Conceded)

6 (5)
4 (2)
0 (0)

Team Statistics

Starting Line-Ups

Manchester City: Thatcher, Musampa, Distin, Reyna, Vassell, James, Davies, Faye (Campo), Dunne, Barton (Ireland), Sibierski, Mills D, Sinclair (Jihai)

Bolton Wanderers: Stelios (Gardner), Ben Haim, Nolan, Jaidi, Jaaskelainen, N'Gotty, Speed, Diouf (Nakata), Pedersen

4 / 4 / 1 / 1   **4 / 5 / 1**

Unused Sub: De Vlieger, Onuoha, Fowler   Unused Sub: Walker, Borgetti

Premiership Totals

Premiership Totals	○ Man City	Bolton ○
Premiership Appearances	1,887	1,626
Team Appearances	669	1,029
Goals Scored	122	196
Assists	129	145
Clean Sheets (goalkeepers)	126	37
Yellow Cards	226	228
Red Cards	15	11
Full Internationals	8	12

Age/Height

Manchester City Age	Bolton Wanderers Age
28 yrs, 3 mo	**29 yrs, 1 mo**

Manchester City Height	Bolton Wanderers Height
6'	**6'**

Match Statistics

League Table after Fixture

		Played	Won	Drawn	Lost	For	Against	Pts
● 1	Chelsea	6	6	0	0	12	0	18
● 2	Charlton	5	4	0	1	8	3	12
↑ 3	Man Utd	5	3	2	0	6	1	11
↑ 4	Bolton	6	3	2	1	7	4	11
↓ 5	Man City	6	3	2	1	7	5	11
↓ 6	West Ham	5	3	1	1	10	4	10
↓ 7	Tottenham	6	2	3	1	5	3	9
● 8	Middlesbrough	6	2	2	2	6	7	8
↑ 9	Wigan	5	2	1	2	4	4	7

Statistics

Statistics	○ Man City	Bolton ○
Goals	0	1
Shots on Target	8	2
Shots off Target	9	4
Hit Woodwork	4	0
Possession %	56	44
Corners	7	5
Offsides	3	5
Fouls	14	16
Disciplinary Points	4	4

1-0

Bolton Wanderers ○
Portsmouth ○

Premiership
24.09.05

▶ Hidetoshi Nakata gets a shot away

Event Line

10 ○ ⇄	O'Brien > Speed
25 ○ ⊕	Nolan / RF / OP / IA
	Assist: Davies
Half time 1-0	
52 ○ ▪	Ben Haim
66 ○ ⇄	Karadas > Taylor
73 ○ ⇄	Songo'o > O'Neil
74 ○ ▪	Stefanovic
75 ○ ⇄	Giannakopoulos > Okocha
85 ○ ⇄	Todorov > Silva
90 ○ ▪	Giannakopoulos
90 ○ ⇄	Diouf > Hunt
90 ○ ▪	Priske
Full time 1-0	

Kevin Nolan struck an amazing 'goal of the season contender' to send Bolton Wanderers to the Barclays Premiership's third spot.

The midfielder hit a spectacular overhead volley past Pompey 'keeper Jamie Ashdown midway through the first-half to make it four Premier League wins out of five for Sam Allardyce's men, who also managed to claim their fourth clean-sheet of the campaign.

The Wanderers boss made four changes to his side for the visit of the south coast club

Jay Jay Okocha returned to captain the side after recuperating from the ankle injury he suffered which prevented his inclusion in the previous week's 1-0 victory against Manchester City. Nicky Hunt and Ricardo Gardner also returned to the starting XI, while new signing Hidetoshi Nakata enjoyed his first league start since joining the Club.

Quote

❻ Sam Allardyce

It was a great goal by Kevin Nolan, demonstrating his superb technique and quality.

Venue:	Reebok Stadium	Referee:	M.Clattenburg - 05/06	**Bolton Wanderers**
Attendance:	23,134	Matches:	8	**Portsmouth**
Capacity:	28,101	Yellow Cards:	33	
Occupancy:	82%	Red Cards:	2	

Form Coming into Fixture

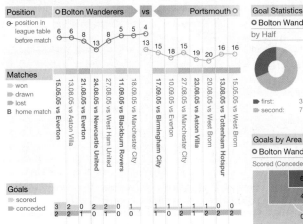

Position	O Bolton Wanderers	vs	Portsmouth O

G- position in league table before match

Bolton: 6 6 8 13 8 5 5 4
Portsmouth: 13 15 18 15 19 20 16 16

Matches
- won
- drawn
- lost
- B home match

Bolton:
- 15.05.05 vs Everton **B**
- 13.08.05 vs Aston Villa
- 21.08.05 vs Everton
- 24.08.05 vs Newcastle United
- 27.08.05 vs West Ham United
- 11.09.05 vs Blackburn Rovers
- 18.09.05 vs Manchester City

Portsmouth:
- 17.09.05 vs Birmingham City
- 10.09.05 vs Everton
- 27.08.05 vs Manchester City
- 23.08.05 vs Aston Villa
- 20.08.05 vs West Brom
- 13.08.05 vs Tottenham Hotspur
- 15.05.05 vs West Brom

Goals
	scored													
scored	3	2	0	2	2	0	1		1	1	1	1	1	0	0
conceded	2	2	1	0	1	0	0		1	0	2	1	2	2	2

Goal Statistics

O Bolton Wanderers

by Half   by Situation
- first: 3
- second: 7
- set piece: 5
- open play: 5

O Portsmouth

by Half   by Situation
- first: 2
- second: 3
- set piece: 3
- open play: 1
- own goals: 1

Goals by Area

O Bolton Wanderers
Scored (Conceded)

6 (4)
4 (2)
0 (0)

O Portsmouth
Scored (Conceded)

3 (1)
0 (9)
2 (0)

Team Statistics

Starting Line-Ups

Bolton Wanderers: Jaaskelainen; Pedersen, Gardner, N'Gotty, Ben Haim; Nakata, Speed/O'Brien, Davies, Okocha/Stelios; Hunt/Diouf, Nolan

Portsmouth: Ashdown; O'Neil/Songo'o, Priske, Diao, O'Brien; Robert, Silva/Todorov, Hughes, Stefanovic; Taylor/Karadas, Vignal

4/5/1 **4/4/1/1**

Unused Sub: Walker, Borgetti   Unused Sub: Westerveld, Skopelitis

Premiership Totals	O Bolton	Portsmouth O
Premiership Appearances	1,672	686
Team Appearances	1,075	252
Goals Scored	198	44
Assists	165	68
Clean Sheets (goalkeepers)	38	3
Yellow Cards	218	82
Red Cards	10	8
Full Internationals	10	9

Age/Height

Bolton Wanderers Age: **28 yrs**
Portsmouth Age: **26 yrs, 4 mo**
Bolton Wanderers Height: **5'11"**
Portsmouth Height: **6'**

Match Statistics

League Table after Fixture

		Played	Won	Drawn	Lost	For	Against	Pts
● 1	Chelsea	7	7	0	0	14	1	21
● 2	Charlton	6	5	0	1	10	4	15
↑ 3	Bolton	7	4	2	1	8	4	14
↑ 4	West Ham	6	3	2	1	10	4	11
↓ 5	Man Utd	6	3	2	1	7	3	11
↓ 6	Man City	7	3	2	2	7	6	11
● 7	Arsenal	6	3	1	2	9	4	10
...	...	...	...	...	...	...	...	...
↓ 17	Portsmouth	7	1	2	4	5	9	5

Statistics	O Bolton	Portsmouth O
Goals	1	0
Shots on Target	2	4
Shots off Target	9	2
Hit Woodwork	0	0
Possession %	52	48
Corners	7	3
Offsides	4	2
Fouls	9	6
Disciplinary Points	8	8

1-2

PFC Lokomotiv Plovdiv ○
Bolton Wanderers ○

▶ Kevin Nolan is the matchwinner for Bolton

Event Line
Half time 0-0

51 ○ ⊕	Iliev G / RF / OP / OA
52 ○ ▪	Iliev G
56 ○ ⇄	Davies > Borgetti
56 ○ ⇄	Nolan > Fernandes
63 ○ ⇄	Stoynev > Vandev
66 ○ ⇄	Nakata > O'Brien
75 ○ ▪	Nakata
79 ○ ⊕	Tunchev / RF / OG / IA
	Assist: Pedersen
80 ○ ⇄	Halimi > Krizmanic
86 ○ ⊕	Nolan / RF / OP / OA
	Assist: Davies
90 ○ ▪	Jancevski

Full time 1-2

Sam Allardyce's selection gamble paid dividends as Bolton Wanderers once again left it late to beat Lokomotiv Plovdiv and therefore advance into the group stages of the UEFA Cup.

Georgi Iliev's stunning strike threatened to end Wanderers' debut European adventure almost as soon as it had begun but a bizarre own goal from Alexander Tunchev and a great, winning strike from substitute Kevin Nolan ensured that their name was in the hat for the group draw,

With the losses, through injury, of Nicky Hunt, Ivan Campo, Gary Speed and Radhi Jaidi, and also with the prospect of playing Wigan Athletic on Sunday in the Barclays Premiership, Sam Allardyce faced a major selection headache.

Former England goalkeeper Ian Walker made his debut and, Joey O'Brien, Fabrice Fernandes and Jared Borgetti all started a game for the first time in their Wanderers' careers, while Stelios, El-Hadji Diouf and Abdoulaye Faye all returned following the 1-0 win against Portsmouth at the weekend.

The game started with a fitting tribute to former Plovdiv president, Georgi Iliev, who was shot dead several weeks before the first leg. The home supporters held up posters of their president and displayed messages of condolence.

Venue:	Lokomotiv Stadium	Referee:	J.Hyytia (FIN)

Attendance: 14,000
Capacity: 18,600
Occupancy: 75%

PFC Lokomotiv Plovdiv
Bolton Wanderers

▶ The teams emerge in Bulgaria

Match Statistics

Starting Line-Ups

▶ 5/3/2   ▶ 4/5/1

Unused Sub: Kamburov, Mihaylov, Georgiev, Hristev, Zlatinov

Unused Sub: Jaaskelainen, Gardner, Fojut, Vaz Te

Statistics	Loko Plovdiv	Bolton
Goals	1	2
Shots on Target	2	2
Shots off Target	3	4
Hit Woodwork	0	0
Possession %	50	50
Corners	6	1
Offsides	3	4
Fouls	19	18
Disciplinary Points	8	4

Quote

🔓 **Sam Allardyce**

I took a walk along the beachfront and saw more Bolton Wanderers shirts than anything else this side of Bulgaria.

37

2-1

Wigan Athletic ○
Bolton Wanderers ○

▶ Kevin Davies brushes aside Stephane Henchoz

Event Line

7 ○ ▪	Nakata
22 ○ ⇄	Taylor > Chimbonda
Half time 0-0	
48 ○ ⊕	Camara / LF / OP / IA
54 ○ ⇄	Giannakopoulos > Okocha
57 ○ ⇄	Diouf > Gardner
63 ○ ⊕	McCulloch / RF / OP / IA
	Assist: Camara
66 ○ ▪	N'Gotty
68 ○ ⊕	Jaidi / H / OP / IA
	Assist: Giannakopoulos
84 ○ ⇄	Borgetti > Nakata
90 ○ ⇄	Connolly > Camara
Full time 2-1	

Wigan Athletic won the bragging rights in this local derby thanks to goals from Henri Camara and Lee McCulloch and in doing so denied Bolton Wanderers the opportunity of moving into the Barclays Premiership's second spot.

Wanderers pulled a goal back through Radhi Jaidi and fought all the way in the hope of rescuing a point, but the hosts hung on to claim their first victory over their neighbours in 15 years.

Sam Allardyce's Bolton Wanderers had a more familiar look about them following the previous week's UEFA Cup triumph in Bulgaria.

Gary Speed and Radhi Jaidi both passed fitness tests, and Kevin Nolan, Kevin Davies, Jussi Jaaskelainen and Hide Nakata all came back into the fold for Wanderers' first clash against Wigan Athletic since 1993 – and their first-ever trip to the JJB Stadium.

Quote

❝ Sam Allardyce

After going 2-0 down we created a huge amount of chances, but there was not enough quality finishing in their box.

Venue:	JJB Stadium	Referee:	A.G.Wiley - 05/06		Wigan Athletic
Attendance:	20,553	Matches:	8		Bolton Wanderers
Capacity:	25,023	Yellow Cards:	24		
Occupancy:	82%	Red Cards:	2		

Form Coming into Fixture

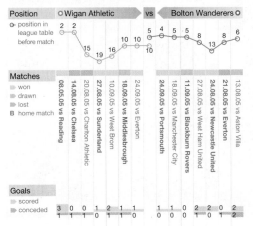

Goal Statistics

○ Wigan Athletic

by Half · by Situation

- first: 4
- second: 4
- set piece: 1
- open play: 7

○ Bolton Wanderers

by Half · by Situation

- first: 4
- second: 4
- set piece: 3
- open play: 5

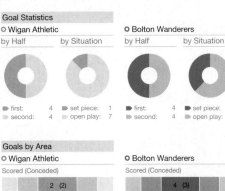

Goals by Area

○ Wigan Athletic

Scored (Conceded)

| 2 (2) |
| 5 (1) |
| 1 (2) |

○ Bolton Wanderers

Scored (Conceded)

| 4 (3) |
| 4 (1) |
| 0 (0) |

Team Statistics

Starting Line-Ups

Wigan Athletic: Filan; Baines, McCulloch, Henchoz, Francis, Kavanagh, Roberts, Camara Connolly, Chimbonda Taylor, Bullard; Nolan

4 / 4 / 2

Unused Sub: Pollitt, Jackson, McMillan

Bolton Wanderers: Jaaskelainen; Ben Haim, Jaidi, N'Gotty, Pedersen, Okocha Stelios, Davies, Speed, Nakata Borgetti, Gardner Diouf

4 / 5 / 1

Unused Sub: Walker, Faye

Premiership Totals	○ Wigan	Bolton ○
Premiership Appearances	553	1,652
Team Appearances	60	1,055
Goals Scored	32	203
Assists	21	162
Clean Sheets (goalkeepers)	13	39
Yellow Cards	72	211
Red Cards	1	10
Full Internationals	8	12

Age/Height

Wigan Athletic Age: **28 yrs, 4 mo**

Bolton Wanderers Age: **29 yrs, 6 mo**

Wigan Athletic Height: **5'11"**

Bolton Wanderers Height: **5'11"**

Match Statistics

League Table after Fixture

		Played	Won	Drawn	Lost	For	Against	Pts
●	1 Chelsea	8	8	0	0	18	2	24
●	2 Charlton	7	5	0	2	12	7	15
●	3 Tottenham	8	4	3	1	9	5	15
●	4 Man Utd	7	4	2	1	10	5	14
●	5 Bolton	8	4	2	2	9	6	14
↑	6 Man City	8	4	2	2	9	6	14
↑	7 Arsenal	7	4	1	2	10	4	13
↑	8 Wigan	7	4	1	2	7	5	13
↓	9 West Ham	7	3	3	1	11	5	12

Statistics	○ Wigan	Bolton ○
Goals	2	1
Shots on Target	9	4
Shots off Target	7	9
Hit Woodwork	0	0
Possession %	48	52
Corners	4	8
Offsides	6	4
Fouls	11	14
Disciplinary Points	0	8

5-1

Chelsea ○
Bolton Wanderers ○

▶ Radhi Jaidi and Tal Ben Haim put Didier Drogba under pressure

Event Line

4 ○ ⊕	Giannakopoulos / RF / OP / IA	
	Assist: Diouf	
33 ○ ▢	Drogba	
41 ○ ▢	Essien	
42 ○ ⇄	Gardner > Pedersen	

Half time 0-1

46 ○ ⇄	Gudjohnsen > Del Horno	
46 ○ ⇄	Nakata > Speed	
51 ○ ▢	Jaidi	
52 ○ ⊕	Drogba / RF / IFK / IA	
	Assist: Lampard	
55 ○ ⊕	Lampard / RF / OP / IA	
	Assist: Drogba	
58 ○ ▢	Gardner	
	Handball	
59 ○ ⊕	Lampard / RF / DFK / OA	
59 ○ ⇄	Ferreira > Cole J	
61 ○ ⊕	Drogba / RF / C / IA	
	Assist: Lampard	
65 ○ ▢	Nolan	
74 ○ ⊕	Gudjohnsen / RF / OP / IA	
	Assist: Makelele	
74 ○ ⇄	Cole C > Wright-Phillips	
75 ○ ⇄	Fernandes > Davies	

Full time 5-1

Two goals each from Didier Drogba and Frank Lampard plus a strike from former Wanderers star Eidur Gudjohnsen maintained Chelsea's winning start to the season with a comfortable victory against ten-man Bolton Wanderers.

A devastating ten-minute display of attacking football, just after half-time, from the defending champions put paid to Wanderers' hopes of causing an upset at Stamford Bridge.

Stelios' fourth-minute opener for the visitors threatened to put Chelsea's 100% start to the season in jeopardy - and for the remainder of the half this still appeared to be the case.

But seven minutes after the restart, Drogba instigated the comeback in which Jose Mourinho's men netted four goals and witnessed Wanderers substitute Ricardo Gardner get sent off for handball.

Gudjohnsen struck later in the game to complete his former club's heaviest defeat in three seasons.

Quote

❝ **Sam Allardyce**

Michael Essien should have been given a straight red card for his tackle on Tal Ben Haim and that was a key moment.

Premiership Milestone

▶ **150**

Kevin Nolan made his 150th Premiership appearance.

Venue:	Stamford Bridge	Referee:	R.Styles - 05/06		Chelsea
Attendance:	41,775	Matches:	9		Bolton Wanderers
Capacity:	42,449	Yellow Cards:	25		
Occupancy:	98%	Red Cards:	1		

Form Coming into Fixture

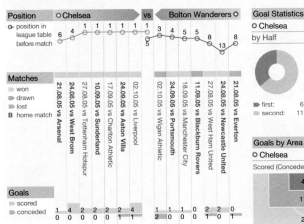

Position ○ Chelsea vs Bolton Wanderers ○

○- position in league table before match

Chelsea: 6 4 1 1 1 1 1
Bolton Wanderers: 3 5 4 5 5 8 13 8

Matches
- won
- drawn
- lost
- B home match

21.08.05 vs Arsenal
24.08.05 vs West Brom
27.08.05 vs Tottenham Hotspur
10.09.05 vs Sunderland
17.09.05 vs Charlton Athletic
24.09.05 vs Aston Villa
02.10.05 vs Liverpool

02.10.05 vs Wigan Athletic
24.09.05 vs Portsmouth
18.09.05 vs Manchester City
11.09.05 vs Blackburn Rovers
27.08.05 vs West Ham United
24.08.05 vs Newcastle United
21.08.05 vs Everton

Goals
| scored | 1 | 4 | 2 | 2 | 2 | 4 | | 1 | 1 | 1 | 0 | 2 | 2 | 0 |
| conceded | 0 | 0 | 0 | 0 | 1 | 1 | | 2 | 0 | 0 | 1 | 0 | 1 |

Goal Statistics

○ Chelsea

by Half | by Situation

- first: 6 — set piece: 6
- second: 11 — open play: 11

○ Bolton Wanderers

by Half | by Situation

- first: 2 — set piece: 2
- second: 5 — open play: 5

Goals by Area

○ Chelsea
Scored (Conceded)

4 (0)
11 (2)
2 (0)

○ Bolton Wanderers
Scored (Conceded)

3 (1)
4 (3)
0 (0)

Team Statistics

Starting Line-Ups

Del Horno / Gudjohnsen
Cole J / Ferreira
Stelios
Ben Haim
Lampard
Nolan
Terry
Jaidi
Cech
Makelele
Drogba
Davies / Fernandes
Faye
Jaaskelainen
Carvalho
N'Gotty
Essien
Speed / Nakata
Gallas
Wright-Phillips / Cole C
Diouf
Pedersen / Gardner

▶ 4/3/3 **▶ 4/5/1**

Unused Sub: Cudicini, Huth
Unused Sub: Walker, Borgetti

Premiership Totals	○ Chelsea	Bolton ○
Premiership Appearances	1,364	1,652
Team Appearances	928	964
Goals Scored	197	196
Assists	164	158
Clean Sheets (goalkeepers)	29	39
Yellow Cards	130	212
Red Cards	5	10
Full Internationals	13	11

Age/Height

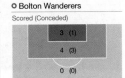

Chelsea Age	Bolton Wanderers Age
▶ 25 yrs, 11 mo	▶ 28 yrs, 9 mo
Chelsea Height	Bolton Wanderers Height
▶ 6'	▶ 5'11"

Match Statistics

League Table after Fixture

			Played	Won	Drawn	Lost	For	Against	Pts
●	1	Chelsea	9	9	0	0	23	3	27
↑	2	Tottenham	9	5	3	1	11	5	18
↑	3	Man Utd	8	5	2	1	13	6	17
↑	4	Wigan	8	5	1	2	8	5	16
↓	5	Charlton	7	5	0	2	12	7	15
●	6	Man City	8	4	2	2	9	6	14
↓	7	Bolton	9	4	2	3	10	11	14
↓	8	Arsenal	8	4	1	3	11	6	13
●	9	West Ham	7	3	3	1	11	5	12

Statistics	○ Chelsea	Bolton ○
Goals	5	1
Shots on Target	8	2
Shots off Target	9	2
Hit Woodwork	0	1
Possession %	60	40
Corners	5	3
Offsides	6	0
Fouls	10	17
Disciplinary Points	8	20

41

1-1

Besiktas JK ○
Bolton Wanderers ○

▶ Jared Borgetti is on target in Turkey

Event Line

7 ○ ⊕ Ailton / LF / OP / OA	
Assist: Metin	
29 ○ ⊕ Borgetti / LF / OP / IA	
Assist: Diouf	
36 ○ ⇄ Uzulmez > Metin	
Half time 1-1	
46 ○ ⇄ Zan > Toraman	
59 ○ ⇄ Nolan > Fernandes	
70 ○ ⇄ Dogan > Zan	
Full time 1-1	

Sam Allardyce's injury-ravaged Bolton Wanderers got the result they wanted as they battled from behind to earn a point in their opening match of the UEFA Cup group stage.

Brazilian striker Ailton put Besiktas in front after seven minutes but Wanderers fought their way back into the game thanks to Jared Borgetti's immaculate finish just before the half-hour mark.

Located on the banks of the Bosphorus, the Inonu Stadium was swimming in a sea of passion. The small travelling army of Bolton Wanderers supporters added to the atmosphere generated by the vociferous Besiktas supporters.

Numerous injuries had forced the Wanderers boss into making seven changes to his side, and with the Barclays Premiership match against West Bromwich Albion on Sunday, the Wanderers boss also rested several key players, who found themselves on the bench.

► El-Hadji Diouf takes a tumble

Match Statistics

Starting Line-Ups

▶ 4/4/1/1   ▶ 4/5/1

Unused Sub: Sahin, Gunes, Cihan,
Dursun Ah

Unused Sub: Jaaskelainen, N'Gotty,
Pedersen, Fojut, Vaz Te, Davies

Statistics	○ Besiktas	Bolton ○
Goals	1	1
Shots on Target	1	2
Shots off Target	4	3
Hit Woodwork	0	0
Possession %	55	45
Corners	7	8
Offsides	4	5
Fouls	15	23
Disciplinary Points	0	0

Quote

❝ **Sam Allardyce**

We gave away a stupid early goal to let Besiktas get their tails up, but I thought we did extremely well after that.

2-0

Bolton Wanderers ○
West Bromwich Albion ○

► Henrik Pedersen battles for possession

Event Line	
Half time 0-0	
64 ○ ⇄	Kanu > Horsfield
69 ○ ▨	Albrechtsen
73 ○ ▨	Nolan
81 ○ ⊕	Nakata / RF / DFK / OA
	Assist: Nakata
82 ○ ▨	Diouf
84 ○ ⇄	Fadiga > Diouf
84 ○ ⇄	Earnshaw > Clement
86 ○ ▨	Carter
90 ○ ⊕	Nolan / RF / OP / OA
Full time 2-0	

Hidetoshi Nakata grabbed his first goal in Bolton Wanderers colours to put his side on course for a 2-0 victory against West Bromwich Albion.

The Japan international ended a match of frustration for the home side when he fired an 81st minute free-kick past Baggies on-loan 'keeper Chris Kirkland.

Stand-in captain Kevin Nolan confirmed Wanderers superior advantage by curling home his fourth goal of the campaign in injury time.

Aiming to avoid a post-European malaise, following his side's midweek draw against Besiktas in Istanbul, and a third successive Barclays Premiership defeat, Sam Allardyce made six changes to his side.

Joey O'Brien, who played a starring role in Turkey, was handed his first league start for the Club in the unfamiliar position of right-back. Bruno N'Gotty returned to partner Tal Ben Haim in the centre of defence, while Jussi Jaaskelainen, Henrik Pedersen, Kevin Davies, Stelios and Nolan were recalled.

The personnel change was effective for Allardyce as none of his players looked jaded from their recent hectic schedule.

Quote	Premiership Milestone
❝ **Sam Allardyce**	► **25**
Hidetoshi Nakata's overall play is beginning to get better and better and if he continues like that he will be a good capture for us.	Kevin Nolan netted his 25th Premiership goal.

Venue:	Reebok Stadium	Referee:	M.L.Dean - 05/06		Bolton Wanderers
Attendance:	24,151	Matches:	7		West Bromwich Albion
Capacity:	28,101	Yellow Cards:	21		
Occupancy:	86%	Red Cards:	0		

Form Coming into Fixture

Position ○ Bolton Wanderers vs West Bromwich Albion ○

- position in league table before match

Bolton: 13, 8, 5, 5, 4, 3, 5
West Brom: 16, 8, 19, 18, 17, 17, 15, 12, 7

Matches
- won
- drawn
- lost
- B home match

Bolton matches: 24.08.05 vs Newcastle United, 27.08.05 vs West Ham United, 11.09.05 vs Blackburn Rovers, 18.09.05 vs Manchester City, 24.09.05 vs Portsmouth, 02.10.05 vs Wigan Athletic, 15.10.05 vs Chelsea

West Brom matches: 15.10.05 vs Arsenal, 01.10.05 vs Blackburn Rovers, 24.09.05 vs Charlton Athletic, 17.09.05 vs Sunderland, 10.09.05 vs Wigan Athletic, 27.08.05 vs Birmingham City, 24.08.05 vs Chelsea

Goals
- scored
- conceded

Bolton: scored 2 2 0 1 1 1 1 / conceded 0 1 0 0 0 2 5
West Brom: scored 2 0 1 1 1 2 0 / conceded 1 2 2 1 2 3 4

Goal Statistics

○ Bolton Wanderers
by Half / by Situation
- first: 3
- second: 5
- set piece: 2
- open play: 6

○ West Bromwich Albion
by Half / by Situation
- first: 3
- second: 4
- set piece: 3
- open play: 4

Goals by Area
○ Bolton Wanderers — Scored (Conceded)
3 (0) / 5 (7) / 0 (1)

○ West Bromwich Albion — Scored (Conceded)
1 (3) / 4 (11) / 2 (1)

Team Statistics

Starting Line-Ups

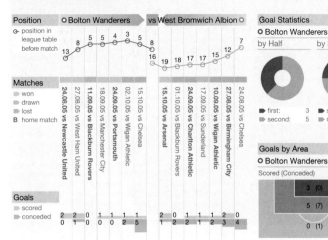

Bolton: Jaaskelainen; N'Gotty, Faye, Ben Haim, O'Brien; Pedersen, Nakata, Davies, Nolan, Stelios; Diouf/Fadiga; Horsfield/Kanu, Kamara

West Brom: Kirkland; Albrechtsen, Greening, Davies C, Watson, Moore; Carter, Clement/Earnshaw, Robinson

4/5/1 (Bolton)
Unused Sub: Walker, Jaidi, Fernandes, Borgetti

5/3/2 (West Brom)
Unused Sub: Kuszczak, Scimeca, Chaplow

Premiership Totals	○ Bolton	West Brom ○
Premiership Appearances	962	1,092
Team Appearances	779	370
Goals Scored	112	103
Assists	84	86
Clean Sheets (goalkeepers)	39	9
Yellow Cards	130	100
Red Cards	7	5
Full Internationals	9	5

Age/Height
Bolton Wanderers Age: **27 yrs, 10 mo**
West Bromwich Albion Age: **26 yrs, 8 mo**
Bolton Wanderers Height: **6'**
West Bromwich Albion Height: **6'1"**

Match Statistics

League Table after Fixture

		Played	Won	Drawn	Lost	For	Against	Pts
● 1	Chelsea	10	9	1	0	24	4	28
● 2	Charlton	9	6	1	2	15	9	19
● 3	Tottenham	10	5	4	1	12	6	19
● 4	Wigan	9	6	1	2	10	5	19
● 5	Man Utd	9	5	3	1	14	7	18
● 6	Man City	10	5	2	3	11	8	17
↑ 7	Bolton	10	5	2	3	12	11	17
...		...	...	...	...	...	...	...
● 16	West Brom	10	2	2	6	9	18	8

Statistics	○ Bolton	West Brom ○
Goals	2	0
Shots on Target	12	1
Shots off Target	7	3
Hit Woodwork	0	0
Possession %	52	48
Corners	10	1
Offsides	5	1
Fouls	13	16
Disciplinary Points	8	8

1-0

Bolton Wanderers ○
West Ham United ○

➡ Jared Borgetti celebrates his winning goal

Event Line

17 ○ ▪	Diagne-Faye	
45 ○ ▪	Ben Haim	
Half time 0-0		
46 ○ ⇄	Djetou > Diagne-Faye	
59 ○ ⇄	Pedersen > Giannakopoulos	
64 ○ ⊕	Borgetti / H / OP / 6Y	
	Assist: Fadiga	
72 ○ ⇄	Newton > Clarke	
73 ○ ⇄	Aliadiere > Sheringham	
75 ○ ▪	Dailly	
79 ○ ⇄	N'Gotty > Fernandes	
86 ○ ⇄	Fletcher > Harewood	
Full time 1-0		

Jared Borgetti hit a second-half winner to put Bolton Wanderers into the last 16 of the Carling Cup at the expense of their Barclays Premiership rivals West Ham United.

Mexico's all-time leading scorer hit his third goal of the campaign in the 64th minute when he nodded in Khalilou Fadiga's deep cross at the far post.

The striker was one of six players recalled to Sam Allardyce's starting line-up as the Wanderers manager continued with his rotation policy amid a frenetic schedule of Premier League and UEFA Cup fixtures.

Ian Walker, Khalilou Fadiga, Radhi Jaidi and Ricardo Gardner were the other changes from the side that beat West Brom on Sunday.

► Kevin Nolan shakes the hand of Shaka Hislop

Match Statistics

Starting Line-Ups

▶ **4/5/1**

Unused Sub: Jaaskelainen, Nakata

▶ **4/4/2**

Unused Sub: Bywater, Williams

Statistics	○ Bolton	West Ham ○
Goals	1	0
Shots on Target	4	10
Shots off Target	3	5
Hit Woodwork	0	0
Possession %	46	54
Corners	3	8
Offsides	4	2
Fouls	12	11
Disciplinary Points	8	4

Age/Height

Bolton Wanderers Age	West Ham United Age
▶ **28 yrs, 8 mo**	▶ **27 yrs, 8 mo**
Bolton Wanderers Height	West Ham United Height
▶ **6'**	▶ **6'**

Quote

🔟 **Sam Allardyce**

We produced the all-important bit of quality that we needed and that was the only difference between the sides.

0-1

Charlton Athletic ○
Bolton Wanderers ○

▶ Kevin Davies tries to stop Jonathan Spector

Event Line

41 ○ ▪ Murphy	
Half time 0-0	
60 ○ ⇄ Hughes > Smertin	
62 ○ ⇄ Johansson > Rommedahl	
68 ○ ⇄ Borgetti > Davies	
72 ○ ⊕ Nolan / RF / OP / 6Y	
Assist: Nakata	
77 ○ ⇄ Holland > Kishishev	
83 ○ ⇄ Okocha > Diouf	
86 ○ ⇄ Ben Haim > Nakata	
Full time 0-1	

Kevin Nolan played a true captain's role by netting the only goal of the game to give Bolton Wanderers another victory at The Valley.

The midfielder retained the skipper's armband despite the inclusion of stand-in skipper Gary Speed, who returned to the starting line-up following a period on the sidelines with a back injury, and hit his fifth goal of the campaign to maintain his side's excellent recent form.

The versatility of Sam Allardyce's squad was once again highly visible at the Valley, as the Wanderers manager made wholesale changes to his side.

With campaigns firmly underway on three fronts, Allardyce reverted to a more orthodox Barclays Premiership line-up following last Wednesday's Carling Cup victory against West Ham United.

In came Jussi Jaaskelainen, Bruno N'Gotty, Speed, Kevin Davies, Hidetoshi Nakata and El-Hadji Diouf at the expense of Ian Walker, Tal Ben Haim, Khalilou Fadiga, Fabrice Fernandes, Jared Borgetti and Stelios.

Regular captain Jay Jay Okocha passed a fitness test to find himself on the bench.

Quote

❻ Sam Allardyce

We let people say what they like about us and we do the playing and get the results.

48

Venue:	The Valley	Referee:	M.Clattenburg - 05/06	**Charlton Athletic**
Attendance:	26,175	Matches:	13	**Bolton Wanderers**
Capacity:	27,111	Yellow Cards:	47	
Occupancy:	97%	Red Cards:	3	

Form Coming into Fixture

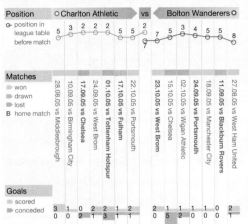

Position ○ Charlton Athletic vs Bolton Wanderers ○
- position in league table before match

5 3 2 2 2 5 5 2 7 5 3 4 5 5 8

Matches
- won
- drawn
- lost
- B home match

28.08.05 vs Middlesbrough
10.09.05 vs Birmingham City
17.09.05 vs Chelsea
24.09.05 vs West Brom
01.10.05 vs Tottenham Hotspur
17.10.05 vs Fulham
22.10.05 vs Portsmouth

23.10.05 vs West Brom
15.10.05 vs Chelsea
02.10.05 vs Wigan Athletic
24.09.05 vs Portsmouth
18.09.05 vs Manchester City
11.09.05 vs Blackburn Rovers
27.08.05 vs West Ham United

Goals
- scored: 3 1 0 2 2 1 2 — 2 1 1 1 1 0 2
- conceded: 0 0 2 1 3 1 1 — 0 5 2 0 0 0 1

Goal Statistics

○ Charlton Athletic

by Half		by Situation	
first:	5	set piece:	2
second:	6	open play:	9

○ Bolton Wanderers

by Half		by Situation	
first:	2	set piece:	3
second:	6	open play:	5

Goals by Area

○ Charlton Athletic — Scored (Conceded)

1 (1)
9 (7)
1 (0)

○ Bolton Wanderers — Scored (Conceded)

1 (0)
5 (7)
2 (1)

Team Statistics

Starting Line-Ups

Spector · Ambrose · Nolan · O'Brien
Murphy · Nakata / Ben Haim
Hreidarsson · Jaidi
Andersen · Kishishev / Holland · Bothroyd · Davies / Borgetti · Faye · Jaaskelainen
Perry · N'Gotty
Smertin / Hughes · Speed
Young · Rommedahl / Johansson · Diouf / Okocha · Gardner

4 / 5 / 1 **4 / 5 / 1**

Unused Sub: Kiely, El Karkouri
Unused Sub: Walker, Djetou

Premiership Totals

	○ Charlton	Bolton ○
Premiership Appearances	1,621	1,507
Team Appearances	756	910
Goals Scored	111	176
Assists	107	146
Clean Sheets (goalkeepers)	3	40
Yellow Cards	173	204
Red Cards	5	11
Full Internationals	10	11

Age/Height

Charlton Athletic Age **27 yrs, 9 mo**
Bolton Wanderers Age **28 yrs, 6 mo**

Charlton Athletic Height **5'11"**
Bolton Wanderers Height **6'**

Match Statistics

League Table after Fixture

		Played	Won	Drawn	Lost	For	Against	Pts
● 1	Chelsea	11	10	1	0	28	6	31
↑ 2	Wigan	10	7	1	2	11	5	22
● 3	Tottenham	11	5	5	1	13	7	20
↑ 4	Bolton	11	6	2	3	13	11	20
↓ 5	Charlton	10	6	1	3	15	10	19
↓ 6	Man Utd	10	5	3	2	15	11	18
↑ 7	Arsenal	10	5	2	3	13	7	17
↓ 8	Man City	10	5	2	3	11	8	17
● 9	West Ham	10	4	3	3	14	10	15

Statistics

	○ Charlton	Bolton ○
Goals	0	1
Shots on Target	4	7
Shots off Target	3	4
Hit Woodwork	0	0
Possession %	46	54
Corners	4	2
Offsides	1	0
Fouls	11	13
Disciplinary Points	4	0

1-0

Bolton Wanderers ○
Zenit St.Petersburg ○

▶ Stelios tries to find space

Event Line

24 ○ ⊕ Nolan / RF / IFK / 6Y	
Assist: Giannakopoulos	
25 ○ ⇄ Gorshkov > Skrtel	
37 ○ ▨ Hagen	
Half time 1-0	
62 ○ ▨ Flachbart	
66 ○ ⇄ Okocha > Nakata	
74 ○ ⇄ Borgetti > Davies	
85 ○ ⇄ Diouf > Nolan	
90 ○ ⇄ Kozlov > Vlasov	
Full time 1-0	

Torrential rain failed to dampen Bolton Wanderers as they saw off Russian outfit Zenit St Petersburg thanks to Kevin Nolan's sixth goal of the season.

The stand-in skipper stabbed home from close-range in the 24th minute to give his side a priceless victory on a waterlogged pitch and put them ever closer to the last 32 of the UEFA Cup.

Wanderers manager Sam Allardyce made just two changes from the side that beat Charlton Athletic at the Valley on Saturday with Tal Ben Haim and Stelios returning to the starting line-up at the expense of Radhi Jaidi and El-Hadji Diouf, who dropped to the bench.

Venue:	Reebok Stadium	Referee:	M.Trefoloni (ITA)		**Bolton Wanderers**
Attendance:	15,905				**Zenit St.Petersburg**
Capacity:	28,101				
Occupancy:	57%				

▶ Tal Ben Haim finds himself under pressure

Match Statistics

Starting Line-Ups

Statistics	o Bolton	Zenit o
Goals	1	0
Shots on Target	3	3
Shots off Target	4	7
Hit Woodwork	0	0
Possession %	44	56
Corners	0	4
Offsides	4	1
Fouls	16	18
Disciplinary Points	0	8

▶ **4/5/1**

▶ **4/4/2**

Unused Sub: Walker, Jaidi, Fojut, Vaz Te

Unused Sub: Malafeev, Stroev, Kozhanov, Cadikovski, Poskus

Quote

❝ **Sam Allardyce**

Jussi Jaaskelainen is playing at the top of his game. He made a couple of vital saves in the second half to help keep a clean sheet.

1-0

Bolton Wanderers ⚪
Tottenham Hotspur ⚪

▶ Hidetoshi Nakata prepares to control the ball

Event Line

32 ⚪ ⊕ Nolan / RF / OP / OA	
Assist: Davies	
Half time 1-0	
49 ⚪ ⇄ Borgetti > Davies	
59 ⚪ ⇄ Nakata > Giannakopoulos	
62 ⚪ ⇄ Keane > Lee	
71 ⬜ Dawson	
84 ⚪ ⇄ Brown > Jenas	
84 ⚪ ⇄ N'Gotty > Diouf	
Full time 1-0	

Captain Kevin Nolan hit his seventh goal of the season to send Bolton Wanderers to third place in the Barclays Premiership.

The Wanderers midfielder fired the game's only goal in the 31st minute to give Wanderers their sixth successive league victory against an in-form Spurs, who were undefeated on their travels in the league this season.

And what a goal it was – an unstoppable strike that flew beyond England 'keeper Paul Robinson, which would surely have impressed the watching England head coach Sven-Goran Eriksson.

Sam Allardyce made two changes to his side following Thursday night's UEFA Cup victory against Zenit St Petersburg. El-Hadji Diouf and Radhi Jaidi came in at the expense of Hidetoshi Nakata and Bruno N'Gotty, who were both named among the substitutes.

Quote

 Sam Allardyce

A little good fortune is always needed. They threw everything at us and we had to defend correctly.

Venue:	Reebok Stadium	Referee:	H.M.Webb - 05/06	**Bolton Wanderers**
Attendance:	26,634	Matches:	11	**Tottenham Hotspur**
Capacity:	28,101	Yellow Cards:	33	
Occupancy:	95%	Red Cards:	1	

Form Coming into Fixture

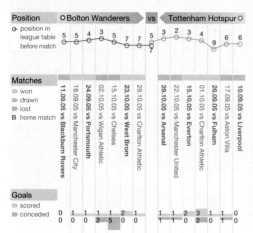

Position

O Bolton Wanderers vs Tottenham Hotspur O

position in league table before match

Bolton: 5 5 4 3 5 7 7 5 7
Tottenham: 3 2 3 4 9 6 6 6

Matches
- won
- drawn
- lost
- B home match

	vs Blackburn Rovers	vs Manchester City	vs Portsmouth	vs Wigan Athletic	vs Chelsea	vs West Brom	vs Charlton Athletic	vs Arsenal	vs Manchester United	vs Everton	vs Charlton Athletic	vs Fulham	vs Aston Villa	vs Liverpool
	11.09.05	18.09.05	24.09.05	02.10.05	15.10.05	23.10.05	29.10.05	29.10.05	22.10.05	15.10.05	01.10.05	26.09.05	17.09.05	10.09.05

Goals
- scored
- conceded

scored: 0 1 1 1 1 2 1 | 1 1 2 3 1 0
conceded: 0 0 0 2 5 0 0 | 1 1 0 2 0 1 0

Goal Statistics

O Bolton Wanderers

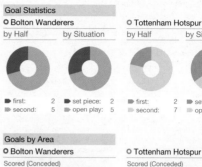

by Half · by Situation

- first: 2
- second: 5
- set piece: 2
- open play: 5

O Tottenham Hotspur

by Half · by Situation

- first: 2
- second: 7
- set piece: 3
- open play: 6

Goals by Area

O Bolton Wanderers

Scored (Conceded)

1 (0)
4 (6)
2 (1)

O Tottenham Hotspur

Scored (Conceded)

1 (1)
7 (3)
1 (1)

Team Statistics

Starting Line-Ups

Bolton: Jaaskelainen; Gardner, Diouf, N'Gotty, Speed, Jaidi, Faye, Davies, Borgetti, Ben Haim, Nolan, O'Brien, Stelios, Nakata

Tottenham: Stalteri, Jenas, Brown, Dawson, Mido, Tainio, Carrick, Robinson, Defoe, King, Davids, Lee, Keane

4/5/1

Unused Sub: Walker, Okocha

4/4/2 (Diamond)

Unused Sub: Cerny, Kelly, Reid

Premiership Totals

	O Bolton	Tottenham O
Premiership Appearances	1,490	995
Team Appearances	893	517
Goals Scored	175	136
Assists	140	95
Clean Sheets (goalkeepers)	41	36
Yellow Cards	209	76
Red Cards	11	4
Full Internationals	11	11

Age/Height

Bolton Wanderers Age **28 yrs, 6 mo**

Tottenham Hotspur Age **25 yrs, 9 mo**

Bolton Wanderers Height **6'**

Tottenham Hotspur Height **5'11"**

Match Statistics

League Table after Fixture

		Played	Won	Drawn	Lost	For	Against	Pts
● 1	Chelsea	12	10	1	1	28	7	31
● 2	Wigan	11	8	1	2	13	5	25
↑ 3	Bolton	12	7	2	3	14	11	23
↓ 4	Man Utd	11	6	3	2	16	11	21
↓ 5	Arsenal	11	6	2	3	16	8	20
↓ 6	Tottenham	12	5	5	2	13	8	20
↓ 7	Man City	12	6	2	4	15	11	20
● 8	Charlton	11	6	1	4	16	14	19
● 9	West Ham	11	5	3	3	15	10	18

Statistics

	O Bolton	Tottenham O
Goals	1	0
Shots on Target	8	7
Shots off Target	1	2
Hit Woodwork	1	1
Possession %	50	50
Corners	6	5
Offsides	2	5
Fouls	13	9
Disciplinary Points	0	4

1-1

Vitoria Guimaraes SC ○
Bolton Wanderers ○

▶ The travelling fans make their presence felt

Event Line	
Half time 0-0	
59 ○ ⇄ Speed > Nakata	
60 ○ ⇄ Targino > Monteiro	
64 ○ ⇄ Diouf > Borgetti	
65 ○ ■ Dragoner	
79 ○ ■ Jaaskelainen	
82 ○ ⇄ Paulo Sergio > Neca	
86 ○ ⊕ Saganowski / H / OP / IA	
	Assist: Targino
87 ○ ⇄ Vaz Te > Okocha	
88 ○ ⊕ Vaz Te / RF / OP / IA	
	Assist: Diouf
89 ○ ■ O'Brien	
89 ○ ■ Targino	
Full time 1-1	

Substitute Ricardo Vaz Te hit a wonder goal in his homeland less than 60 seconds after replacing Jay Jay Okocha to earn Bolton Wanderers a priceless point in Portugal.

Wanderers once again had to come back from behind in the UEFA Cup when Marek Saganowski put the hosts in front with a diving header as late as the 86th minute.

But the 19 year-old substitute grabbed the headlines with his second professional goal to put Wanderers on course for qualification to the last 32.

Jared Borgetti came into the starting line-up at the expense of Kevin Davies, who failed to travel with the team to Portugal after suffering a recurrence of a rib injury he picked up in Wanderers' last UEFA Cup outing against Zenit St Petersburg.

Sam Allardyce made a total of four changes from his side's last game – against Spurs over a fortnight ago – with Hidetoshi Nakata, Jay Jay Okocka and Bruno N'Gotty coming in for Gary Speed, El Hadji Diouf and Radhi Jaidi.

Wanderers went into the game in buoyant mood courtesy of five successive wins.

Venue: Estadio D.Afonso Henriques   Referee: L.Duhamel (FRA)
Attendance: 20,000
Capacity: 30,000
Occupancy: 67%

Vitoria Guimaraes SC
Bolton Wanderers

▶ Ricardo Vaz Te celebrates his late leveller

Match Statistics

Starting Line-Ups

▶ **4/4/2** (Diamond)   ▶ **4/5/1**

Unused Sub: Freitas, Geromel,
Zezinho, Moreno, Manoel

Unused Sub: Walker, Hunt, Jaidi,
Fadiga

Statistics	○ Guimaraes	Bolton ○
Goals	1	1
Shots on Target	5	2
Shots off Target	6	5
Hit Woodwork	0	0
Possession %	55	45
Corners	5	3
Offsides	0	9
Fouls	17	18
Disciplinary Points	8	8

Quote

❝ **Sam Allardyce**

I thought Ricardo Vaz Te's first
touch could have been a little
better, but then he struck an
absolutely fantastic goal.

2-1

Fulham ○
Bolton Wanderers ○

➡ Tal Ben Haim closes down Collins John

Event Line

4 ○ ⊕ McBride / RF / OP / IA	
Assist: Radzinski	
18 ○ ⊕ McBride / RF / OP / IA	
Assist: Crossley	
32 ○ ⇄ N'Gotty > Jaidi	
38 ○ Speed	
42 ○ Ben Haim	
45 ○ Davies	
Half time 2-0	
51 ○ Rosenior	
53 ○ ⇄ Okocha > Nakata	
59 ○ ⇄ Djetou > Diagne-Faye	
61 ○ ⇄ Legwinski > Boa Morte	
68 ○ Okocha	
83 ○ Nolan	
86 ○ O'Brien	
88 ○ Bocanegra	
89 ○ ⇄ Helguson > John	
90 ○ ◢ Diouf	
2nd Bookable Offence	
90 ○ ⊕ Legwinski / RF / OG / IA	
Assist: Nolan	
Full time 2-1	

A Brian McBride brace consigned Bolton Wanderers to their first defeat in eight games as the USA international's first-half double proved to be enough for Fulham.

Although Cottagers substitute Sylvain Legwinski struck the ball past team-mate Mark Crossley in the 90th minute to give Wanderers a consolation, the writing was effectively on the wall for Wanderers midway through the opening 45 minutes.

Wanderers' great run of three successive Barclays Premiership clean sheets also came to end as McBride netted his first of the afternoon on four minutes. The big American then doubled his tally and his side's lead 14 minutes later to effectively put the result beyond doubt.

Following on from their 1-1 draw against Vitoria Guimaraes in the UEFA Cup just three days earlier, Wanderers manager Sam Allardyce made four changes to his side. Kevin Davies returned from a rib injury to lead the line, while Gary Speed, Radhi Jaidi and Diouf were recalled to the starting line-up.

Bruno N'Gotty and Jay Jay Okocha started from the bench, while Jared Borgetti was omitted from the squad and Stelios sidelined with an ankle injury.

Quote

🔊 **Sam Allardyce**

You have to be in control of your emotions and anyone who got booked for mouthing off will be dealt with and fined.

Premiership Milestone

➡ **50**

Gary Speed made his 50th Premiership appearance in the colours of Bolton.

Venue:	Craven Cottage	Referee:	G.Poll - 05/06	**Fulham**
Attendance:	19,768	Matches:	15	**Bolton Wanderers**
Capacity:	22,646	Yellow Cards:	57	
Occupancy:	87%	Red Cards:	2	

Form Coming into Fixture

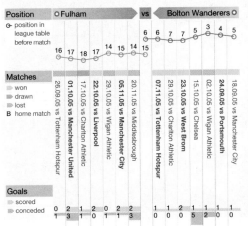

Position

- o Fulham
- vs
- Bolton Wanderers o

G- position in league table before match

Fulham: 16 17 18 17 14 15 14 15
Bolton: 6 6 7 7 5 3 4 5

Matches

- won
- drawn
- lost
- B home match

Fulham:
26.09.05 vs Tottenham Hotspur
01.10.05 vs Manchester United
17.10.05 vs Charlton Athletic
22.10.05 vs Liverpool
29.10.05 vs Wigan Athletic
05.11.05 vs Manchester City
20.11.05 vs Middlesbrough

Bolton:
07.11.05 vs Tottenham Hotspur
29.10.05 vs Charlton Athletic
23.10.05 vs West Brom
15.10.05 vs Chelsea
02.10.05 vs Wigan Athletic
24.09.05 vs Portsmouth
18.09.05 vs Manchester City

Goals
- scored
- conceded

Fulham scored: 0 2 1 2 0 2 2
Fulham conceded: 1 3 1 0 1 1 3

Bolton scored: 1 1 2 1 1 1 1
Bolton conceded: 0 0 0 5 2 0 0

Goal Statistics

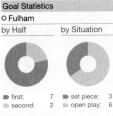

o Fulham
by Half | by Situation
- first: 7 / set piece: 3
- second: 2 / open play: 6

o Bolton Wanderers
by Half | by Situation
- first: 3 / set piece: 2
- second: 5 / open play: 6

Goals by Area

o Fulham
Scored (Conceded)
- 0 (2)
- 8 (8)
- 1 (0)

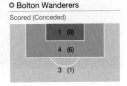

o Bolton Wanderers
Scored (Conceded)
- 1 (0)
- 4 (6)
- 3 (1)

Team Statistics

Starting Line-Ups

Fulham: Rosenior, Radzinski, Boa Morte (Legwinski), Bocanegra, Crossley, Diop, McBride, Goma, Malbranque, Volz, John (Helguson)

Bolton: Nolan, O'Brien, Nakata (Okocha), Ben Haim, Davies, Faye (Djetou), Jaidi (N'Gotty), Speed, Diouf, Gardner, Jaaskelainen

Fulham: 4/5/1
Bolton: 4/5/1

Unused Sub: Warner, Knight, Pearce
Unused Sub: Walker, Vaz Te

Premiership Totals	o Fulham	Bolton o
Premiership Appearances	1,232	1,579
Team Appearances	860	931
Goals Scored	134	179
Assists	118	149
Clean Sheets (goalkeepers)	49	42
Yellow Cards	145	209
Red Cards	11	11
Full Internationals	9	11

Age/Height

Fulham Age: **28 yrs, 4 mo**
Bolton Wanderers Age: **28 yrs, 6 mo**
Fulham Height: **5'10"**
Bolton Wanderers Height: **5'11"**

Match Statistics

League Table after Fixture

		Played	Won	Drawn	Lost	For	Against	Pts
● 6	Bolton	13	7	2	4	15	13	23
● 7	Liverpool	12	6	4	2	13	8	22
● 8	Man City	14	6	3	5	15	12	21
● 9	West Ham	13	5	4	4	17	13	19
↑ 10	Middlesbrough	14	5	4	5	20	20	19
↓ 11	Charlton	13	6	1	6	17	18	19
● 12	Newcastle	14	5	3	6	12	14	18
● 13	Blackburn	14	5	3	6	15	18	18
↑ 14	Fulham	14	4	3	7	16	20	15

Statistics	o Fulham	Bolton o
Goals	2	1
Shots on Target	7	3
Shots off Target	3	2
Hit Woodwork	0	0
Possession %	45	55
Corners	3	6
Offsides	1	6
Fouls	17	18
Disciplinary Points	8	34

2-1

Bolton Wanderers ○
Leicester City ○

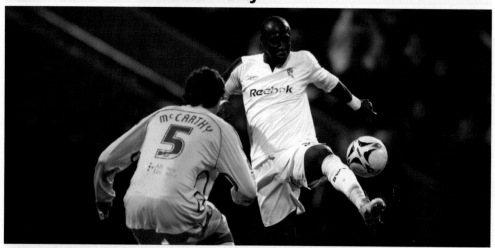

▶ Khalilou Fadiga brings the ball down

Event Line	
Half time 0-0	
46 ○ ⇄ Campo > Speed	
51 ○ ⇄ Fadiga > Okocha	
62 ○ ▢ Davies	
70 ○ ⇄ Sylla > Hughes	
83 ○ ⇄ Borgetti > Davies	
84 ○ ⇄ McCarthy > Tiatto	
104 ○ ⊕ Borgetti / LF / IFK / 6Y	
Assist: Djetou	
106 ○ ⊕ Vaz Te / RF / OP / IA	
Assist: Hunt	
109 ○ ⇄ Sheehan > Stearman	
110 ○ ⊕ Williams / RF / OP / OA	
Assist: Gudjonsson	
111 ○ ▢ McCarthy	
Full time 2-1	

Wanderers progressed to the quarter-finals of the Carling Cup – but only after Championship outfit Leicester City bravely held them until extra time.

Goals from substitute Jared Borgetti and Ricardo Vaz Te put the Barclays Premiership outfit in the hat, but a consolation strike from Gareth Williams ensured that the tie ended in dramatic fashion.

Sam Allardyce made four changes from the side that lost to Fulham on Sunday. Martin Djetou and Vaz Te started for the first time this season, while Nicky Hunt returned to action after recovering from the broken leg he suffered in September. Jay Jay Okocha was the other alteration.

Venue:	Reebok Stadium	Referee:	D.J.Gallagher - 05/06	**Bolton Wanderers**
Attendance:	13,067	Matches:	16	**Leicester City**
Capacity:	28,101	Yellow Cards:	36	
Occupancy:	47%	Red Cards:	3	

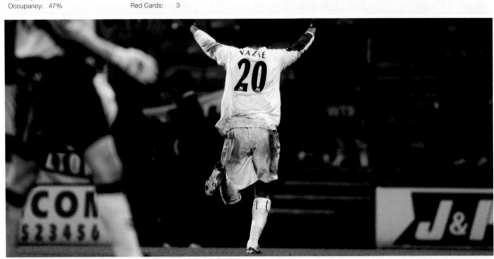

► Ricardo Vaz Te celebrates his decisive strike

Match Statistics

Starting Line-Ups

► **4**/**5**/**1**   ► **4**/**5**/**1**

Unused Sub: Howarth, N'Gotty   Unused Sub: Gerrbrand, Kisnorbo

Statistics	○ Bolton	Leicester ○
Goals	2	1
Shots on Target	6	2
Shots off Target	13	7
Hit Woodwork	0	0
Possession %	60	40
Corners	3	2
Offsides	9	0
Fouls	14	22
Disciplinary Points	4	4

Age/Height

Bolton Wanderers Age

► **28 yrs, 11 mo**

Bolton Wanderers Height

► **6'**

Leicester City Age

► **26 yrs, 4 mo**

Leicester City Height

► **6'**

Quote

🄶 **Sam Allardyce**

I didn't want extra-time, but I'm glad we got through and we can now look forward to the draw.

2-0

Bolton Wanderers ○
Arsenal ○

▶ El-Hadji Diouf takes on Gilberto

Event Line

20 ○ ⊕	Diagne-Faye / H / C / IA
	Assist: Giannakopoulos
32 ○ ⊕	Giannakopoulos / RF / OP / IA
	Assist: Davies
Half time 2-0	
47 ○	Diagne-Faye
50 ○	Lauren
68 ○ ⇄	Reyes > Fabregas
68 ○ ⇄	Bergkamp > van Persie
73 ○ ⇄	Eboue > Lauren
81 ○ ⇄	Vaz Te > Giannakopoulos
86 ○ ⇄	Jaidi > Diagne-Faye
90 ○	Cygan
Full time 2-0	

Goals from Abdoulaye Faye and Stelios extended Bolton Wanderers' awesome home record and put a major dent in Arsenal's championship hopes.

Wanderers were simply too good for Arsene Wenger's men and bettered them in every department.

The hosts had gone six successive league games without conceding a single goal at the Reebok Stadium and, courtesy of the result, moved on equal points with their opponents.

Although Thierry Henry hit the post on two occasions, Wanderers were excellent value for their second consecutive home win against the Gunners.

Faye, who was awesome throughout, hit his first goal for the club, after securing a permanent move earlier in the week, to put his side on course for three points, while Stelios, who netted the only goal of the game in last season's corresponding fixture, struck Wanderers' second.

Quote

🔟 **Sam Allardyce**

We put Arsenal under severe pressure and they made mistakes that we capitalised on.

Premiership Milestone

▶ **First Goal**

Abdoulaye Faye netted his first Premiership goal.

Venue:	Reebok Stadium	Referee:	H.M.Webb - 05/06		Bolton Wanderers
Attendance:	26,792	Matches:	14		Arsenal
Capacity:	28,101	Yellow Cards:	43		
Occupancy:	95%	Red Cards:	1		

Form Coming into Fixture

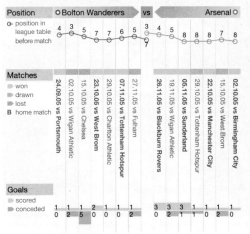

Position — Bolton Wanderers vs Arsenal

G- position in league table before match

Matches:
- won
- drawn
- lost
- B home match

Bolton Wanderers positions: 4, 3, 5, 7, 7, 6, 5, 3/7
Arsenal positions: 4, 5, 8, 8, 8, 7, 8

Bolton matches:
- 24.09.05 vs Portsmouth
- 02.10.05 vs Wigan Athletic
- 15.10.05 vs Chelsea
- 23.10.05 vs West Brom
- 29.10.05 vs Charlton Athletic
- 07.11.05 vs Tottenham Hotspur
- 27.11.05 vs Fulham

Arsenal matches:
- 26.11.05 vs Blackburn Rovers
- 19.11.05 vs Wigan Athletic
- 05.11.05 vs Sunderland
- 29.10.05 vs Tottenham Hotspur
- 22.10.05 vs Manchester City
- 15.10.05 vs West Brom
- 02.10.05 vs Birmingham City

Goals
- scored
- conceded

Bolton scored: 1, 1, 1, 2, 1, 1, 1
Bolton conceded: 0, 2, 5, 0, 0, 0, 2
Arsenal scored: 3, 3, 3, 1, 1, 1, 1
Arsenal conceded: 0, 2, 1, 1, 0, 2, 0

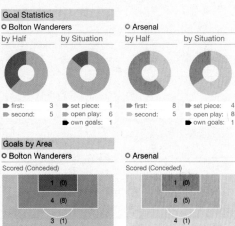

Goal Statistics

Bolton Wanderers

by Half | by Situation

- first: 3
- second: 5
- set piece: 1
- open play: 6
- own goals: 1

Arsenal

by Half | by Situation

- first: 8
- second: 5
- set piece: 4
- open play: 8
- own goals: 1

Goals by Area

Bolton Wanderers — Scored (Conceded)

1 (0)
4 (8)
3 (1)

Arsenal — Scored (Conceded)

1 (0)
8 (5)
4 (1)

Team Statistics

Starting Line-Ups

Bolton Wanderers:
- Jaaskelainen
- Gardner
- Stelios Vaz Te
- Speed
- N'Gotty
- Faye / Jaidi
- Davies
- Ben Haim
- Nolan
- O'Brien
- Diouf

Arsenal:
- Lehmann
- Ljungberg
- Lauren / Eboue
- Gilberto Silva
- Toure
- van Persie / Bergkamp
- Henry
- Fabregas / Reyes
- Campbell
- Pires
- Cygan

4/5/1 **4/4/2**

Unused Sub: Walker, Fadiga, Okocha   Unused Sub: Almunia, Senderos

Premiership Totals	Bolton	Arsenal
Premiership Appearances	1,511	1,866
Team Appearances	914	1,611
Goals Scored	175	391
Assists	140	327
Clean Sheets (goalkeepers)	42	32
Yellow Cards	214	179
Red Cards	12	7
Full Internationals	9	12

Age/Height

	Bolton Wanderers	Arsenal
Age	27 yrs, 6 mo	28 yrs, 1 mo
Height	6'	6'

Match Statistics

League Table after Fixture

		Played	Won	Drawn	Lost	For	Against	Pts
↓ 5	Arsenal	14	8	2	4	22	12	26
↑ 6	Bolton	14	8	2	4	17	13	26
↓ 7	Wigan	14	8	1	5	16	13	25
• 8	Man City	14	6	3	5	15	12	21
• 9	West Ham	13	5	4	4	17	13	19
• 10	Middlesbrough	15	5	4	6	20	21	19
• 11	Charlton	13	6	1	6	17	18	19
• 12	Newcastle	15	5	4	6	13	15	19
• 13	Blackburn	15	5	3	7	15	20	18

Statistics	Bolton	Arsenal
Goals	2	0
Shots on Target	9	3
Shots off Target	1	5
Hit Woodwork	0	2
Possession %	53	47
Corners	9	3
Offsides	5	0
Fouls	16	15
Disciplinary Points	4	8

1-1

Bolton Wanderers ○
Aston Villa ○

➡ Ricardo Vaz Te bursts forward

Event Line
Half time 0-0

57	○ ▨	Ben Haim
64	○ ▨	Diouf
66	○ ⇄	Okocha > Davies
73	○ ▨	Milner
74	○ ▨	Baros
76	○ ⇄	Moore > Baros
80	○ ⇄	Vaz Te > Giannakopoulos
82	○ ⊕	Diouf / RF / OP / IA
		Assist: Vaz Te
83	○ ⇄	Davis > Milner
84	○ ▨	McCann
84	○ ⇄	Angel > Hendrie
86	○ ▨	Bakke
88	○ ⊕	Angel / LF / OP / 6Y
		Assist: Moore

Full time 1-1

Bolton Wanderers had to settle for a point despite taking the lead through El-Hadji Diouf when Aston Villa substitute Juan Pablo Angel netted a late equaliser four minutes after coming on to the field.

Diouf's third goal of the season, in the 82nd minute, appeared to have given Sam Allardyce's men their fifth straight Barclays Premiership victory at the Reebok Stadium. But Angel capitalised on fellow substitute Luke Moore's persistence to bundle the ball past Jussi Jaaskelainen to earn under-pressure David O'Leary some breathing space.

Buoyed by the home victory against Arsenal seven days earlier, Allardyce opted not to make any chances to his starting line-up.

Villa, in contrast, made two changes, and an alteration in formation from their customary 4-4-2 to a 4-5-1 line-up with former Liverpool striker Milan Baros the sole striker.

Quote

❝ Sam Allardyce

We always knew our home run would come to an end at some stage, but I am disappointed to drop two points to Villa.

Venue:	Reebok Stadium	Referee:	P.Dowd - 05/06	**Bolton Wanderers**
Attendance:	23,646	Matches:	17	**Aston Villa**
Capacity:	28,101	Yellow Cards:	64	
Occupancy:	84%	Red Cards:	3	

Form Coming into Fixture

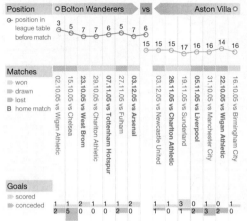

Position
- ⊕ position in league table before match

Bolton Wanderers: 3 5 7 7 6 5 7 6
Aston Villa: 15 15 15 17 16 16 14 16

Matches
- ▶ won
- ▶ drawn
- ▶ lost
- B home match

02.10.05 vs Wigan Athletic
15.10.05 vs Chelsea
23.10.05 vs West Brom
29.10.05 vs Charlton Athletic
07.11.05 vs Tottenham Hotspur
27.11.05 vs Fulham
03.12.05 vs Arsenal

03.12.05 vs Newcastle United
26.11.05 vs Charlton Athletic
19.11.05 vs Sunderland
05.11.05 vs Liverpool
31.10.05 vs Manchester City
22.10.05 vs Wigan Athletic
16.10.05 vs Birmingham City

Goals
- ▶ scored
- ▶ conceded

scored: 1 1 2 1 1 1 2 | 1 1 3 0 1 0 1
conceded: 2 5 0 0 0 2 0 | 1 0 1 2 3 2 0

Goal Statistics

○ Bolton Wanderers

by Half
- ▶ first: 4
- ▶ second: 5

by Situation
- ▶ set piece: 2
- ▶ open play: 6
- ▶ own goals: 1

○ Aston Villa

by Half
- ▶ first: 1
- ▶ second: 6

by Situation
- ▶ set piece: 1
- ▶ open play: 6

Goals by Area

○ Bolton Wanderers
Scored (Conceded)

1 (0)
5 (8)
3 (1)

○ Aston Villa
Scored (Conceded)

3 (1)
3 (5)
1 (3)

Team Statistics

Starting Line-Ups

Bolton Wanderers:
Gardner, Diouf, Speed, N'Gotty, Jaaskelainen, Faye, Davies (Okocha), Baros (Moore), Ben Haim, Nolan, O'Brien, Stelios (Vaz Te)

▶ 4/5/1

Unused Sub: Walker, Jaidi, Nakata

Aston Villa:
Milner (Davis), Hughes, McCann, Mellberg, Sorensen, Hendrie (Angel), Ridgewell, Bakke, Barry, Bouma

▶ 4/5/1

Unused Sub: Taylor, Samuel

Premiership Totals

	○ Bolton	Aston Villa ○
Premiership Appearances	1,593	1,787
Team Appearances	996	1,068
Goals Scored	184	143
Assists	158	142
Clean Sheets (goalkeepers)	43	62
Yellow Cards	219	213
Red Cards	12	8
Full Internationals	9	11

Age/Height

Bolton Wanderers Age
▶ 27 yrs, 8 mo

Aston Villa Age
▶ 25 yrs, 6 mo

Bolton Wanderers Height
▶ 5'11"

Aston Villa Height
▶ 5'11"

Match Statistics

League Table after Fixture

		Played	Won	Drawn	Lost	For	Against	Pts
●	1 Chelsea	16	14	1	1	35	7	43
↑	2 Liverpool	15	9	4	2	20	8	31
↓	3 Man Utd	14	9	3	2	24	13	30
●	4 Tottenham	15	7	6	2	19	12	27
↑	5 Bolton	15	8	3	4	18	14	27
↓	6 Arsenal	15	8	2	5	22	13	26
●	7 Wigan	15	8	1	6	14	14	25
...	...	...	...	...	...	...	...	...
↑	14 Aston Villa	16	4	5	7	16	24	17

Statistics

	○ Bolton	Aston Villa ○
Goals	1	1
Shots on Target	7	3
Shots off Target	6	3
Hit Woodwork	0	0
Possession %	49	51
Corners	6	3
Offsides	6	4
Fouls	16	22
Disciplinary Points	8	16

1-1

Bolton Wanderers ○
Sevilla ○

▶ Hidetoshi Nakata gets a boot to the ball

Event Line	
35 ○ ■ Nakata	
Half time 0-0	
46 ○ ⇄ N'Gotty > Gardner	
55 ○ ⇄ Speed > Diagne-Faye	
58 ○ ⇄ Ocio > Pablo	
65 ○ ⊕ N'Gotty / RF / C / 6Y	
Assist: Vaz Te	
65 ○ ⇄ Vaz Te > Davies	
67 ○ ⇄ Adriano > Lopez	
73 ○ ⇄ Saviola > Kepa	
74 ○ ■ Adriano	
74 ○ ⊕ Adriano / RF / OP / IA	
Assist: Marti	
89 ○ ■ Puerta	
Full time 1-1	

Bruno N'Gotty's first goal in almost two years helped Bolton Wanderers to earn the point against Sevilla that was required to secure their progression to the last 32 of the UEFA Cup.

The veteran Frenchman came off the bench to put Wanderers in the driving seat, only for Sevilla substitute Adriano to grab an equaliser.

Besiktas 3-1 victory against Guimaraes in Portugal was immaterial as Sam Allardyce's men secured the third and final qualifying berth in Group H.

Allardyce made six changes to the side that drew against Aston Villa on Saturday, with Ian Walker, Nicky Hunt, Radhi Jaidi, Hidetoshi Nakata, Khalilou Fadiga and Jay Jay Okocha all starting.

Regular captain Kevin Nolan was on the bench, which allowed Ricardo Gardner the opportunity of skippering the club he joined in 1998.

Venue:	Reebok Stadium	Referee:	M.Weiner (GER)	**Bolton Wanderers**

Attendance: 15,623
Capacity: 28,101
Occupancy: 56%

Bolton Wanderers
Sevilla

▶ Bruno N'Gotty fires Bolton in front

Match Statistics

Starting Line-Ups

Gardner   Diouf
N'Gotty
Fadiga
Jaidi
Walker   Faye   Davies
Speed   Vaz Te
Ben Haim
Okocha
Hunt   Nakata

Lopez   Crespo
Adriano
Pablo   Prieto
Ocio
Fabiano
Notario
Kepa   Marti   Alfaro
Saviola
Puerta   Dragutinovic

▶ **4/5/1**   ▶ **4/4/2**

Unused Sub: Jaaskelainen, Nolan, Stelios, Borgetti

Unused Sub: Palop, Navas, Capel, Kanoute

Statistics	○ Bolton	Sevilla ○
Goals	1	1
Shots on Target	2	3
Shots off Target	5	3
Hit Woodwork	0	1
Possession %	53	47
Corners	10	1
Offsides	8	5
Fouls	20	9
Disciplinary Points	4	8

0-4

Everton ○
Bolton Wanderers ○

▶ Kevin Nolan in midfield action

Event Line

1 ○ ■	Davies	
23 ○ ■	Hibbert	
27 ○ ■	Diagne-Faye	
32 ○ ⊕	Davies / H / IFK / IA	
	Assist: Nolan	
Half time 0-1		
67 ○ ■	Neville	
67 ○ ⇄	Hunt > Okocha	
73 ○ ⇄	Vaz Te > Diouf	
75 ○ ⊕	Giannakopoulos / RF / OP / IA	
	Assist: Vaz Te	
77 ○ ⇄	Osman > Hibbert	
79 ○ ⊕	Speed / LF / P / IA	
	Assist: Davies	
80 ○ ⊕	Giannakopoulos / RF / OP / IA	
	Assist: Speed	
84 ○ ⇄	Djetou > Diagne-Faye	
Full time 0-4		

Christmas came eight days early for Bolton Wanderers as they comprehensively demolished Everton at Goodison Park.

Goals from Stelios (2), Kevin Davies and a Gary Speed penalty comfortably secured the three points for Sam Allardyce's men, who destroyed their hosts in a frantic five-minute spell 15 minutes from the end.

Ricardo Gardner failed to recover from the hamstring injury he sustained during Wednesday's UEFA Cup tie against Sevilla, which led to Gary Speed playing in the unusual role of left-back.

Allardyce also had to make another defensive reshuffle when he brought in Radhi Jaidi to cover the suspended Tal Ben Haim.

In total the Wanderers boss made six changes from the Sevilla game with captain Kevin Nolan, Jussi Jaaskelainen, Bruno N'Gotty, Joey O'Brien, Stelios and Speed all returning to the starting line-up.

Quote

❝ **Sam Allardyce**

When Everton tired we picked them off, which is a sign of growing confidence and of a team getting used to what it takes to win a game.

Venue:	Goodison Park	Referee:	A.G.Wiley - 05/06		Everton
Attendance:	34,500	Matches:	19		Bolton Wanderers
Capacity:	40,569	Yellow Cards:	54		
Occupancy:	85%	Red Cards:	3		

Form Coming into Fixture

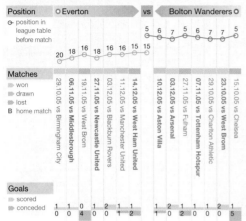

Position ○ Everton vs Bolton Wanderers ○

position in league table before match

Everton: 20, 18, 16, 18, 16, 16, 15, 15
Bolton: 5, 6, 7, 5, 6, 7, 7, 5

Matches
- won
- drawn
- lost
- B home match

Everton matches:
29.10.05 vs Birmingham City
06.11.05 vs Middlesbrough
19.11.05 vs West Brom
27.11.05 vs Newcastle United
03.12.05 vs Blackburn Rovers
11.12.05 vs Manchester United
14.12.05 vs West Ham United

Bolton matches:
10.12.05 vs Aston Villa
03.12.05 vs Arsenal
27.11.05 vs Fulham
07.11.05 vs Tottenham Hotspur
29.10.05 vs Charlton Athletic
23.10.05 vs West Brom
15.10.05 vs Chelsea

Goals
- scored
- conceded

Everton scored: 1 1 0 1 2 1 1
Everton conceded: 0 0 4 0 0 1 2

Bolton scored: 1 2 1 1 1 2 1
Bolton conceded: 1 0 2 0 0 0 5

Goal Statistics

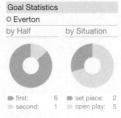

○ Everton — by Half / by Situation
- first: 6
- second: 1
- set piece: 2
- open play: 5

● Bolton Wanderers — by Half / by Situation
- first: 4
- second: 5
- set piece: 2
- open play: 6
- own goals: 1

Goals by Area

○ Everton — Scored (Conceded)
1 (2)
4 (3)
2 (2)

○ Bolton Wanderers — Scored (Conceded)
1 (1)
5 (6)
3 (1)

Team Statistics

Starting Line-Ups

Everton:
Wright
Hibbert (Osman), Yobo, Weir, Valente
Arteta, Cahill, Neville, Davies
McFadden (Beattie)
Beattie

Bolton:
Jaaskelainen
Stelios, N'Gotty, Jaidi, O'Brien
Okocha (Hunt), Faye (Djetou), Nolan, Speed
Diouf (Vaz Te), Davies

4/4/2 — **4/5/1**

Unused Sub: Turner, Kroldrup, Kilbane, Bent M
Unused Sub: Walker, Nakata

Premiership Totals

	○ Everton	Bolton ○
Premiership Appearances	1,345	1,595
Team Appearances	703	947
Goals Scored	125	187
Assists	97	155
Clean Sheets (goalkeepers)	27	43
Yellow Cards	148	216
Red Cards	9	9
Full Internationals	9	9

Age/Height

Everton Age: **27 yrs, 1 mo**   Bolton Wanderers Age: **28 yrs, 1 mo**

Everton Height: **5'11"**   Bolton Wanderers Height: **6'**

Match Statistics

League Table after Fixture

		Played	Won	Drawn	Lost	For	Against	Pts
● 1	Chelsea	16	14	1	1	35	7	43
● 2	Man Utd	17	11	4	2	31	14	37
● 3	Liverpool	15	9	4	2	20	8	31
● 4	Tottenham	16	8	6	2	22	13	30
● 5	Bolton	16	9	3	4	22	14	30
↑ 6	Wigan	17	9	1	7	19	18	28
↑ 7	Man City	17	8	3	6	24	17	27
...	...	...	...	...	...	...	...	...
↓ 16	Everton	17	5	2	10	9	23	17

Statistics

	○ Everton	Bolton ○
Goals	0	4
Shots on Target	10	6
Shots off Target	3	2
Hit Woodwork	0	0
Possession %	67	33
Corners	10	0
Offsides	2	0
Fouls	13	15
Disciplinary Points	8	8

2-0   Wigan Athletic ○
Bolton Wanderers ○

➡ Kevin Nolan applauds the away support

Event Line

40 ○ ⊕ Roberts / RF / OP / IA	
	Assist: Johansson
45 ○ ⊕ Roberts / RF / OP / IA	
	Assist: Mahon
Half time 2-0	
56 ○ ▪ Kavanagh	
57 ○ ⇄ Vaz Te > Giannakopoulos	
61 ○ ⇄ Diouf > Nakata	
69 ○ ⇄ Camara > Johansson	
69 ○ ⇄ Teale > Mahon	
71 ○ ⇄ Okocha > Diagne-Faye	
81 ○ ▪ Nolan	
86 ○ ⇄ Chimbonda > Taylor	
90 ○ ▪ Diouf	
Full time 2-0	

Bolton Wanderers' hopes of taking part in another Carling Cup final were put on hold for another year after they failed to recover from Jason Roberts' first-half brace.

Sam Allardyce's men seemed out of sorts as they tasted defeat at the JJB Stadium for a second time this season.

Two goals from the former West Brom striker in the final five minutes of the opening period went without reply as Wigan Athletic advanced to the semi-finals of the competition for the first time in their history.

Venue:	JJB Stadium	Referee:	M.L.Dean - 05/06		Wigan Athletic
Attendance:	13,401	Matches:	17		Bolton Wanderers
Capacity:	25,023	Yellow Cards:	47		
Occupancy:	54%	Red Cards:	4		

▶ Joey O'Brien and Abdoulaye Faye try to stop Jason Roberts

Match Statistics

Starting Line-Ups

▶ 4/4/2

Unused Sub: Filan, Connolly

▶ 4/5/1

Unused Sub: Walker, Hunt

Statistics	○ Wigan	Bolton ○
Goals	2	0
Shots on Target	6	7
Shots off Target	4	5
Hit Woodwork	0	0
Possession %	50	50
Corners	7	9
Offsides	3	4
Fouls	15	13
Disciplinary Points	4	8

Age/Height

Wigan Athletic Age

▶ 28 yrs, 5 mo

Wigan Athletic Height

▶ 5'11"

Bolton Wanderers Age

▶ 27 yrs, 6 mo

Bolton Wanderers Height

▶ 5'11"

Quote

🏻 **Sam Allardyce**

We have missed a magnificent opportunity to get through to the semi-finals.

0-0 Sunderland ○
Bolton Wanderers ○

► Gary Speed gets to grips with Julio Arca

Event Line

17 ○ ▪	Fadiga	
30 ○ ▪	Gray	
34 ○ ▪	Giannakopoulos	
36 ○ ▪	Ben Haim	
Half time 0-0		
57 ○ ⇄	Campo > Djetou	
69 ○ ⇄	Murphy D > Gray	
69 ○ ⇄	Le Tallec > Stead	
76 ○ ⇄	Borgetti > Diouf	
81 ○ ⇄	Okocha > Fadiga	
81 ○ ⇄	Stubbs > Bassila	
Full time 0-0		

In a dour affair at the Stadium of Light Wanderers started their festive period of four matches with a goalless draw against the Premiership's basement club Sunderland.

Wanderers rested Kevin Nolan and Kevin Davies, who are both on four bookings, in a side which featured six changes from the one which started the Carling Cup quarter-final defeat at Wigan in midweek. They had the better of a scrappy game, but did not create enough to claim all three points.

The Wearsiders, who finally ended their 10-game losing run by picking up a first point since October 1, rarely troubled Jaaskelainen even with the impressive Julio Arca at times justifying the faith invested in him by the club's supporters.

Quote

❝ **Sam Allardyce**

We have four games in eight days and we would be foolish not to use the potential of our squad.

Venue:	Stadium of Light	Referee:	M.Atkinson - 05/06		Sunderland
Attendance:	32,232	Matches:	18		Bolton Wanderers
Capacity:	48,300	Yellow Cards:	40		
Occupancy:	67%	Red Cards:	1		

Form Coming into Fixture

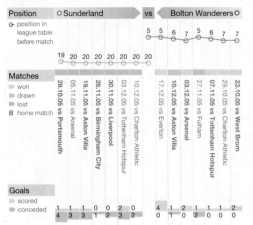

Position	○ Sunderland	vs	Bolton Wanderers ○

position in league table before match

Sunderland: 19 20 20 20 20 20 20 20
Bolton Wanderers: 5 5 6 7 5 6 6 7 7

Matches
- won
- drawn
- lost
- B home match

Sunderland matches:
29.10.05 vs Portsmouth · 05.11.05 vs Arsenal · 19.11.05 vs Aston Villa · 26.11.05 vs Birmingham City · 30.11.05 vs Liverpool · 03.12.05 vs Charlton Athletic · 10.12.05 vs Tottenham Hotspur

Bolton matches:
17.12.05 vs Everton · 10.12.05 vs Aston Villa · 03.12.05 vs Arsenal · 27.11.05 vs Fulham · 07.11.05 vs Tottenham Hotspur · 29.10.05 vs Charlton Athletic · 23.10.05 vs West Brom

Goals

	scored	1	1	1	0	0	2	0		4	1	2	1	1	1	2
	conceded	4	3	3	1	2	3	2		0	1	0	2	0	0	0

Goal Statistics

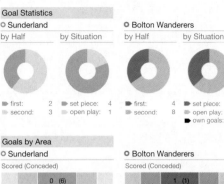

○ Sunderland

by Half / by Situation

- first: 2
- second: 3
- set piece: 4
- open play: 1

○ Bolton Wanderers

by Half / by Situation

- first: 4
- second: 8
- set piece: 4
- open play: 7
- own goals: 1

Goals by Area

○ Sunderland

Scored (Conceded)

| 0 (6) |
| 4 (10) |
| 1 (2) |

○ Bolton Wanderers

Scored (Conceded)

| 1 (1) |
| 8 (2) |
| 3 (0) |

Team Statistics

Starting Line-Ups

Collins D, Arca, Stelios, Hunt
Caldwell, Bassila/Stubbs, Stead/Le Tallec, Vaz Te, Fadiga/Okocha, Ben Haim
Davis, Gray/Murphy D, Djetou/Campo, N'Gotty
Breen, Whitehead, Speed
Hoyte, Lawrence, Diouf/Borgetti, Gardner

▶ 4/4/2 **▶ 4/5/1**

Unused Sub: Alnwick, Woods   Unused Sub: Walker, Jaidi

Premiership Totals

	○ Sunderland	Bolton ○
Premiership Appearances	635	1,457
Team Appearances	217	937
Goals Scored	32	132
Assists	29	128
Clean Sheets (goalkeepers)	1	44
Yellow Cards	64	190
Red Cards	2	12
Full Internationals	4	12

Age/Height

Sunderland Age	Bolton Wanderers Age
▶ 25 yrs, 11 mo	▶ 29 yrs, 3 mo
Sunderland Height	Bolton Wanderers Height
▶ 6'	▶ 5'11"

Match Statistics

League Table after Fixture

		Played	Won	Drawn	Lost	For	Against	Pts
● 1	Chelsea	18	16	1	1	40	9	49
● 2	Man Utd	18	12	4	2	34	14	40
● 3	Liverpool	16	10	4	2	22	8	34
● 4	Tottenham	18	9	7	2	27	16	34
● 5	Bolton	17	9	4	4	22	14	31
● 6	Wigan	18	10	1	7	23	21	31
↑ 7	Arsenal	17	9	2	6	23	15	29
...		...	...	...	...	...	...	...
● 20	Sunderland	18	1	3	14	14	35	6

Statistics

	○ Sunderland	Bolton ○
Goals	0	0
Shots on Target	7	1
Shots off Target	4	7
Hit Woodwork	0	0
Possession %	49	51
Corners	1	4
Offsides	0	2
Fouls	16	12
Disciplinary Points	4	12

4-1

Manchester United ○
Bolton Wanderers ○

▶ Jussi Jaaskelainen closes down Louis Saha

Event Line

8 ○ ⊕	N'Gotty / LF / OG / 6Y	
	Assist: Richardson	
29 ○ ▪	Diagne-Faye	
33 ○ ⊕	Speed / H / OP / 6Y	
	Assist: Diagne-Faye	
44 ○ ⊕	Saha / LF / OP / 6Y	
Half time 2-1		
46 ○ ⇄	Vaz Te > Ben Haim	
55 ○ ▪	Gardner	
62 ○ ▪	Richardson	
62 ○ ▪	Vaz Te	
68 ○ ⊕	Ronaldo / RF / OP / 6Y	
	Assist: Rooney	
69 ○ ▪	Ronaldo	
73 ○ ⇄	van Nistelrooy > Saha	
76 ○ ⇄	Fadiga > Giannakopoulos	
79 ○ ⇄	Park > Rooney	
86 ○ ⇄	Pique > Fletcher	
90 ○ ⊕	Ronaldo / LF / OP / IA	
	Assist: van Nistelrooy	
90 ○ ▪	Davies	
90 ○ ▪	Nolan	
Full time 4-1		

Wanderers ended 2005 in disappointment as they lost to neighbours Manchester United at Old Trafford.

Although Gary Speed cancelled out Bruno N'Gotty's unfortunate own-goal, further goals from Louis Saha and Cristiano Ronaldo (2) ensured that the three points went to the home side.

Sam Allardyce reverted back to his strongest line-up for the last game of 2005, making five changes from the side that shared a goalless draw with Sunderland on Boxing Day.

Kevin Nolan, Kevin Davies, Abdoulaye Faye, Joey O'Brien and Jay Jay Okocha all came back into the fray at the expense of Nicky Hunt, Khalilou Fadiga, Ricardo Vaz Te, Martin Djetou and the suspended El-Hadji Diouf.

United, missing the services of Paul Scholes, Alan Smith and Ruud van Nistelrooy, started the game at a frenetic pace with veteran Ryan Giggs the main protagonist.

Quote

❝ **Sam Allardyce**

Right from the start we weren't doing the correct things defensively and they took full advantage of that.

Venue:	Old Trafford	Referee:	S.G.Bennett - 05/06	**Manchester United**
Attendance:	67,858	Matches:	21	**Bolton Wanderers**
Capacity:	73,006	Yellow Cards:	75	
Occupancy:	93%	Red Cards:	7	

Form Coming into Fixture

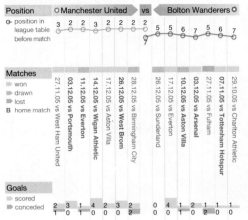

Position

O Manchester United vs Bolton Wanderers O

position in league table before match

Manchester United: 3 2 2 3 2 2 2 2 (7)
Bolton Wanderers: 5 5 6 7 5 6 7

Matches
- won
- drawn
- lost
- **B** home match

27.11.05 vs West Ham United
03.12.05 vs Portsmouth
11.12.05 vs Everton
14.12.05 vs Wigan Athletic
17.12.05 vs Aston Villa
26.12.05 vs West Brom
28.12.05 vs Birmingham City

26.12.05 vs Sunderland
17.12.05 vs Everton
10.12.05 vs Aston Villa
03.12.05 vs Arsenal
27.11.05 vs Fulham
07.11.05 vs Tottenham Hotspur
29.10.05 vs Charlton Athletic

Goals
- scored
- conceded

2	3	1	4	2	3	2		0	4	1	2	1	1
1	0	1	0	0	0	2		0	0	1	0	2	0	0

Goal Statistics

O Manchester United

by Half
- first: 8
- second: 9

by Situation
- set piece: 5
- open play: 12

O Bolton Wanderers

by Half
- first: 4
- second: 6

by Situation
- set piece: 3
- open play: 6
- own goals: 1

Goals by Area

O Manchester United
Scored (Conceded)

| 2 (1) |
| 15 (3) |
| 0 (0) |

O Bolton Wanderers
Scored (Conceded)

| 1 (1) |
| 8 (2) |
| 1 (0) |

Team Statistics

Starting Line-Ups

Manchester United:
Richardson, Giggs
Silvestre, O'Shea
van der Sar
Saha, van Nistelrooy
Ferdinand, Fletcher, Pique
Neville, Ronaldo
Rooney / Park

Bolton Wanderers:
Nolan, O'Brien
Okocha
Ben Haim / Vaz Te
Davies, Faye
Jaaskelainen
N'Gotty
Speed
Stelios / Fadiga, Gardner

4/4/2

Unused Sub: Howard, Bardsley

4/5/1

Unused Sub: Walker, Jaidi, Nakata

Premiership Totals

	O Man Utd	Bolton O
Premiership Appearances	2,037	1,534
Team Appearances	1,566	992
Goals Scored	286	175
Assists	311	144
Clean Sheets (goalkeepers)	51	45
Yellow Cards	164	200
Red Cards	7	10
Full Internationals	13	9

Age/Height

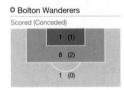

Manchester United Age
25 yrs, 11 mo

Bolton Wanderers Age
28 yrs, 2 mo

Manchester United Height
6'

Bolton Wanderers Height
5'11"

Match Statistics

League Table after Fixture

		Played	Won	Drawn	Lost	For	Against	Pts
● 2	Man Utd	20	13	5	2	40	17	44
● 3	Liverpool	18	12	4	2	26	9	40
● 4	Tottenham	20	10	7	3	29	18	37
● 5	Wigan	20	11	1	8	25	24	34
● 6	Arsenal	19	10	3	6	27	15	33
● 7	Bolton	18	9	4	5	23	18	31
● 8	Man City	20	8	4	8	27	22	28
↑ 9	Blackburn	19	8	3	8	24	24	27
↓ 10	West Ham	20	7	5	8	26	27	26

Statistics

	O Man Utd	Bolton O
Goals	4	1
Shots on Target	9	2
Shots off Target	9	2
Hit Woodwork	2	0
Possession %	56	44
Corners	7	1
Offsides	2	4
Fouls	9	22
Disciplinary Points	8	20

2-2

Bolton Wanderers ○
Liverpool ○

► Captains Kevin Nolan and Steven Gerrard complete the pre-match formalities

Event Line

10○	⊕	Jaidi / H / IFK / 6Y
38○	■	Diagne-Faye
41○	■	Crouch
42○	■	Carragher
Half time 1-0		
48○	■	Nolan
58○	■	Sissoko
62○	⇄	Garcia > Sinama-Pongolle
64○	⇄	Alonso > Hamann
67○	⊕	Gerrard / RF / P / IA
		Assist: Gerrard
71○	⊕	Diouf / H / OP / 6Y
		Assist: Davies
82○	⊕	Garcia / LF / OP / IA
		Assist: Alonso
83○	⇄	Cisse > Sissoko
83○	⇄	Ben Haim > Diouf
90○	⇄	Fadiga > Speed
Full time 2-2		

Luis Garcia denied Bolton Wanderers their first three points of 2006 with a late equaliser for Liverpool at the Reebok Stadium.

The Spain international came off the bench to cancel out El Hadji Diouf's strike after the former Liverpool man appeared to have netted the winner.

Wanderers, though, will be kicking themselves at not picking up a victory after they had taken the lead twice against the in-form Reds.

Radhi Jaidi opened the scoring only to see Steven Gerrard equalise from the penalty spot, before Diouf netted what should have been the winner.

Jaidi and Diouf returned to the starting line-up as Sam Allardyce made two changes from the side that suffered defeat at Manchester United on New Year's Eve.

With Liverpool looking to stretch their winning streak to 11 successive games against a Wanderers side that was virtually impregnable at the Reebok Stadium, the match was always going to be played in a passionate manner.

Quote

🎙 **Sam Allardyce**

People talk about us being tough, but Steven Gerrard stamped on Kevin Nolan and Mohamed Sissoko did the same thing to El-Hadji Diouf.

Premiership Milestone

▶ **100**

El-Hadji Diouf marked his 100th Premiership appearance with a goal against his old club.

Venue:	Reebok Stadium	Referee:	M.Clattenburg - 05/06
Attendance:	27,604	Matches:	22
Capacity:	28,101	Yellow Cards:	74
Occupancy:	98%	Red Cards:	4

Bolton Wanderers
Liverpool

Form Coming into Fixture

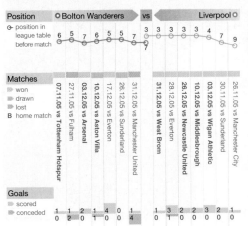

Goal Statistics

○ Bolton Wanderers

by Half	by Situation

■ first: 5 ■ set piece: 3
■ second: 5 ■ open play: 6
■ own goals: 1

○ Liverpool

by Half	by Situation

■ first: 8 ■ set piece: 1
■ second: 6 ■ open play: 13

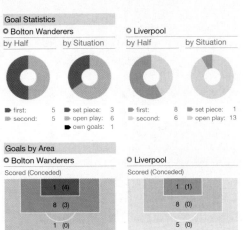

Goals by Area

○ Bolton Wanderers
Scored (Conceded)

1 (4)
8 (3)
1 (0)

○ Liverpool
Scored (Conceded)

1 (1)
8 (0)
5 (0)

Team Statistics

Starting Line-Ups

▶ **4/5/1**   ▶ **4/4/2**

Unused Sub: Walker, Borgetti, Vaz Te   Unused Sub: Carson, Riise

Premiership Totals

	○ Bolton	Liverpool ○
Premiership Appearances	1,560	1,654
Team Appearances	963	1,316
Goals Scored	183	169
Assists	146	173
Clean Sheets (goalkeepers)	45	14
Yellow Cards	225	184
Red Cards	12	12
Full Internationals	10	13

Age/Height

Bolton Wanderers Age	Liverpool Age
▶ **28 yrs, 6 mo**	▶ **26 yrs, 3 mo**
Bolton Wanderers Height	Liverpool Height
▶ **6'**	▶ **6'1"**

Match Statistics

League Table after Fixture

		Played	Won	Drawn	Lost	For	Against	Pts
● 3	Liverpool	19	12	5	2	28	11	41
● 4	Tottenham	20	10	7	3	29	18	37
● 5	Wigan	21	11	1	9	25	26	34
● 6	Arsenal	19	10	3	6	27	15	33
● 7	Bolton	19	9	5	5	25	20	32
↑ 8	Blackburn	20	9	3	8	26	25	30
↓ 9	Man City	20	8	4	8	27	22	28
● 10	West Ham	21	7	5	9	27	30	26
● 11	Newcastle	20	7	5	8	20	23	26

Statistics

	○ Bolton	Liverpool ○
Goals	2	2
Shots on Target	7	8
Shots off Target	5	8
Hit Woodwork	0	0
Possession %	57	43
Corners	3	5
Offsides	6	2
Fouls	16	14
Disciplinary Points	8	12

0-3

Watford ○
Bolton Wanderers ○

▶ Ricardo Vaz Te makes forward progress at Vicarage Road

Event Line
11 ○ ⊕ Borgetti / LF / OP / IA
34 ○ ⊕ Giannakopoulos / RF / OP / IA
　　　Assist: Vaz Te
Half time 0-2
72 ○ ⇄ Gill > Henderson
73 ○ ⊕ Vaz Te / RF / OP / OA
　　　Assist: Nakata
79 ○ ⇄ Fojut > Fadiga
84 ○ ⇄ Sissons > N'Gotty
90 ○ ⇄ Ashton > Borgetti
Full time 0-3

Goals from Jared Borgetti, Stelios and Ricardo Vaz Te helped Bolton Wanderers cruise into the FA Cup Fourth Round with an emphatic victory against Championship high-fliers Watford.

Wanderers, with a total of nine senior players absent through injuries, suspensions and international call-ups, were too classy for their opponents who rarely troubled Ian Walker.

Such were Sam Allardyce's selection problems that he named a side that contained five players from the club's Academy on the bench.

Goalkeeper Sam Ashton, defender Jaroslaw Fojut, midfielders James Sinclair and Robert Sissons, and forward Bedi Buval were named as substitutes, while the starting XI comprised of the only professionals available to the Wanderers manager.

Khalilou Fadiga shook off a virus concern to start in midfield alongside Jay Jay Okocha and Hidetoshi Nakata, while the front three consisted of Stelios, Borgetti and Vaz Te.

Allardyce was able to name his first choice defence with Joey O'Brien, Tal Ben Haim, Bruno N'Gotty and stand-in captain Ricardo Gardner charged with the task of shutting out the Hornets' front men.

Ian Walker returned between the sticks at the expense of Jussi Jaaskelainen, who was rested.

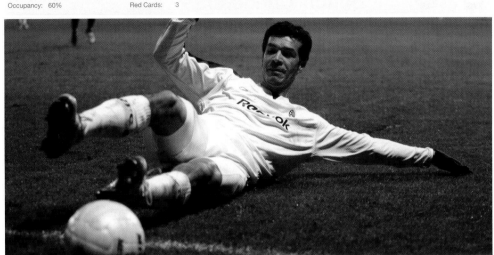

▶ Jared Borgetti follows the ball out of play

Match Statistics

Starting Line-Ups

▶ 4/4/2   ▶ 4/5/1

Unused Sub: Chamberlain, DeMerit, Bouazza, Grant

Unused Sub: Buval, Sinclair

Statistics	○ Watford	Bolton ○
Goals	0	3
Shots on Target	3	5
Shots off Target	7	2
Hit Woodwork	0	1
Possession %	42	58
Corners	7	1
Offsides	1	9
Fouls	12	12
Disciplinary Points	0	0

Age/Height

Watford Age
▶ 24 yrs

Bolton Wanderers Age
▶ 26 yrs, 5 mo

Watford Height
▶ 6'

Bolton Wanderers Height
▶ 5'11"

Quote

❝ **Sam Allardyce**

We didn't have anything on the bench to strengthen the side, but thankfully we didn't need to.

0-0

Blackburn Rovers ○
Bolton Wanderers ○

▶ Bruno N'Gotty competes with Robbie Savage

Event Line

31 ○ ■	Fadiga	
33 ○ ◪	Nakata	
	2nd Bookable Offence	
36 ○ ⇄	Campo > Borgetti	
39 ○ ■	O'Brien	
45 ○ ■	Reid	

Half time 0-0

62 ○ ⇄	Vaz Te > Giannakopoulos	
64 ○ ⇄	Kuqi > Emerton	
70 ○ ⇄	Bellamy > Dickov	
70 ○ ■	N'Gotty	
78 ○ ■	Jaaskelainen	
78 ○ ⇄	Jansen > Fadiga	
90 ○ ■	Bentley	

Full time 0-0

Ten-man Bolton Wanderers survived a second-half onslaught from Blackburn Rovers to claim a point at Ewood Park.

Despite playing the majority of the game with a man less than their opponents, following Hidetoshi Nakata's first-half dismissal, a dogged Wanderers clung on to a scoreless draw with some determined defending.

Wanderers were looking to get their league campaign back on track following last week's FA Cup victory at Watford.

Jared Borgetti was handed his first Premiership start for the club, while Khalilou Fadiga and Nakata were given rare starts.

Quote

⓰ Sam Allardyce

We showed real resilience and determination to get something out of the game against the odds. We've performed miracles and I'm proud.

Premiership Milestone

▶ Debut

Matt Jansen made his first Premiership appearance in the colours of Bolton, against his former employers.

Venue:	Ewood Park	Referee:	M.A.Riley - 05/06		Blackburn Rovers
Attendance:	18,180	Matches:	22		Bolton Wanderers
Capacity:	31,367	Yellow Cards:	71		
Occupancy:	58%	Red Cards:	4		

Form Coming into Fixture

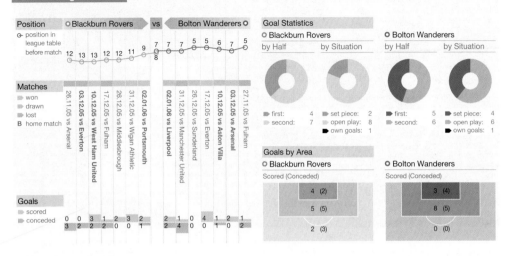

Position

○ Blackburn Rovers vs Bolton Wanderers ○

⊙ position in league table before match

12 13 13 12 12 11 9 8 / 7 7 7 5 5 6 7 5

Matches
- won
- drawn
- lost
- B home match

26.11.05 vs Arsenal
03.12.05 vs Everton
10.12.05 vs West Ham United
17.12.05 vs Fulham
26.12.05 vs Middlesbrough
31.12.05 vs Wigan Athletic
02.01.06 vs Portsmouth
02.01.06 vs Liverpool
31.12.05 vs Manchester United
26.12.05 vs Sunderland
17.12.05 vs Everton
10.12.05 vs Aston Villa
03.12.05 vs Arsenal
27.11.05 vs Fulham

Goals
scored	0	0	3	1	2	3	2		2	1	0	4	1	2	1
conceded	3	2	2	2	0	0	1		2	4	0	0	1	0	2

Goal Statistics

○ Blackburn Rovers

by Half
- first: 4
- second: 7

by Situation
- set piece: 2
- open play: 8
- own goals: 1

○ Bolton Wanderers

by Half
- first: 5
- second: 6

by Situation
- set piece: 4
- open play: 6
- own goals: 1

Goals by Area

○ Blackburn Rovers
Scored (Conceded)

4 (2)
5 (5)
2 (3)

○ Bolton Wanderers
Scored (Conceded)

3 (4)
8 (5)
0 (0)

Team Statistics

Starting Line-Ups

Gray Pedersen Davies O'Brien
Nolan
Nelson Savage Ben Haim
Dickov
Bellamy Jaaskelainen
Friedel Borgetti Fadiga
Campo Jansen
Todd Reid Bentley
N'Gotty
Nakata
Neill Emerton Stelios Gardner
Kuqi Vaz Te

4/4/1/1   **4/5/1**

Unused Sub: Enckelman, Khizanishvili, Tugay

Unused Sub: Walker, Hunt

Premiership Totals

	○ Blackburn	Bolton ○
Premiership Appearances	1,521	1,174
Team Appearances	757	955
Goals Scored	136	120
Assists	137	93
Clean Sheets (goalkeepers)	58	45
Yellow Cards	227	163
Red Cards	11	10
Full Internationals	11	9

Age/Height

Blackburn Rovers Age
28 yrs, 7 mo

Bolton Wanderers Age
28 yrs

Blackburn Rovers Height
5'11"

Bolton Wanderers Height
6'

Match Statistics

League Table after Fixture

		Played	Won	Drawn	Lost	For	Against	Pts
● 1	Chelsea	21	19	1	1	46	10	58
● 2	Man Utd	22	13	6	3	41	20	45
● 3	Liverpool	20	13	5	2	29	11	44
● 4	Tottenham	22	11	7	4	31	19	40
● 5	Arsenal	21	11	4	6	34	15	37
● 6	Wigan	21	11	1	9	25	26	34
● 7	Bolton	20	9	6	5	25	20	33
↑ 8	Man City	22	9	4	9	30	25	31
↓ 9	Blackburn	21	9	4	8	26	25	31

Statistics

	○ Blackburn	Bolton ○
Goals	0	0
Shots on Target	3	1
Shots off Target	15	2
Hit Woodwork	1	0
Possession %	53	47
Corners	11	1
Offsides	4	2
Fouls	21	16
Disciplinary Points	8	26

2-0

Bolton Wanderers ○
Manchester City ○

▶ Kevin Nolan executes a quick change of direction

Event Line

22 ○ ⇄	Vaz Te > Fadiga
37 ○ ⊕	Borgetti / RF / OP / IA
	Assist: Giannakopoulos
41 ○ ⊕	Nolan / RF / IFK / IA
Half time 2-0	
58 ○ ▢	Davies
67 ○ ⇄	Fowler > Cole
67 ○ ⇄	Sibierski > Riera
76 ○ ⇄	Croft > Vassell
79 ○ ⇄	Jansen > Borgetti
86 ○ ▢	Jihai
88 ○ ▢	Ben Haim
90 ○ ▢	Sinclair
90 ○ ⇄	Hunt > Vaz Te
Full time 2-0	

First-half goals from Jared Borgetti and Kevin Nolan gave Sam Allardyce his 100th league win as manager when his Bolton Wanderers side outclassed opponents Manchester City.

A dominant Wanderers were simply too good for their rivals who trudged off the field at the end of the match without even troubling Jussi Jaaskelainen.

It was a great occasion for Borgetti, who is looking to get a regular run in the side in a bid to spearhead Mexico's World Cup bid in the summer, as he marked his first league start at the Reebok Stadium with the game's opening goal.

Skipper Nolan completed the victory just a few minutes later with his eighth strike of the campaign.

Allardyce made only one change from the side that held Blackburn Rovers at Ewood Park seven days earlier, drafting in Ivan Campo at the expense of the suspended Hidetoshi Nakata. It was a shrewd move by the Wanderers boss, who saw Campo return to his best form.

Quote

⓬ Sam Allardyce

Our strength in depth has been excellent this season and that is why we have achieved so much.

Premiership Milestone

▶ First Goal

Jared Borgetti netted his first Premiership goal.

Venue:	Reebok Stadium	Referee:	R.Styles - 05/06	Bolton Wanderers
Attendance:	26,466	Matches:	26	Manchester City
Capacity:	28,101	Yellow Cards:	88	
Occupancy:	94%	Red Cards:	3	

Form Coming into Fixture

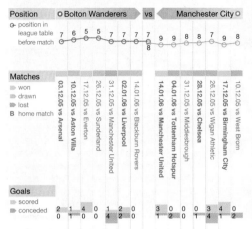

Goal Statistics

Bolton Wanderers

by Half
- first: 5
- second: 5

by Situation
- set piece: 4
- open play: 6

Manchester City

by Half
- first: 6
- second: 4

by Situation
- set piece: 4
- open play: 6

Goals by Area

Bolton Wanderers

Scored (Conceded)

3 (4)

7 (3)

0 (0)

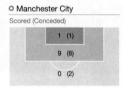

Manchester City

Scored (Conceded)

1 (1)

9 (8)

0 (2)

Team Statistics

Starting Line-Ups

4/5/1

Unused Sub: Walker, Fojut

4/4/2

Unused Sub: Onuoha, Musampa

Premiership Totals	O Bolton	Man City O
Premiership Appearances	1,247	2,338
Team Appearances	1,028	831
Goals Scored	120	458
Assists	97	258
Clean Sheets (goalkeepers)	46	129
Yellow Cards	177	224
Red Cards	10	16
Full Internationals	8	7

Age/Height

Bolton Wanderers Age
▶ 27 yrs, 7 mo

Manchester City Age
▶ 27 yrs, 7 mo

Bolton Wanderers Height
▶ 6'

Manchester City Height
▶ 6'

Match Statistics

League Table after Fixture

		Played	Won	Drawn	Lost	For	Against	Pts
● 1	Chelsea	22	20	1	1	48	11	61
● 2	Man Utd	22	13	6	3	41	20	45
● 3	Liverpool	20	13	5	2	29	11	44
● 4	Tottenham	23	11	8	4	31	19	41
● 5	Arsenal	22	11	4	7	34	16	37
● 6	Wigan	23	12	1	10	28	29	37
● 7	Bolton	21	10	6	5	27	20	36
↑ 8	Blackburn	22	10	4	8	27	25	34
↓ 9	Man City	23	9	4	10	30	27	31

Statistics	O Bolton	Man City O
Goals	2	0
Shots on Target	6	2
Shots off Target	5	7
Hit Woodwork	0	0
Possession %	51	49
Corners	4	5
Offsides	4	3
Fouls	8	17
Disciplinary Points	8	8

81

1-0

Bolton Wanderers ○
Arsenal ○

FA Cup
28.01.06

► Kevin Davies goes in bravely

Event Line	
5 ○ ■ Reyes	
Half time 0-0	
48 ○ ■ Diaby	
50 ○ ■ Davies	
51 ○ ■ Senderos	
54 ○ ⇄ Vaz Te > Campo	
62 ○ ■ van Persie	
73 ○ ⇄ Jansen > Borgetti	
82 ○ ■ Gilbert	
84 ○ ⊕ Giannakopoulos / H / OP	
Assist: Gardner	
89 ○ ⇄ Hunt > Giannakopoulos	
Full time 1-0	

Stelios hit the only goal of the game with six minutes remaining to dump holders Arsenal out of the FA Cup and secure Bolton Wanderers' passage into the Fifth Round draw.

The Greece international headed the outstanding Ricardo Gardner's left-wing cross beyond Manuel Almunia to leave Arsene Wenger's men dejected in the North West for the second time in a week following their Carling Cup exit at Wigan in midweek.

The Arsenal boss opted to rest Thierry Henry, Dennis Bergkamp, Lauren and Gilberto Silva, and instead handed some first team experience to the younger end of his squad.

Sam Allardyce, however, made just one change from the side that beat Manchester City seven days earlier, bringing in Hidetoshi Nakata, who was back from suspension, for the injured Khalilou Fadiga.

➡ Matt Jansen sees a shot blocked

Match Statistics

Starting Line-Ups

➡ **4/5/1**

Unused Sub: Walker, Fojut

➡ **4/5/1**

Unused Sub: Poom, Larsson, Muamba, Bendtner, Lupoli

Statistics	○ Bolton	Arsenal ○
Goals	1	0
Shots on Target	5	7
Shots off Target	6	4
Hit Woodwork	0	2
Possession %	49	51
Corners	3	10
Offsides	7	2
Fouls	11	19
Disciplinary Points	4	20

Age/Height

Bolton Wanderers Age

➡ **27 yrs, 5 mo**

Arsenal Age

➡ **23 yrs, 7 mo**

Bolton Wanderers Height

➡ **6'**

Arsenal Height

➡ **6'**

Quote

🔊 **Sam Allardyce**

We wore them down and pulled out an absolutely wonderful goal to get us through to the next round.

83

1-1

Portsmouth ○
Bolton Wanderers ○

➡ Matt Jansen is unable to get to Pedro Mendes

Event Line

15 ○ ⇄	Griffin > Stefanovic
Half time 0-0	
46 ○ ⇄	Todorov > O'Neil
60 ○ ⇄	Vaz Te > Hunt
69 ○ ⊕	Fadiga / LF / DFK / OA
	Assist: Giannakopoulos
81 ○ ⇄	Karadas > Mwaruwari
85 ○ ⊕	Karadas / RF / OP / IA
	Assist: Routledge
86 ○ ⇄	Fojut > Fadiga
Full time 1-1	

Substitute Azar Karadas earned Portsmouth a late point after Khalilou Fadiga's first goal in Wanderers colours appeared to have given his side a victory.

The on-loan Norwegian midfielder adeptly finished Wayne Routledge's centre with six minutes of the game remaining to earn Harry Redknapp's men a priceless point in their battle to avoid relegation.

Wanderers though will be ruing their luck after Fadiga found the back of the net after atoning for his first-half penalty miss.

Matt Jansen made his full debut for Wanderers as Sam Allardyce made three changes from the side that knocked Arsenal out of the FA Cup.

Jared Borgetti made way for the former Blackburn Rovers player and occupied the bench alongside Hidetoshi Nakata, who was replaced by the fit-again Fadiga.

Ivan Campo's absence through injury was accommodated by a positional switch with Joey O'Brien moving into a more accustomed role in the centre of midfield. Nicky Hunt returned to right full back.

Quote

❝ Sam Allardyce

We have thrown two points away and should have killed the game off.

Premiership Milestone

➡ First Goal

Khalilou Fadiga netted his first Premiership goal.

Venue:	Fratton Park	Referee:	D.J.Gallagher - 05/06		Portsmouth
Attendance:	19,128	Matches:	26		Bolton Wanderers
Capacity:	20,288	Yellow Cards:	63		
Occupancy:	94%	Red Cards:	7		

Form Coming into Fixture

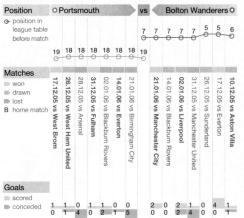

Position ○ Portsmouth vs Bolton Wanderers ○

○ position in league table before match

Portsmouth: 19 18 18 18 18 18 18 19
Bolton: 7 7 7 7 7 5 5 6

Matches
- won
- drawn
- lost
- B home match

Portsmouth matches: 17.12.05 vs West Brom, 26.12.05 vs West Ham United, 28.12.05 vs Arsenal, 31.12.05 vs Fulham, 02.01.06 vs Blackburn Rovers, 14.01.06 vs Everton, 21.01.06 vs Birmingham City

Bolton matches: 21.01.06 vs Manchester City, 14.01.06 vs Blackburn Rovers, 02.01.06 vs Liverpool, 31.12.05 vs Manchester United, 26.12.05 vs Sunderland, 17.12.05 vs Everton, 10.12.05 vs Aston Villa

Goals
- scored
- conceded

Portsmouth scored: 1 1 0 1 1 0 0
Portsmouth conceded: 0 1 4 0 2 1 5

Bolton scored: 2 0 2 1 0 4 1
Bolton conceded: 0 0 2 4 0 0 1

Goal Statistics

○ Portsmouth — by Half / by Situation

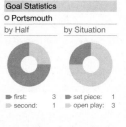

- first: 3 | set piece: 1
- second: 1 | open play: 3

○ Bolton Wanderers — by Half / by Situation

- first: 5 | set piece: 4
- second: 5 | open play: 6

Goals by Area

○ Portsmouth — Scored (Conceded)

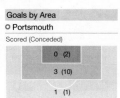

0 (2)
3 (10)
1 (1)

○ Bolton Wanderers — Scored (Conceded)

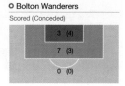

3 (4)
7 (3)
0 (0)

Team Statistics

Starting Line-Ups

Portsmouth: Taylor, O'Neil, Todorov, Stefanovic, Griffin, Davis, Mwaruwari, Karadas, Kiely, Jansen, D'Alessandro, O'Brien, Mendes, Primus, Routledge

Bolton: Davies, Hunt, Vaz Te, O'Brien, Ben Haim, Jaaskelainen, Fadiga, Fojut, N'Gotty, Nolan, Stelios, Gardner

4/4/1/1   **4/5/1**

Unused Sub: Ashdown, Hughes

Unused Sub: Walker, Nakata, Borgetti

Premiership Totals

	○ Portsmouth	Bolton ○
Premiership Appearances	1,039	1,147
Team Appearances	364	928
Goals Scored	39	113
Assists	49	95
Clean Sheets (goalkeepers)	52	47
Yellow Cards	108	153
Red Cards	7	9
Full Internationals	8	6

Age/Height

Portsmouth Age ▶ **27 yrs**

Bolton Wanderers Age ▶ **26 yrs, 2 mo**

Portsmouth Height ▶ **5'11"**

Bolton Wanderers Height ▶ **6'**

Match Statistics

League Table after Fixture

		Played	Won	Drawn	Lost	For	Against	Pts
● 1	Chelsea	24	20	3	1	50	13	63
● 2	Man Utd	24	14	6	4	45	24	48
● 3	Liverpool	22	13	6	3	30	13	45
● 4	Tottenham	24	11	8	5	31	20	41
● 5	Wigan	24	12	2	10	29	30	38
● 6	Arsenal	23	11	4	8	36	19	37
● 7	Bolton	22	10	7	5	28	21	37
...	...	...	...	...	...	...	...	...
● 19	Portsmouth	24	4	6	14	17	40	18

Statistics

	○ Portsmouth	Bolton ○
Goals	1	1
Shots on Target	5	2
Shots off Target	8	7
Hit Woodwork	0	0
Possession %	50	50
Corners	6	4
Offsides	1	5
Fouls	12	9
Disciplinary Points	0	0

1-1 Bolton Wanderers ○
Wigan Athletic ○

➡ Stelios sends over a cross

Event Line

16 ○ ▢ Mellor	
23 ○ ⇄ Hunt > Fadiga	
Half time 0-0	
46 ○ ⇄ Vaz Te > Jansen	
53 ○ ⇄ Borgetti > Davies	
63 ○ ⊕ Giannakopoulos / RF / IFK / 6Y	
Assist: Vaz Te	
65 ○ ⇄ Thompson > Baines	
65 ○ ⇄ Johansson > Mellor	
77 ○ ⊕ Johansson / RF / IFK / 6Y	
Assist: Ziegler	
80 ○ Chimbonda	
82 ○ Henchoz	
85 ○ Thompson	
Full time 1-1	

Honours ended up even in this local derby as Andreas Johannson cancelled out a Stelios strike to earn Wigan Athletic a point at the Reebok Stadium.

The Swedish midfielder, who was a second-half substitute, netted his first Barclays Premiership goal after 77 minutes following the Greece international's eighth goal of the campaign 14 minutes earlier.

But Wanderers suffered a major blow during the match after losing the services of Khalilou Fadiga for the remainder of the season.

Sam Allardyce made one change to his side with Hidetoshi Nakata replacing Nicky Hunt in the starting XI.

Quote

⑤ Sam Allardyce

It was a disappointing result, but the squad put in a tremendous effort considering the number of players we were without.

Venue:	Reebok Stadium	Referee:	S.G.Bennett - 05/06		Bolton Wanderers
Attendance:	25,854	Matches:	27		Wigan Athletic
Capacity:	28,101	Yellow Cards:	91		
Occupancy:	92%	Red Cards:	9		

Form Coming into Fixture

Position

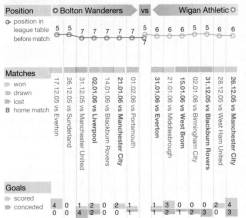

o- position in league table before match

Bolton Wanderers vs **Wigan Athletic** o

5 5 7 7 7 7 7 5 / 7 6 6 6 5 5 6 6

Matches
- won
- drawn
- lost
- B home match

17.12.05 vs Everton
26.12.05 vs Sunderland
31.12.05 vs Manchester United
02.01.06 vs Liverpool
14.01.06 vs Blackburn Rovers
21.01.06 vs Manchester City
01.02.06 vs Portsmouth
31.01.06 vs Everton
21.01.06 vs Middlesbrough
15.01.06 vs West Brom
02.01.06 vs Birmingham City
31.12.05 vs Blackburn Rovers
28.12.05 vs West Ham United
26.12.05 vs Manchester City

Goals
scored	4	0	1	2	0	2	1		1	3	0	0	2	4
conceded	0	0	4	2	0	0	1		1	2	1	2	3	3

Goal Statistics

o Bolton Wanderers

by Half — by Situation

- first: 5
- second: 5
- set piece: 5
- open play: 5

o Wigan Athletic

by Half — by Situation

- first: 8
- second: 2
- set piece: 2
- open play: 8

Goals by Area

o Bolton Wanderers
Scored (Conceded)

3 (3)
6 (4)
1 (0)

o Wigan Athletic
Scored (Conceded)

2 (5)
8 (6)
0 (1)

Team Statistics

Starting Line-Ups

Gardner	Stelios	Teale	Chimbonda
Nakata		Bullard	
N'Gotty			Henchoz
Jaaskelainen	Fadiga Hunt	Davies Borgetti	Mellor Johansson	Kavanagh	Pollitt
Ben Haim			De Zeeuw
Nolan		Scharner	
O'Brien	Jansen Vaz Te	Ziegler	Baines Thompson

4/5/1   **4/5/1**

Unused Sub: Walker, Fojut

Unused Sub: Walsh, Jackson, Francis

Premiership Totals
	o Bolton	Wigan o
Premiership Appearances	1,177	665
Team Appearances	958	177
Goals Scored	116	27
Assists	98	38
Clean Sheets (goalkeepers)	47	3
Yellow Cards	154	101
Red Cards	10	3
Full Internationals	8	5

Age/Height
Bolton Wanderers Age	Wigan Athletic Age
27 yrs, 5 mo	**27 yrs, 10 mo**
Bolton Wanderers Height	Wigan Athletic Height
6'	**5'11"**

Match Statistics

League Table after Fixture
		Played	Won	Drawn	Lost	For	Against	Pts
↓ 6	Wigan	25	12	3	10	30	31	39
● 7	Bolton	23	10	8	5	29	22	38
↑ 8	West Ham	25	11	5	9	36	34	38
↓ 9	Blackburn	24	11	4	9	31	30	37
● 10	Man City	25	10	4	11	33	28	34
↑ 11	Everton	25	10	3	12	18	32	33
↑ 12	Aston Villa	25	7	9	9	31	33	30
↓ 13	Charlton	22	9	3	10	27	31	30
↓ 14	Fulham	25	8	5	12	30	36	29

Statistics
	o Bolton	Wigan o
Goals	1	1
Shots on Target	9	4
Shots off Target	3	3
Hit Woodwork	0	0
Possession %	55	45
Corners	4	1
Offsides	4	2
Fouls	12	12
Disciplinary Points	0	16

1-1

Arsenal ○
Bolton Wanderers ○

▶ Tempers flare at Highbury

Event Line

12 ○ ⊕ Nolan / RF / OP / IA	
Assist: Jansen	
28 ○ ▨ Gilberto Silva	
30 ○ ▨ Diagne-Faye	
32 ○ ⇄ Pires > Reyes	
Half time 0-1	
46 ○ ⇄ Ljungberg > Diaby	
68 ○ ▨ Fabregas	
73 ○ ⇄ Bergkamp > Larsson	
75 ○ ⇄ Hunt > Diagne-Faye	
82 ○ ⇄ Vaz Te > Jansen	
85 ○ ▨ Davies	
90 ○ ⊕ Gilberto Silva / RF / OP / IA	
Assist: Fabregas	
90 ○ ⇄ Okocha > Giannakopoulos	
Full time 1-1	

Gilberto snatched a last minute leveller to prevent Wanderers from claiming a memorable hat-trick of wins against Arsenal.

The Brazilian ghosted in to volley past the previously unbeatable Jussi Jaaskelainen to cancel out Kevin Nolan's first-half opener.

Wanderers almost grabbed the lead on two occasions inside the opening 60 seconds. Kevin Nolan's side-footed volley from Matt Jansen's cross was denied by a diving save by Jens Lehmann. From the resulting set-play, Bruno N'Gotty towered above everybody at the far post but his header rebounded off the bar.

There was a penalty scare moments later when Jose Reyes made a meal out of Tal Ben Haim's challenge, but a goal kick was correctly awarded by Howard Webb.

But the visitors' early pressured paid off in the 11th minute, captain Nolan collecting in space before adeptly lobbing the advancing Lehmann with the outside of his right boot to claim his ninth goal of the season.

But, five minutes into time added on, the Brazilian midfielder volleyed past Jussi Jaaskelainen to steal a point for the hosts.

Quote

 Sam Allardyce

Our tremendous performance warranted three points, but it's our own fault for wasting golden chances to extend the lead.

Venue:	Highbury	Referee:	H.M.Webb - 05/06	Arsenal
Attendance:	38,193	Matches:	28	Bolton Wanderers
Capacity:	38,419	Yellow Cards:	68	
Occupancy:	99%	Red Cards:	3	

Form Coming into Fixture

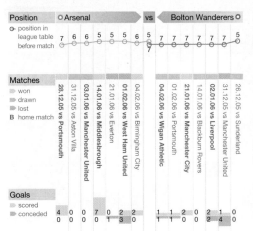

Position — Arsenal vs Bolton Wanderers

O- position in league table before match

Arsenal: 7 6 6 5 5 5 6 5 7 (below)
Bolton: 5 7 7 7 7 7 7 5

Matches
- won
- drawn
- lost
- B home match

Arsenal:
28.12.05 vs Portsmouth
31.12.05 vs Aston Villa
03.01.06 vs Manchester United
14.01.06 vs Middlesbrough
21.01.06 vs Everton
01.02.06 vs West Ham United
04.02.06 vs Birmingham City

Bolton:
04.02.06 vs Wigan Athletic
01.02.06 vs Portsmouth
21.01.06 vs Manchester City
14.01.06 vs Blackburn Rovers
02.01.06 vs Liverpool
31.12.05 vs Manchester United
26.12.05 vs Sunderland

Goals
- scored
- conceded

Arsenal: scored 4 0 0 7 0 2 2 | conceded 0 0 0 0 1 3 0
Bolton: scored 1 1 2 0 2 1 0 | conceded 1 1 0 0 2 4 0

Goal Statistics

Arsenal

by Half / by Situation
- first: 10
- second: 5
- set piece: 3
- open play: 12

Bolton Wanderers

by Half / by Situation
- first: 4
- second: 3
- set piece: 4
- open play: 3

Goals by Area

Arsenal — Scored (Conceded)
2 (0)
12 (4)
1 (0)

Bolton Wanderers — Scored (Conceded)
4 (4)
2 (4)
1 (0)

Team Statistics

Starting Line-Ups

Arsenal
Larsson, Reyes (Bergkamp, Pires)
Senderos, Gilberto Silva
Henry
Lehmann
Djourou, Diaby (Ljungberg), Adebayor
Flamini, Fabregas

Bolton Wanderers
Davies, O'Brien
Nolan
Ben Haim
Jansen (Vaz Té), Faye (Hunt)
N'Gotty
Nakata
Jääskeläinen
Stelios (Okocha), Gardner

4/4/2 — 4/5/1

Unused Sub: Almunia, Song
Unused Sub: Walker, Borgetti

Premiership Totals

	Arsenal	Bolton
Premiership Appearances	1,278	1,291
Team Appearances	1,278	1,072
Goals Scored	368	129
Assists	315	118
Clean Sheets (goalkeepers)	38	47
Yellow Cards	125	163
Red Cards	4	10
Full Internationals	9	8

Age/Height

	Arsenal	Bolton Wanderers
Age	25 yrs, 6 mo	27 yrs, 2 mo
Height	6'	5'11"

Match Statistics

League Table after Fixture

		Played	Won	Drawn	Lost	For	Against	Pts
● 5	Arsenal	25	12	5	8	39	20	41
↑ 6	Bolton	24	10	9	5	30	23	39
↓ 7	Wigan	26	12	3	11	30	32	39
● 8	West Ham	25	11	5	9	36	34	38
● 9	Blackburn	25	11	4	10	31	31	37
↑ 10	Everton	26	11	3	12	19	32	36
↓ 11	Man City	25	10	4	11	33	28	34
↓ 12	Charlton	24	10	3	11	30	34	33
↑ 13	Fulham	26	9	5	12	36	37	32

Statistics

	Arsenal	Bolton
Goals	1	1
Shots on Target	10	3
Shots off Target	6	2
Hit Woodwork	0	1
Possession %	47	53
Corners	8	6
Offsides	2	6
Fouls	14	12
Disciplinary Points	8	8

0-0

Bolton Wanderers ○
Olympique de Marseille ○

▶ Ricardo Gardner takes on Franck Ribery

Event Line	
31 ○ ■ Oruma	
Half time 0-0	
47 ○ ■ Cana	
60 ○ ⇄ Speed > Okocha	
62 ○ ■ Cesar	
67 ○ ⇄ Vaz Te > Borgetti	
70 ○ ■ Barthez	
73 ○ ■ Ferreira	
73 ○ ⇄ Gimenez > Nasri	
90 ○ ⇄ Cantareil > Niang	
Full time 0-0	

Bolton Wanderers were denied two valid penalty shouts as Marseille held them to a scoreless draw at the Reebok Stadium in the first-leg of their UEFA Cup Round of 32 tie.

A place in the last 16 of the competition was all the more likely after they kept a clean-sheet, but Wanderers were left cursing their luck at not being able to break a stoic Marseille defence.

However, Portuguese referee Olegario Buenquerenca waved away two clear-cut penalty shouts to leave Sam Allardyce and his men feeling frustrated.

The Wanderers boss made two changes from the side that drew against Arsenal at the weekend with Jared Borgetti and Jay Jay Okocha replacing the rested Matt Jansen and the suspended Hidetoshi Nakata.

Venue:	Reebok Stadium	Referee:	O.Benquerenca (POR)
Attendance:	19,288		
Capacity:	28,101		
Occupancy:	69%		

Bolton Wanderers
Olympique de Marseille

➡ Sam Allardyce makes some tactical adjustments

Match Statistics

Starting Line-Ups

➡ **4/5/1**   ➡ **5/3/2**

Unused Sub: Walker, Hunt, Jaidi, Fojut, Perez

Unused Sub: Carrasso, Meite, Civelli, Delfim, Deruda

Statistics	○ Bolton	Marseille ○
Goals	0	0
Shots on Target	7	3
Shots off Target	4	7
Hit Woodwork	0	0
Possession %	51	49
Corners	7	2
Offsides	3	1
Fouls	14	12
Disciplinary Points	0	20

Quote

❝ Sam Allardyce

We had a couple of chances that we missed and a number of penalty decisions that went against us.

0-0

Bolton Wanderers ○
West Ham United ○

► Ricardo Gardner tries to outwit Teddy Sheringham

Event Line

Half time 0-0

62 ○ ⇄ Zamora > Harewood

70 ○ ⇄ Vaz Te > Giannakopoulos

76 ○ ⇄ Sheringham > Ashton

82 ○ ⇄ Dailly > Benayoun

85 ○ ⇄ Borgetti > Davies

Full time 0-0

A replay at Upton Park was required to determine the winner of this FA Cup Fifth Round tie after a goalless stalemate was reached at the Reebok Stadium – but Wanderers will be frustrated after Stelios appeared to have a perfectly legitimate goal disallowed.

The Greek star found a way beyond Hammers' 'keeper Shaka Hislop just after the hour mark, but a flag robbed the midfielder of a goal despite television replays suggesting otherwise.

Wanderers, who had now faced the Hammers on three occasions this term, were poised to face a tough encounter in east London in ten days' time.

The hosts were by far the better side and enjoyed superior swathes of possession. They created chances but failed to break down the industrious West Ham defence, while Jussi Jaaskelainen wasn't tested by the Hammers' front-line.

Sam Allardyce made three changes; handing Gary Speed his first start in six weeks following an injury lay-off, while Radhi Jaidi and Hidetoshi Nakata also returned. Bruno N'Gotty was rested, presumable with Thursday's UEFA trip to Marseille in mind, and Jared Borgetti and Abdoulaye Faye sat on the bench.

West Ham were chasing their eighth successive victory in what has been an impressive season, and as such, Alan Pardew named an unchanged line-up from the side that thumped Birmingham City on Monday.

Venue:	Reebok Stadium	Referee:	C.J.Foy - 05/06		Bolton Wanderers
Attendance:	17,120	Matches:	28		West Ham United
Capacity:	28,101	Yellow Cards:	62		
Occupancy:	61%	Red Cards:	6		

▶ Ricardo Vaz Te attempts to shrug off Hayden Mullins

Match Statistics

Starting Line-Ups

▶ 4/5/1   ▶ 4/4/2

Unused Sub: Walker, Hunt, Faye   Unused Sub: Bywater, Collins

Statistics	○ Bolton	West Ham ○
Goals	0	0
Shots on Target	6	1
Shots off Target	11	3
Hit Woodwork	0	0
Possession %	47	53
Corners	4	3
Offsides	6	2
Fouls	9	11
Disciplinary Points	0	0

Age/Height

Bolton Wanderers Age
▶ **28 yrs, 2 mo**

West Ham United Age
▶ **27 yrs, 3 mo**

Bolton Wanderers Height
▶ **5'11"**

West Ham United Height
▶ **5'11"**

Quote

❝ **Sam Allardyce**

We have produced so much and come away with so little. We did not win the game because of our poor finishing.

2-1 Olympique de Marseille ○
Bolton Wanderers ○

➤ Stelios celebrates opening the scoring

Event Line

25 ○ ⊕	Giannakopoulos / RF / OP / 6Y	
39 ○ ■	Diagne-Faye	
45 ○ ⊕	Ribery / H / OP / IA	
	Assist: Nasri	

Half time 1-1

52 ○ ■	Beye	
66 ○ ⇄	Deruda > Ferreira	
67 ○ ■	Nolan	
68 ○ ⊕	Ben Haim / LF / OG / 6Y	
	Assist: Beye	
73 ○ ⇄	Pedersen > Diagne-Faye	
80 ○ ⇄	Cantareil > Ribery	
84 ○ ⇄	Vaz Te > Speed	
84 ○ ■	Cana	
87 ○ ⇄	Borgetti > Pedersen	
90 ○ ⇄	Civelli > Cana	

Full time 2-1

Wanderers' European dream ended in disappointment as they battled valiantly in the south of France.

Although Stelios' first-half opener put them on course for progression, the hosts fought back twice through Franck Ribery and a Tal Ben Haim own-goal to set themselves up for a quarter-final tie in St Petersburg.

Pre-match worries of Sam Allardyce's absence through illness were assuaged when the Wanderers boss landed at Marseille Airport four hours before kick off.

Allardyce was still suffering from the effects of a heavy chest infection as he jetted into the south of France but was able to pick his team and deliver the team-talk.

Bruno N'Gotty and Abdoulaye Faye returned to the starting line-up after being rested for the FA Cup tie against West Ham at the weekend. The pair who made way, Hidetoshi Nakata and Radhi Jaidi, occupied the bench, where a fit-again Henrik Pedersen sat.

▶ Kevin Nolan surges past Abdoulaye Meite

Match Statistics

Starting Line-Ups

▶ 5/3/2   ▶ 4/5/1

Unused Sub: Carrasso, Luis,
Gimenez, Begeorgi

Unused Sub: Walker, Hunt, Jaidi,
Nakata

Statistics	Marseille	Bolton
Goals	2	1
Shots on Target	4	4
Shots off Target	11	0
Hit Woodwork	0	0
Possession %	55	45
Corners	7	5
Offsides	0	5
Fouls	15	19
Disciplinary Points	8	8

Quote

❝ **Sammy Lee**

We are disappointed to lose the
game, but this isn't the end of
the journey.

2-1

Bolton Wanderers ○
Fulham ○

➧ Ricardo Gardner puts Moritz Volz under pressure

Event Line

22 ○ ⊕ Helguson / H / IFK / IA	
	Assist: Elliott
36 ○ ▓ Boa Morte	
42 ○ ▓ Nolan	
45 ○ ⊕ Helguson / RF / OG / 6Y	
	Assist: N'Gotty
Half time 1-1	
60 ○ ⇄ Speed > Diagne-Faye	
68 ○ ⊕ Nolan / RF / OP / IA	
	Assist: Davies
75 ○ ⇄ John > McBride	
75 ○ ⇄ Diop > Radzinski	
82 ○ ⇄ Vaz Te > Nakata	
90 ○ ⇄ Ben Haim > Okocha	
Full time 2-1	

Kevin Nolan's second-half strike ensured that Bolton Wanderers bounced back to winning ways following their UEFA Cup exit on Thursday evening.

The Wanderers' skipper completed a resilient fightback for Sam Allardyce's troops as Fulham threatened to pick up their first Premiership away win of the season when Heidar Helgusson put them in front with a fantastic headed goal.

But the Iceland international's bizarre own-goal on the cusp of half-time put the hosts back into the match, and eventually set them up for a win that took them to sixth in the Premiership.

Allardyce made two changes from the side that suffered disappointment in Marseille with Hidetoshi Nakata and Radhi Jaidi coming back into the fray at the expense of Gary Speed and Tal Ben Haim, who both occupied the bench.

Quote

 Sam Allardyce

I challenged the players after Thursday to hit back with a win. The lads were magnificent and showed great character after that defeat.

Form Coming into Fixture

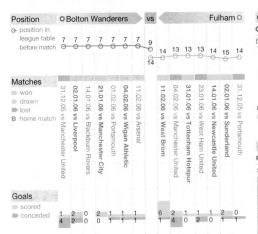

Position

- position in league table before match

Bolton Wanderers vs Fulham

Bolton: 7 7 7 7 7 7 7 9
Fulham: 14 13 13 13 14 15 14
14

Matches
- won
- drawn
- lost
- B home match

Bolton:
- 31.12.05 vs Manchester United
- 02.01.06 vs Liverpool
- 14.01.06 vs Blackburn Rovers
- 21.01.06 vs Manchester City
- 01.02.06 vs Portsmouth
- 04.02.06 vs Wigan Athletic
- 11.02.06 vs Arsenal

Fulham:
- 11.02.06 vs West Brom
- 04.02.06 vs Manchester United
- 31.01.06 vs Tottenham Hotspur
- 23.01.06 vs West Ham United
- 14.01.06 vs Newcastle United
- 02.01.06 vs Sunderland
- 31.12.05 vs Portsmouth

Goals
- scored
- conceded

Bolton: scored 1 2 0 2 1 1 1 / conceded 4 2 0 0 1 1 1
Fulham: scored 6 2 1 1 1 2 0 / conceded 1 4 0 2 0 1 1

Goal Statistics

Bolton Wanderers

by Half | by Situation

- first: 5
- second: 3
- set piece: 4
- open play: 4

Fulham

by Half | by Situation

- first: 5
- second: 8
- set piece: 3
- open play: 9
- own goals: 1

Goals by Area

Bolton Wanderers

Scored (Conceded)

4 (4)
3 (5)
1 (0)

Fulham

Scored (Conceded)

3 (0)
10 (6)
0 (3)

Team Statistics

Starting Line-Ups

Bolton Wanderers:
Gardner, Stelios, Nakata / Vaz Te, N'Gotty, Okocha / Ben Haim, Davies, Jaaskelainen, Jaidi, Faye / Speed, O'Brien, Nolan

Fulham:
Volz, Radzinski / Diop, Knight, McBride / John, Malbranque, Elliott, Warner, Helguson, Bocanegra, Boa Morte, Bridge

4/5/1

4/4/2 (Diamond)

Unused Sub: Walker, Borgetti

Unused Sub: Goma, Jensen N, Rosenior

Premiership Totals

	Bolton	Fulham
Premiership Appearances	1,646	1,185
Team Appearances	1,104	832
Goals Scored	187	150
Assists	153	143
Clean Sheets (goalkeepers)	47	2
Yellow Cards	217	124
Red Cards	11	10
Full Internationals	10	10

Age/Height

Bolton Wanderers Age: **28 yrs, 4 mo**

Fulham Age: **27 yrs, 10 mo**

Bolton Wanderers Height: **5'11"**

Fulham Height: **5'11"**

Match Statistics

League Table after Fixture

		Played	Won	Drawn	Lost	For	Against	Pts
↑ 6	Bolton	25	11	9	5	32	24	42
↓ 7	Arsenal	27	12	5	10	39	22	41
↓ 8	West Ham	26	12	5	9	39	34	41
↓ 9	Wigan	27	12	4	11	32	34	40
• 10	Man City	27	11	4	12	36	31	37
• 11	Newcastle	27	10	6	11	26	29	36
• 12	Everton	27	11	3	13	19	34	36
• 13	Charlton	27	10	5	12	32	37	35
• 14	Fulham	27	9	5	13	37	39	32

Statistics

Statistics	Bolton	Fulham
Goals	2	1
Shots on Target	5	6
Shots off Target	8	4
Hit Woodwork	0	1
Possession %	50	50
Corners	8	5
Offsides	10	1
Fouls	13	13
Disciplinary Points	4	4

3-1

Newcastle United ○
Bolton Wanderers ○

► Radhi Jaidi tries to reach the ball first

Event Line

17 ○ ⇄	Nakata > Okocha
34 ○ ⊕	Solano / RF / DFK / OA
	Assist: Ameobi
45 ○ ⊕	Shearer / H / OP / 6Y
	Assist: N'Zogbia
Half time 2-0	
46 ○ ⇄	Pedersen > N'Gotty
60 ○	Davies
70 ○ ⊕	Ameobi / RF / OP / IA
	Assist: Emre
72 ○ ⊕	Davies / RF / C / 6Y
	Assist: Jaidi
75 ○ ⇄	Vaz Te > Nakata
80 ○	Shearer
82 ○ ⇄	Bowyer > Emre
83 ○ ⇄	Luque > Ameobi
90 ○	Luque
Full time 3-1	

Bolton Wanderers' 47-year wait for a league victory at St James' Park must go on for another season as their seven-game unbeaten Barclays Premiership run came to an end against a rejuvenated Newcastle United.

First-half goals from Nolberto Solano and Alan Shearer caused the damage from which Sam Allardyce's men never truly recovered.

And when Shola Ameobi hit a third in the second-half the writing was on the wall for Wanderers.

Although Kevin Davies pegged a goal back, it was a case of too little too late as far as Wanderers were concerned.

Quote

❻ Sam Allardyce

Our goalkeeper could have saved the first two and we didn't do anything special until we were 2-0 down.

Venue:	St James' Park	Referee:	A.G.Wiley - 05/06		Newcastle United
Attendance:	52,012	Matches:	33		Bolton Wanderers
Capacity:	52,327	Yellow Cards:	100		
Occupancy:	99%	Red Cards:	7		

Form Coming into Fixture

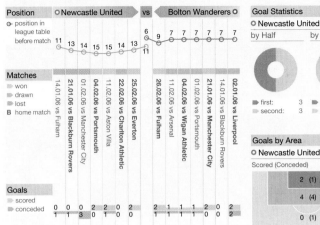

Position
Newcastle United vs Bolton Wanderers

⊙ position in league table before match

Newcastle United: 11, 13, 14, 15, 15, 14, 13
Bolton Wanderers: 6, 9, 11, 7, 7, 7, 7, 7, 7

Matches
- won
- drawn
- lost
- B home match

Newcastle matches:
14.01.06 vs Fulham
21.01.06 vs Blackburn Rovers
01.02.06 vs Manchester City
04.02.06 vs Portsmouth
11.02.06 vs Aston Villa
22.02.06 vs Charlton Athletic
25.02.06 vs Everton

Bolton matches:
26.02.06 vs Fulham
11.02.06 vs Arsenal
04.02.06 vs Wigan Athletic
01.02.06 vs Portsmouth
21.01.06 vs Manchester City
14.01.06 vs Blackburn Rovers
02.01.06 vs Liverpool

Goals
- scored
- conceded

Newcastle: scored 0 0 0 2 2 0 2 / conceded 1 1 3 0 1 0 0
Bolton: scored 2 1 1 1 2 0 2 / conceded 1 1 1 1 0 0 2

Goal Statistics

⊙ Newcastle United
by Half | by Situation
- first: 3 — set piece: 1
- second: 3 — open play: 5

⊙ Bolton Wanderers
by Half | by Situation
- first: 5 — set piece: 4
- second: 4 — open play: 4
- own goals: 1

Goals by Area

⊙ Newcastle United — Scored (Conceded)
2 (1)
4 (4)
0 (1)

⊙ Bolton Wanderers — Scored (Conceded)
4 (1)
4 (5)
1 (0)

Team Statistics

Starting Line-Ups

Newcastle United:
Babayaro, N'Zogbia
Elliott, Emre (Bowyer), Ameobi (Luque)
Given
Boumsong, Parker, Shearer
Ramage, Solano

4/4/2

Unused Sub: Harper, Clark, Faye

Bolton Wanderers:
Nolan, O'Brien
Okocha (Nakata), Jaidi
Davies, Faye, Jaaskelainen
N'Gotty (Pedersen)
Speed
Stelios, Gardner

4/5/1

Unused Sub: Walker, Ben Haim

Premiership Totals

	⊙ Newcastle	Bolton ⊙
Premiership Appearances	1,932	1,729
Team Appearances	1,269	1,187
Goals Scored	389	207
Assists	253	163
Clean Sheets (goalkeepers)	78	47
Yellow Cards	242	209
Red Cards	16	11
Full Internationals	9	11

Age/Height

Newcastle United Age: **27 yrs, 6 mo**
Bolton Wanderers Age: **28 yrs, 10 mo**

Newcastle United Height: **5'11"**
Bolton Wanderers Height: **6'**

Match Statistics

League Table after Fixture

		Played	Won	Drawn	Lost	For	Against	Pts
↑ 2	Liverpool	28	16	7	5	33	17	55
↓ 3	Man Utd	26	16	6	4	52	27	54
● 4	Tottenham	27	12	10	5	37	24	46
↑ 5	Arsenal	28	13	5	10	43	22	44
↓ 6	Blackburn	27	13	4	10	34	31	43
↓ 7	Bolton	26	11	9	6	33	27	42
● 8	West Ham	27	12	6	9	41	36	42
● 9	Wigan	27	12	4	11	32	34	40
↑ 10	Newcastle	28	11	6	11	29	30	39

Statistics

	⊙ Newcastle	Bolton ⊙
Goals	3	1
Shots on Target	5	3
Shots off Target	4	8
Hit Woodwork	1	0
Possession %	62	38
Corners	11	5
Offsides	3	4
Fouls	18	14
Disciplinary Points	8	4

4-1

Bolton Wanderers ○
West Ham United ○

▶ Stelios looks to get beyond Anton Ferdinand

Event Line

12 ○ ⊕ Giannakopoulos / RF / OP / IA	
Assist: Vaz Te	
33 ○ ⊕ Giannakopoulos / RF / OP / IA	
Assist: Nolan	
45 ○ ⊕ Speed / LF / IFK / IA	
Assist: Gardner	
Half time 3-0	
46 ○ ⇄ Benayoun > Newton	
46 ○ ⇄ Dailly > Ward	
47 ○ Scaloni	
67 ○ ⇄ Hunt > O'Brien	
73 ○ Sheringham	
75 ○ ⇄ Pedersen > Giannakopoulos	
79 ○ ⊕ Sheringham / RF / OP / 6Y	
Assist: Benayoun	
81 ○ ⊕ Pedersen / LF / OP / OA	
Assist: Vaz Te	
83 ○ Konchesky	
84 ○ ⇄ Nakata > Okocha	
85 ○ Dailly	
87 ○ Vaz Te	
88 ○ Ferdinand	
Full time 4-1	

Bolton Wanderers bounced back to winning ways with an emphatic victory over Wednesday night's FA Cup replay opponents West Ham.

Goals from Stelios (2), Gary Speed and Henrik Pedersen completed a glorious win over their fellow European hopefuls and put the previous Saturday's disappointing defeat against Newcastle United to the back of their minds in memorable fashion.

Ricardo Vaz Te was handed only his second start of the campaign as Wanderers manager Sam Allardyce made two changes from the side that lost to Newcastle United seven days' earlier.

The Portuguese under-21 international replaced Abdoulaye Faye, who was absent with a viral infection. Tal Ben Haim also came into the starting XI to replace the rested Bruno N'Gotty.

Hammers' boss Alan Pardew picked his side with a view to Wednesday night's FA Cup contest at Upton Park. Veteran Teddy Sheringham was recalled into the attack to partner Bobby Zamora, with regular duo Marlon Harewood and Dean Ashton dropping to the bench.

Quote

❝ **Sam Allardyce**

The first 45 minutes were probably the best we've produced all season in terms of flair, ability, passing and movement.

Venue:	Reebok Stadium	Referee:	M.L.Dean - 05/06	**Bolton Wanderers**
Attendance:	24,461	Matches:	28	**West Ham United**
Capacity:	28,101	Yellow Cards:	76	
Occupancy:	87%	Red Cards:	7	

Form Coming into Fixture

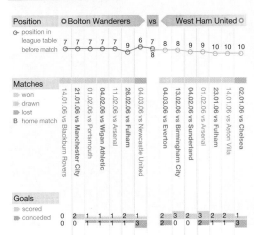

Position

○ Bolton Wanderers vs West Ham United ○

position in league table before match: 7 7 7 7 7 9 6 8 7 8 8 9 9 10 10 10 10

Matches
- won
- drawn
- lost
- B home match

14.01.06 vs Blackburn Rovers
21.01.06 vs Manchester City
01.02.06 vs Portsmouth
04.02.06 vs Wigan Athletic
11.02.06 vs Arsenal
25.02.06 vs Fulham
04.03.06 vs Newcastle United
04.03.06 vs Everton
13.02.06 vs Birmingham City
04.02.06 vs Sunderland
01.02.06 vs Arsenal
23.01.06 vs Fulham
14.01.06 vs Aston Villa
02.01.06 vs Chelsea

Goals
scored	0	2	1	1	1	2	1		2	3	2	3	2	2	1
conceded	0	0	1	1	1	1	3		2	0	0	2	1	1	3

Goal Statistics

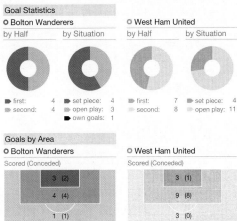

○ Bolton Wanderers

by Half | by Situation
- first: 4
- second: 4
- set piece: 4
- open play: 3
- own goals: 1

○ West Ham United

by Half | by Situation
- first: 7
- second: 8
- set piece: 4
- open play: 11

Goals by Area

○ Bolton Wanderers
Scored (Conceded)
- 3 (2)
- 4 (4)
- 1 (1)

○ West Ham United
Scored (Conceded)
- 3 (1)
- 9 (8)
- 3 (0)

Team Statistics

Starting Line-Ups

Bolton Wanderers:
Jaaskelainen
Gardner, Vaz Te
Speed
Jaidi
Okocha (Nakata), Davies
Ben Haim
Nolan
O'Brien (Hunt), Stelios (Pedersen)

▶ 4/5/1

Unused Sub: Walker, Borgetti

West Ham United:
Newton, Scaloni
Benayoun
Ferdinand, Gabbidon
Sheringham
Hislop
Zamora
Mullins, Ward (Dailly)
Etherington, Konchesky

▶ 4/4/2

Unused Sub: Bywater, Ashton, Harewood

Premiership Totals
	○ Bolton	West Ham ○
Premiership Appearances	1,702	1,248
Team Appearances	1,160	425
Goals Scored	204	167
Assists	163	140
Clean Sheets (goalkeepers)	47	56
Yellow Cards	215	105
Red Cards	9	6
Full Internationals	10	7

Age/Height
Bolton Wanderers Age	West Ham United Age
▶ 27 yrs, 9 mo	▶ 28 yrs
Bolton Wanderers Height	West Ham United Height
▶ 5'11"	▶ 5'11"

Match Statistics

League Table after Fixture
		Played	Won	Drawn	Lost	For	Against	Pts
● 1	Chelsea	29	24	3	2	58	18	75
● 2	Man Utd	27	17	6	4	54	28	57
● 3	Liverpool	28	16	7	5	33	17	55
● 4	Tottenham	29	13	10	6	41	28	49
↑ 5	Blackburn	29	14	4	11	38	34	46
↑ 6	Bolton	27	12	9	6	37	28	45
↓ 7	Arsenal	28	13	5	10	43	22	44
↑ 8	Wigan	29	13	4	12	34	36	43
↓ 9	West Ham	28	12	6	10	42	40	42

Statistics
	○ Bolton	West Ham ○
Goals	4	1
Shots on Target	10	5
Shots off Target	9	4
Hit Woodwork	1	0
Possession %	50	50
Corners	7	6
Offsides	5	4
Fouls	12	18
Disciplinary Points	4	20

2-1

West Ham United ○
Bolton Wanderers ○

► Kevin Nolan battles with Paul Konchesky

Event Line

10 ○ ⊕ Jaaskelainen / H / OG / 6Y	
12 ○ ▇ Etherington	
12 ○ ▇ Nolan	
17 ○ ▇ Harewood	
28 ○ ▇ Ben Haim	
31 ○ ⊕ Davies / RF / OP / OA	
Assist: Nolan	
Half time 1-1	
53 ○ ▇ Reo-Coker	
79 ○ ⇄ Pedersen > Diagne-Faye	
96 ○ ⊕ Harewood / RF / OP / 6Y	
Assist: Benayoun	
98 ○ ⇄ Dailly > Reo-Coker	
105 ○ ⇄ Sheringham > Ashton	
105 ○ ⇄ Zamora > Etherington	
105 ○ ▇ Pedersen	
105 ○ ⇄ Vaz Te > Speed	
113 ○ ⇄ Borgetti > Hunt	
Full time 2-1	

Sam Allardyce's FA Cup dream must go on hold for another season after Marlon Harewood's extra time strike put West Ham United into the quarter-final.

The former Forest man hit the winner five minutes into overtime after Kevin Davies cancelled out Jussi Jaaskelainen's own-goal during the first-half.

The Wanderers boss made two changes from his side that thumped West Ham United in the league at the weekend, as both sides took to the field to determine who would play Manchester City in the FA Cup quarter-final at the City of Manchester Stadium on Monday evening.

Nicky Hunt returned to the starting line-up at the expense of the rested Joey O'Brien, while Abdoulaye Faye recovered from a virus to oust Ricardo Vaz Te, who occupied a seat on the bench.

Alan Pardew, the West Ham manager, recalled Dean Ashton, Marlon Harewood and Yossi Benayoun, after his decision to name them on the bench for last Saturday's league clash proved to be costly.

This was the fifth occasion both sides had met this term with Wanderers claiming three victories, to the Hammers' scoreless draw in the cup tie that preceded this fixture.

► Ricardo Gardner races past Lionel Scaloni

Match Statistics

Starting Line-Ups

4/4/2

Unused Sub: Bywater, Clarke

4/5/1

Unused Sub: Al Habsi, N'Gotty

Statistics	○ West Ham	Bolton ○
Goals	2	1
Shots on Target	8	9
Shots off Target	8	10
Hit Woodwork	0	0
Possession %	55	45
Corners	4	8
Offsides	3	5
Fouls	15	17
Disciplinary Points	12	12

Age/Height

West Ham United Age

27 yrs, 4 mo

Bolton Wanderers Age

28 yrs, 7 mo

West Ham United Height

5'11"

Bolton Wanderers Height

6'

Quote

❝ **Sam Allardyce**

We should have put the game away in the first 90 minutes and have ended up paying a heavy price for not doing so.

2-0

Bolton Wanderers ○
Sunderland ○

▶ Kevin Nolan celebrates making sure of the points

Event Line

30 ○ ⇄	Pedersen > Gardner
45 ○ ▢	Kyle
Half time 0-0	
47 ○ ⊕	Davies / H / C / 6Y
	Assist: Giannakopoulos
56 ○	Delap
57 ○ ⇄	Murphy D > Smith
63 ○ ⇄	Brown > Kyle
65 ○ ⇄	Borgetti > Vaz Te
69 ○ ▢	Nolan
72 ○ ⇄	Breen > Leadbitter
76 ○ ▢	Breen
80 ○ ▢	Brown
85 ○ ⊕	Nolan / RF / OP / IA
	Assist: Speed
87 ○ ⇄	Diagne-Faye > Okocha
Full time 2-0	

Kevin Davies and Kevin Nolan were both on the scoresheet as Bolton Wanderers comfortably beat bottom-of-the-table Sunderland.

Davies netted Wanderers' 300th goal in their Premier League history, just after the interval, to set Wanderers on their way, before captain Nolan made sure of the victory with his 11th goal five minutes from time.

Quote

❝ Sam Allardyce

Kevin Nolan is a great example to the team and has a great attitude too.

Premiership Milestone

▶ **300**

Kevin Davies marked his 100th top-flight appearance in the colours of Bolton by netting the club's 300th Premiership goal.

Venue:	Reebok Stadium		Referee:	P.Dowd - 05/06		**Bolton Wanderers**
Attendance:	23,568		Matches:	38		**Sunderland**
Capacity:	28,101		Yellow Cards:	147		
Occupancy:	84%		Red Cards:	5		

Form Coming into Fixture

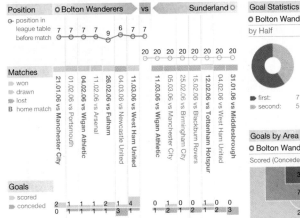

Position

○ Bolton Wanderers vs Sunderland ○

position in league table before match: 7 7 7 7 9 6 7 7 / 20 20 20 20 20 20 20 20

Matches
- won
- drawn
- lost
- B home match

21.01.06 vs Manchester City
01.02.06 vs Portsmouth
04.02.06 vs Wigan Athletic
11.02.06 vs Arsenal
26.02.06 vs Fulham
11.03.06 vs West Ham United
11.03.06 vs Wigan Athletic
05.03.06 vs Manchester City
25.02.06 vs Birmingham City
15.02.06 vs Blackburn Rovers
12.02.06 vs Tottenham Hotspur
04.02.06 vs West Ham United
31.01.06 vs Middlesbrough

Goals
- scored
- conceded

scored	2	1	1	1	2	1	4		0	1	0	0	1	0	0
conceded	0	1	1	1	1	3	1		1	2	1	2	1	2	3

Goal Statistics

○ Bolton Wanderers

by Half / by Situation

- first: 7
- second: 5
- set piece: 5
- open play: 6
- own goals: 1

○ Sunderland

by Half / by Situation

- first: 1
- second: 1
- set piece: 1
- open play: 1

Goals by Area

○ Bolton Wanderers — Scored (Conceded)

3 (3)
7 (4)
2 (1)

○ Sunderland — Scored (Conceded)

2 (3)
0 (7)
0 (2)

Team Statistics

Starting Line-Ups

Gardner, Stelios, Whitehead, Nosworthy
Pedersen
Speed, Miller
N'Gotty, Caldwell
Jaaskelainen, Okocha, Davies, Kyle Brown, Leadbitter Breen, Davis
Faye
Ben Haim, Collins D
Nolan, Delap
O'Brien, Vaz Te, Smith, McCartney
Borgetti, Murphy D

▶ **4/5/1**   ▶ **4/5/1**

Unused Sub: Walker, Nakata
Unused Sub: Alnwick, Bassila

Premiership Totals	○ Bolton	Sunderland ○
Premiership Appearances	1,755	661
Team Appearances	1,213	264
Goals Scored	206	28
Assists	163	33
Clean Sheets (goalkeepers)	47	3
Yellow Cards	218	93
Red Cards	10	6
Full Internationals	11	6

Age/Height

Bolton Wanderers Age ▶ **28 yrs, 8 mo**   Sunderland Age ▶ **25 yrs, 2 mo**

Bolton Wanderers Height ▶ **6'**   Sunderland Height ▶ **6'**

Match Statistics

League Table after Fixture

		Played	Won	Drawn	Lost	For	Against	Pts
● 1	Chelsea	29	24	3	2	58	18	75
● 2	Man Utd	29	19	6	4	58	29	63
● 3	Liverpool	30	17	7	6	39	20	58
● 4	Tottenham	30	14	10	6	43	28	52
● 5	Arsenal	30	15	5	10	48	23	50
● 6	Blackburn	30	15	4	11	41	36	49
● 7	Bolton	28	13	9	6	39	28	48
...		...	...	...	...	...	...	...
● 20	Sunderland	30	2	4	24	19	54	10

Statistics	○ Bolton	Sunderland ○
Goals	2	0
Shots on Target	7	3
Shots off Target	9	3
Hit Woodwork	0	0
Possession %	59	41
Corners	7	6
Offsides	2	3
Fouls	9	18
Disciplinary Points	4	16

4-3

Middlesbrough ○
Bolton Wanderers ○

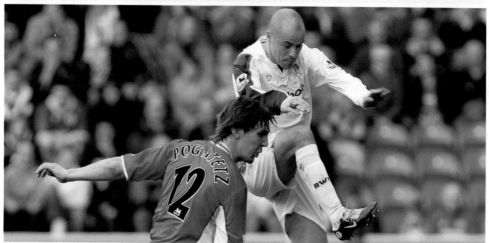

➡ Stelios fires the ball goalwards

Stuart Parnaby condemned Wanderers to a heartbreaking defeat at the Riverside Stadium with an injury-time winner for Middlesbrough.

Wanderers drew first blood after three minutes when Stelios showed superb tenacity to race on to a long ball and fire home right-footed from six yards, but Boro equalised five minutes later through a Jimmy Floyd Hasselbaink penalty

Boro stole ahead on the half hour mark, Hasselbaink chesting the ball directly into the path of onrushing strike partner Mark Viduka to slot home.

Shortly after the restart Boro edged 3-1 ahead after Hasselbaink latched on to a Viduka flick and coolly lifted the ball over the onrushing Jussi Jaaskelainen.

Jay-Jay Okocha blasted a 58th-minute straight at Mark Schwarzer, but was on hand to fire home the rebound. With seven minutes remaining a neat short corner routine saw Bolton level, Radhi Jaidi heading home Ricardo Gardner's dangerous cross.

But just when Wanderers looked to have secured a priceless point in their quest for another season of European football, Parnaby slotted home Yakubu's cross.

Quote

❝ **Sam Allardyce**

We should have prevented three Middlesbrough goals and it is something that is really concerning me.

Venue:	Riverside Stadium	Referee:	H.M.Webb - 05/06	Middlesbrough
Attendance:	25,971	Matches:	35	Bolton Wanderers
Capacity:	35,100	Yellow Cards:	93	
Occupancy:	74%	Red Cards:	4	

Form Coming into Fixture

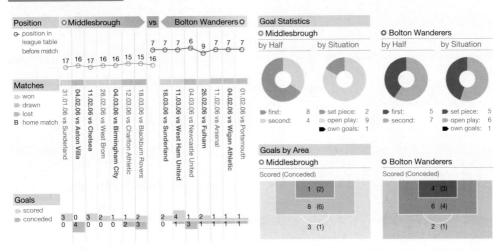

Position ○ Middlesbrough vs Bolton Wanderers ○

G- position in league table before match

Middlesbrough: 17 16 17 16 16 15 15 16
Bolton Wanderers: 7 7 7 6 9 7 7 7

Matches
- won
- drawn
- lost
- B home match

Middlesbrough matches: 31.01.06 vs Sunderland, 04.02.06 vs Aston Villa, 11.02.06 vs Chelsea, 26.02.06 vs West Brom, 04.03.06 vs Birmingham City, 12.03.06 vs Charlton Athletic, 18.03.06 vs Blackburn Rovers

Bolton matches: 18.03.06 vs Sunderland, 11.03.06 vs West Ham United, 04.03.06 vs Newcastle United, 26.02.06 vs Fulham, 11.02.06 vs Arsenal, 04.02.06 vs Wigan Athletic, 01.02.06 vs Portsmouth

Goals
- scored
- conceded

Middlesbrough: scored 3 0 3 2 1 1 2 / conceded 0 4 0 0 0 2 3
Bolton: scored 2 4 1 2 1 1 1 / conceded 0 1 3 1 1 1 1

Goal Statistics

○ Middlesbrough — by Half / by Situation
- first: 8
- second: 4
- set piece: 2
- open play: 9
- own goals: 1

○ Bolton Wanderers — by Half / by Situation
- first: 5
- second: 7
- set piece: 5
- open play: 6
- own goals: —

Goals by Area

○ Middlesbrough — Scored (Conceded)

1 (2)
8 (6)
3 (1)

○ Bolton Wanderers — Scored (Conceded)

4 (3)
6 (4)
2 (1)

Team Statistics

Starting Line-Ups

Middlesbrough: Pogatetz, Rochemback (Downing), Queudrue, Schwarzer, Ehiogu, Boateng, Viduka, Davies, Hasselbaink (Yakubu), Morrison (Cattermole), Parnaby

Bolton Wanderers: Stelios, O'Brien, Nolan (Nakata), Ben Haim, Davies, Okocha, Jaaskelainen, Jaidi, Speed (Faye), Pedersen (Borgetti), Gardner

5/3/2   **4/5/1**

Unused Sub: Jones, Mendieta
Unused Sub: Walker, Diouf

Premiership Totals	○ Boro	Bolton ○
Premiership Appearances	1,775	1,659
Team Appearances	994	1,117
Goals Scored	288	211
Assists	193	159
Clean Sheets (goalkeepers)	76	48
Yellow Cards	207	208
Red Cards	16	9
Full Internationals	9	12

Age/Height

Middlesbrough Age **26 yrs, 1 mo** — Bolton Wanderers Age **29 yrs, 1 mo**

Middlesbrough Height **6'** — Bolton Wanderers Height **5'11"**

Match Statistics

League Table after Fixture

		Played	Won	Drawn	Lost	For	Against	Pts
●	6 Arsenal	30	15	5	10	48	23	50
●	7 Bolton	29	13	9	7	42	32	48
●	8 Wigan	31	14	4	13	36	38	46
●	9 West Ham	30	13	6	11	46	45	45
●	10 Everton	31	13	4	14	29	41	43
↑	11 Charlton	31	12	6	13	37	42	42
↓	12 Man City	31	12	4	15	39	37	40
↓	13 Newcastle	31	11	6	14	31	38	39
↑	14 Middlesbrough	30	10	7	13	43	52	37

Statistics	○ Boro	Bolton ○
Goals	4	3
Shots on Target	12	6
Shots off Target	5	5
Hit Woodwork	0	0
Possession %	56	44
Corners	1	6
Offsides	2	6
Fouls	11	12
Disciplinary Points	8	8

1-2

Bolton Wanderers ○
Manchester United ○

▶ Jay-Jay Okocha tries to keep his balance

Event Line

26 ○ ⊕	Davies / RF / OP / IA
	Assist: Nolan
33 ○ ⊕	Saha / LF / OP / IA
	Assist: Silvestre
Half time 1-1	
61 ○ ⇄	van Nistelrooy > Fletcher
72 ○	Ronaldo
74 ○ ⇄	Hunt > O'Brien
79 ○ ⊕	van Nistelrooy / RF / OP / 6Y
	Assist: Saha
82 ○	Rooney
87 ○ ⇄	Borgetti > Davies
87 ○ ⇄	Diouf > Speed
90 ○ ⇄	Park > Ronaldo
90 ○	Diagne-Faye
Full time 1-2	

Fortress Reebok was breached for the first time since the opening day of the season as Manchester United came from behind to maintain their hopes of catching Chelsea at the top of the Barclays Premiership.

But Wanderers battled every inch of the way, hoping to get back on track following last week's 4-3 reverse against Middlesbrough.

They took the lead through Kevin Davies' sixth of the season only to see Louis Saha cancel the strike out seven minutes later.

Substitute Ruud van Nistelrooy then wrapped up the win with 11 minutes remaining.

Wanderers suffered a blow before the game got underway with the news that Ricardo Gardner was to miss the match through illness. The left-back was replaced by Henrik Pedersen, who started last week's game against Middlesbrough in his familiar forward role. Bruno N'Gotty, who was rested at the Riverside, returned to the starting line-up at the expense of Radhi Jaidi.

Quote

❻ Sam Allardyce

I was pleased with the way we played, but their forward line was very difficult to play against.

Venue:	Reebok Stadium		Referee:	A.G.Wiley - 05/06		**Bolton Wanderers**
Attendance:	27,718		Matches:	38		**Manchester United**
Capacity:	28,101		Yellow Cards:	115		
Occupancy:	99%		Red Cards:	7		

Form Coming into Fixture

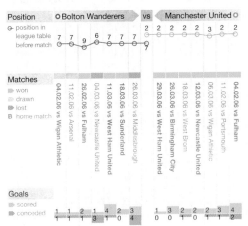

Position ○ Bolton Wanderers ▶ vs ◀ Manchester United ○

position in league table before match

Bolton: 7 7 9 6 7 7 7 7
Man Utd: 2 2 2 2 2 3 2 2

Matches
- won
- drawn
- lost
- B home match

Goals
- scored
- conceded

Bolton scored: 1 1 2 1 4 2 3
Bolton conceded: 1 1 1 3 1 0 4

Man Utd scored: 1 3 2 2 3 4
Man Utd conceded: 0 0 1 0 1 2

Goal Statistics

○ Bolton Wanderers

by Half	by Situation
first: 6	set piece: 6
second: 8	open play: 7
	own goals: 1

○ Manchester United

by Half	by Situation
first: 12	set piece: 3
second: 5	open play: 12
	own goals: 2

Goals by Area

○ Bolton Wanderers
Scored (Conceded)

6 (4)
7 (6)
1 (1)

○ Manchester United
Scored (Conceded)

2 (4)
11 (1)
4 (0)

Team Statistics

Starting Line-Ups

Pedersen, Stelios, Speed (Diouf), N'Gotty, Jaaskelainen, Faye, Davies (Borgetti), Ben Haim, Okocha, O'Brien (Hunt), Nolan

Ronaldo, Neville (Park), Fletcher (van Nistelrooy), Ferdinand, Rooney, van der Sar, Saha, O'Shea, Vidic, Giggs, Silvestre

4/5/1　　**4/4/2**

Unused Sub: Al Habsi, Nakata　　Unused Sub: Howard, Evra, Pique

Premiership Totals	○ Bolton	Man Utd ○
Premiership Appearances	1,788	2,140
Team Appearances	1,191	1,681
Goals Scored	221	306
Assists	172	330
Clean Sheets (goalkeepers)	48	56
Yellow Cards	239	175
Red Cards	9	9
Full Internationals	11	13

Age/Height

Bolton Wanderers Age
▶ 28 yrs, 9 mo

Manchester United Age
▷ 27 yrs

Bolton Wanderers Height
▶ 6'

Manchester United Height
▷ 6'1"

Match Statistics

League Table after Fixture

		Played	Won	Drawn	Lost	For	Against	Pts
● 2	Man Utd	32	22	6	4	64	30	72
● 3	Liverpool	33	20	7	6	47	22	67
● 4	Tottenham	32	15	10	7	46	32	55
↑ 5	Arsenal	31	16	5	10	53	23	53
↓ 6	Blackburn	31	16	4	11	42	36	52
● 7	Bolton	30	13	9	8	43	34	48
● 8	Wigan	31	14	4	13	36	38	46
● 9	West Ham	31	13	6	12	46	46	45
● 10	Everton	32	13	5	14	31	43	44

Statistics	○ Bolton	Man Utd ○
Goals	1	2
Shots on Target	2	10
Shots off Target	5	4
Hit Woodwork	0	0
Possession %	50	50
Corners	3	5
Offsides	2	1
Fouls	17	11
Disciplinary Points	4	8

1-0

Birmingham City ○
Bolton Wanderers ○

▶ Bruno N'Gotty gives Mikael Forssell little room in which to work

Wanderers' aspirations of playing Champions League football next season took a stern blow at St Andrew's as Birmingham City moved out of the relegation zone with a 1-0 win.

Jiri Jarosik's first-half stunner gave Steve Bruce's men a perfect tonic which saw them leapfrog West Midlands rivals West Brom and, more importantly, climb away from the bottom three.

It was Wanderers' third defeat on the trot, and with games against Liverpool and Chelsea on the horizon, Sam Allardyce's men were in urgent need of a lift.

Quote

 Sam Allardyce

One terrific goal from Jiri Jarosik was the difference and Champions League qualification is drifting away rapidly now.

Premiership Milestone

 50

Tal Ben Haim made his 50th Premiership appearance.

Venue:	St Andrew's	Referee:	C.J.Foy - 05/06		**Birmingham City**
Attendance:	26,493	Matches:	35		**Bolton Wanderers**
Capacity:	30,016	Yellow Cards:	82		
Occupancy:	88%	Red Cards:	9		

Form Coming into Fixture

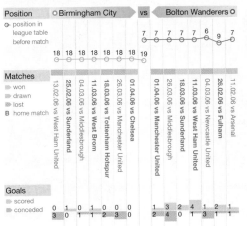

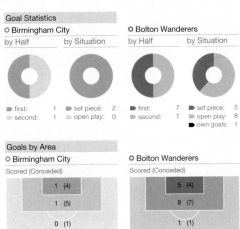

Goal Statistics

○ Birmingham City

by Half · by Situation

- ▶ first: 1
- ▶ second: 1
- ▶ set piece: 2
- ▶ open play: 0

○ Bolton Wanderers

by Half · by Situation

- ▶ first: 7
- ▶ second: 7
- ▶ set piece: 5
- ▶ open play: 8
- ▶ own goals: 1

Goals by Area

○ Birmingham City
Scored (Conceded)

1 (4)	
1 (5)	
0 (1)	

○ Bolton Wanderers
Scored (Conceded)

5 (4)	
8 (7)	
1 (1)	

Team Statistics

Starting Line-Ups

▶ 4/5/1 · ▶ 4/5/1

Unused Sub: Vaesen, Campbell · Unused Sub: Walker, Nakata

Premiership Totals

	○ Birmingham	Bolton ○
Premiership Appearances	2,101	1,349
Team Appearances	879	1,166
Goals Scored	186	150
Assists	211	129
Clean Sheets (goalkeepers)	40	48
Yellow Cards	223	181
Red Cards	16	8
Full Internationals	10	10

Age/Height

Birmingham City Age	Bolton Wanderers Age
▶ **28 yrs, 6 mo**	▶ **27 yrs, 7 mo**
Birmingham City Height	Bolton Wanderers Height
▶ **6'**	▶ **6'**

Match Statistics

League Table after Fixture

		Played	Won	Drawn	Lost	For	Against	Pts
● 1	Chelsea	32	25	4	3	60	19	79
● 2	Man Utd	32	22	6	4	64	30	72
● 3	Liverpool	33	20	7	6	47	22	67
● 4	Tottenham	32	15	10	7	46	32	55
● 5	Arsenal	31	16	5	10	53	23	53
● 6	Blackburn	32	16	5	11	43	37	53
● 7	Bolton	31	13	9	9	43	35	48
...		...	...	...	...	...	...	...
↑ 17	Birmingham	32	7	7	18	24	44	28

Statistics

	○ Birmingham	Bolton ○
Goals	1	0
Shots on Target	2	1
Shots off Target	5	7
Hit Woodwork	0	0
Possession %	47	53
Corners	5	2
Offsides	1	1
Fouls	12	7
Disciplinary Points	4	0

1-0

Liverpool ○
Bolton Wanderers ○

➡ Ivan Campo is stopped in his tracks by Dietmar Hamann

Event Line

20 ○ ■	Diagne-Faye
45 ○ ⊕	Fowler / LF / OP / IA
	Assist: Crouch

Half time 1-0

46 ○ ⇄	Garcia > Cisse
53 ○ ⇄	Pedersen > Giannakopoulos
57 ○ ■	Hyypia
61 ○ ⇄	Jansen > Okocha
74 ○ ⇄	Campo > Diagne-Faye
75 ○ ⇄	Hamann > Fowler
88 ○ ⇄	Traore > Kewell

Full time 1-0

Robbie Fowler's strike seconds before the interval consigned Wanderers to their fourth consecutive defeat as Liverpool maintained their chase with Manchester United for second spot.

The visitors showed a marked improvement from the 1-0 defeat at Birmingham City in midweek, but failed to really test Jose Reina in the Liverpool goal.

Buoyed by the return to fitness of Gary Speed and Ricardo Gardner, Sam Allardyce was able to name his strongest line-up.

Nicky Hunt also came into the starting XI as the Wanderers boss made a total of three changes from the side that lost to Birmingham City in midweek.

Ivan Campo and Matt Jansen, who both enjoyed run-outs for the reserves on Wednesday evening, were named on the bench after recovering from long-term injuries.

Quote

❝ **Sam Allardyce**

We paid the price for creating chances and not taking them.

Venue:	Anfield		Referee:	R.Styles - 05/06
Attendance:	44,194		Matches:	39
Capacity:	45.362		Yellow Cards:	126
Occupancy:	97%		Red Cards:	5

Liverpool
Bolton Wanderers

Form Coming into Fixture

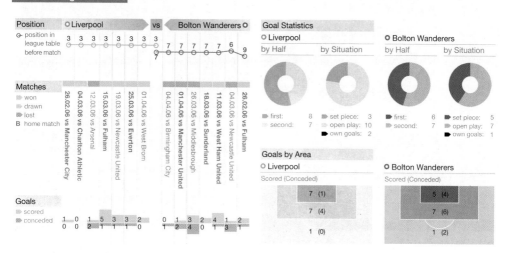

Position ○ Liverpool vs Bolton Wanderers ○

position in league table before match

Liverpool: 3 3 3 3 3 3 3 3 7
Bolton: 7 7 7 7 7 6 9

Matches
- won
- drawn
- lost
- B home match

Liverpool matches:
26.02.06 vs Manchester City
04.03.06 vs Charlton Athletic
12.03.06 vs Arsenal
15.03.06 vs Fulham
19.03.06 vs Newcastle United
25.03.06 vs Everton
01.04.06 vs West Brom

Bolton matches:
04.04.06 vs Birmingham City
01.04.06 vs Manchester United
26.03.06 vs Middlesbrough
18.03.06 vs Sunderland
11.03.06 vs West Ham United
04.03.06 vs Newcastle United
26.02.06 vs Fulham

Goals
- scored
- conceded

Liverpool Goals: 1 0 | 1 5 3 2 | 0
Liverpool conceded: 0 0 | 2 1 1 1 | 0

Bolton Goals: 0 1 3 2 4 1 2
Bolton conceded: 1 2 4 0 1 3 1

Goal Statistics

○ Liverpool

by Half / by Situation

- first: 8
- second: 7
- set piece: 3
- open play: 10
- own goals: 2

○ Bolton Wanderers

by Half / by Situation

- first: 6
- second: 7
- set piece: 5
- open play: 7
- own goals: 1

Goals by Area

○ Liverpool
Scored (Conceded)

7 (1)
7 (4)
1 (0)

○ Bolton Wanderers
Scored (Conceded)

5 (4)
7 (6)
1 (2)

Team Statistics

Starting Line-Ups

Liverpool:
Riise, Kewell (Traore), Nolan, Hunt
Hyypia, Alonso, Okocha (Jansen), Ben Haim
Reina, Fowler (Hamann), Davies, Faye (Campo), Jaaskelainen
Carragher, Gerrard, Crouch, N'Gotty
Speed
Finnan, Cisse (Garcia), Stelios (Pedersen), Gardner

4/4/2   **4/5/1**

Unused Sub: Dudek, Sissoko
Unused Sub: Walker, Borgetti

Premiership Totals

	○ Liverpool	Bolton ○
Premiership Appearances	2,269	2,020
Team Appearances	1,821	1,387
Goals Scored	356	239
Assists	253	181
Clean Sheets (goalkeepers)	18	48
Yellow Cards	222	256
Red Cards	16	11
Full Internationals	14	10

Age/Height

Liverpool Age	Bolton Wanderers Age
27 yrs, 7 mo	**29 yrs, 6 mo**

Liverpool Height	Bolton Wanderers Height
6'1"	**6'**

Match Statistics

League Table after Fixture

		Played	Won	Drawn	Lost	For	Against	Pts
● 3	Liverpool	34	21	7	6	48	22	70
● 4	Tottenham	33	16	10	7	48	33	58
● 5	Blackburn	33	16	6	11	45	39	54
● 6	Arsenal	32	16	5	11	53	25	53
● 7	Bolton	32	13	9	10	43	36	48
● 8	Wigan	33	14	6	13	38	40	48
● 9	West Ham	33	13	7	13	47	50	46
↑ 10	Newcastle	33	13	6	14	36	40	45
↓ 11	Everton	33	13	6	14	31	43	45

Statistics

	○ Liverpool	Bolton ○
Goals	1	0
Shots on Target	7	4
Shots off Target	10	3
Hit Woodwork	1	0
Possession %	53	47
Corners	3	2
Offsides	3	5
Fouls	6	6
Disciplinary Points	4	4

0-2

Bolton Wanderers ○
Chelsea ○

 Kevin Davies forces Petr Cech to punch

Event Line

30 ○ ▨	Gardner
41 ○ ▨	Makelele
44 ○ ⊕	Terry / H / IFK / IA
	Assist: Drogba
Half time 0-1	
46 ○ ⇄	Pedersen > Borgetti
46 ○ ⇄	Giannakopoulos > Vaz Te
51 ○ ▨	Davies
59 ○ ⊕	Lampard / RF / OP / 6Y
	Assist: Crespo
60 ○ ⇄	Robben > Crespo
70 ○ ⇄	Nakata > Speed
82 ○ ▨	Drogba
82 ○ ⇄	Ferreira > Cole J
86 ○ ⇄	Huth > Drogba
87 ○ ▨	Huth
90 ○ ▰	Ben Haim
	2nd Bookable Offence
Full time 0-2	

Bolton Wanderers succumbed to their fifth straight league defeat as Chelsea inched one step closer to their second successive Premier League title with a comfortable victory at the Reebok Stadium.

The hosts fell behind just before the half-time interval thanks to a John Terry header and his side sealed the three points later in the game though a Frank Lampard special.

Although Ricardo Vaz Te hit the post for his side early in the game, Wanderers failed to test Petr Cech as Jose Mourinho's men showed their opponents just how clinical they can be.

Sam Allardyce rang the changes as he aimed to stem his side's four-game losing streak. With an eye on Monday's game at West Bromwich Albion, the Wanderers boss brought in Jared Borgetti, Ricardo Vaz Te and Ivan Campo at the expense of Stelios, Nicky Hunt and Jay Jay Okocha.

Quote

❝ **Sam Allardyce**

To play against Chelsea when you are 1-0 down is difficult. You cannot defend against the free-kick that led to their first goal.

Venue:	Reebok Stadium	Referee:	P.Dowd - 05/06	**Bolton Wanderers**
Attendance:	27,266	Matches:	43	**Chelsea**
Capacity:	28,101	Yellow Cards:	167	
Occupancy:	97%	Red Cards:	7	

Form Coming into Fixture

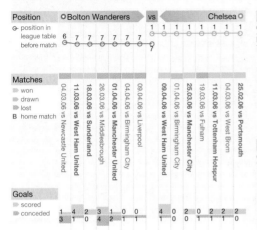

Position

	O Bolton Wanderers	vs	Chelsea
position in league table before match	6 7 7 7 7 7 7		1 1 1 1 1 1 1
	7		

Matches
- won
- drawn
- lost
- B home match

04.03.06 vs Newcastle United
11.03.06 vs West Ham United
18.03.06 vs Sunderland
26.03.06 vs Middlesbrough
01.04.06 vs Manchester United
09.04.06 vs Liverpool
09.04.06 vs West Ham United
01.04.06 vs Birmingham City
25.03.06 vs Manchester City
19.03.06 vs Fulham
11.03.06 vs Tottenham Hotspur
04.03.06 vs West Brom
25.02.06 vs Portsmouth

Goals
- scored: 1 4 2 3 1 0 0 | 4 0 2 0 2 2 2
- conceded: 3 1 0 4 2 1 1 | 1 0 0 1 1 0

Goal Statistics

O Bolton Wanderers

by Half	by Situation
first: 5	set piece: 5
second: 6	open play: 6

O Chelsea

by Half	by Situation
first: 5	set piece: 3
second: 7	open play: 9

Goals by Area

O Bolton Wanderers
Scored (Conceded)

| 4 (4) |
| 6 (6) |
| 1 (2) |

O Chelsea
Scored (Conceded)

| 3 (1) |
| 8 (3) |
| 1 (0) |

Team Statistics

Starting Line-Ups

Jaaskelainen — N'Gotty, Ben Haim, Gardner, Vaz Te / Stelios, Speed / Nakata, Campo, Faye, Nolan, Davies, Borgetti / Pedersen

Cech — Del Horno, Terry, Gallas, Geremi, Makelele, Essien, Cole J / Ferreira, Lampard, Drogba / Huth, Crespo / Robben

▶ 4/5/1

Unused Sub: Walker, Okocha

▶ 4/4/2 (Diamond)

Unused Sub: Cudicini, Wright-Phillips

Premiership Totals

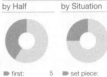

Statistics	O Bolton	Chelsea O
Premiership Appearances	1,795	1,403
Team Appearances	1,253	1,096
Goals Scored	206	187
Assists	155	167
Clean Sheets (goalkeepers)	48	39
Yellow Cards	241	161
Red Cards	12	6
Full Internationals	11	14

Age/Height

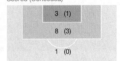

Bolton Wanderers Age	Chelsea Age
▶ 29 yrs, 4 mo	**▶ 26 yrs, 4 mo**
Bolton Wanderers Height	Chelsea Height
▶ 6'	**▶ 6'**

Match Statistics

League Table after Fixture

		Played	Won	Drawn	Lost	For	Against	Pts
●	1 Chelsea	34	27	4	3	66	20	85
●	2 Man Utd	34	23	7	4	66	30	76
●	3 Liverpool	34	21	7	6	48	22	70
●	4 Tottenham	34	17	10	7	49	33	61
●	5 Arsenal	34	17	6	11	57	27	57
●	6 Blackburn	33	16	6	11	45	39	54
↑	7 West Ham	34	14	7	13	48	50	49
↓	8 Bolton	33	13	9	11	43	38	48
↑	9 Newcastle	34	14	6	14	39	41	48

Statistics

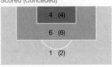

Statistics	O Bolton	Chelsea O
Goals	0	2
Shots on Target	4	3
Shots off Target	3	2
Hit Woodwork	1	0
Possession %	50	50
Corners	4	2
Offsides	1	2
Fouls	19	15
Disciplinary Points	18	12

0-0

West Bromwich Albion ○
Bolton Wanderers ○

■ Hidetoshi Nakata drives the ball towards goal

Half time 0-0

73 ○ Kanu > Campbell

75 ○ ⇄ Nicholson > Kamara

83 ○ ⇄ Vaz Te > Giannakopoulos

Full time 0-0

Bolton Wanderers' losing streak came to an end at the Hawthorns as they ground out a scoreless draw with relegation threatened West Brom.

Sam Allardyce's troops picked up a valuable point after Saturday's defeat at home to Chelsea made it five defeats on the spin.

It was a professional performance by the visitors who endured some shaky moments against a Baggies side that was fighting for its Premiership future. Although captain Kevin Nolan will be left wondering how he failed to score from an injury-time chance created by substitute Ricardo Vaz Te.

Quote

🍌 **Sam Allardyce**

There wasn't a lot of football played, but there was plenty of effort and commitment from both teams.

Venue:	The Hawthorns		Referee:	D.J.Gallagher - 05/06
Attendance:	23,181		Matches:	39
Capacity:	28,003		Yellow Cards:	85
Occupancy:	83%		Red Cards:	9

Form Coming into Fixture

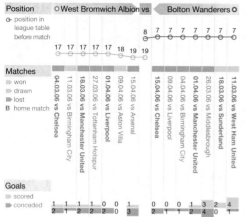

Position

○ West Bromwich Albion vs ◄ Bolton Wanderers ○

⊙ position in league table before match

West Bromwich Albion: 17 17 17 17 17 18 19 19
Bolton Wanderers: 8 7 7 7 7 7 7 7

Matches
- won
- drawn
- lost
- B home match

West Bromwich Albion fixtures:
04.03.06 vs Chelsea
11.03.06 vs Birmingham City
18.03.06 vs Manchester United
27.03.06 vs Tottenham Hotspur
01.04.06 vs Liverpool
09.04.06 vs Aston Villa
15.04.06 vs Arsenal

Bolton Wanderers fixtures:
15.04.06 vs Chelsea
09.04.06 vs Liverpool
04.04.06 vs Birmingham City
01.04.06 vs Manchester United
26.03.06 vs Middlesbrough
18.03.06 vs Sunderland
11.03.06 vs West Ham United

Goals
- scored
- conceded

West Bromwich Albion:
scored: 1 1 1 1 0 0 1
conceded: 2 1 2 2 2 0 3

Bolton Wanderers:
scored: 0 0 0 1 3 2 4
conceded: 2 1 1 2 4 0 1

Goal Statistics

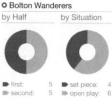

○ West Bromwich Albion — by Half / by Situation
- first: 1
- second: 4
- set piece: 2
- open play: 3

○ Bolton Wanderers — by Half / by Situation
- first: 5
- second: 5
- set piece: 4
- open play: 6

Goals by Area

○ West Bromwich Albion — Scored (Conceded)
- 2 (2)
- 2 (9)
- 1 (1)

○ Bolton Wanderers — Scored (Conceded)
- 3 (4)
- 6 (6)
- 1 (1)

Team Statistics

Starting Line-Ups

West Bromwich Albion (4/4/2):
Kuszczak
Robinson, Greening
Clement, Quashie
Campbell Kanu
Davies C, Johnson
Kamara Nicholson
Watson, Gera

4/4/2

Unused Sub: Albrechtsen, Carter, Inamoto

Bolton Wanderers (4/5/1):
Jaaskelainen
Nolan, Hunt
Nakata
Faye
Davies, Okocha
N'Gotty
Speed
Stelios Vaz Te, Gardner

4/5/1

Unused Sub: Al Habsi, Campo, Borgetti, Pedersen

Premiership Totals	○ West Brom	Bolton ○
Premiership Appearances	1,546	1,708
Team Appearances	542	1,166
Goals Scored	178	190
Assists	147	167
Clean Sheets (goalkeepers)	9	48
Yellow Cards	149	222
Red Cards	6	11
Full Internationals	6	8

Age/Height

West Bromwich Albion Age
▷ 27 yrs, 5 mo

Bolton Wanderers Age
▶ 28 yrs, 11 mo

West Bromwich Albion Height
▷ 6'

Bolton Wanderers Height
▶ 5'11"

Match Statistics

League Table after Fixture

		Played	Won	Drawn	Lost	For	Against	Pts
●	2 Man Utd	35	24	7	4	68	31	79
●	3 Liverpool	35	22	7	6	49	22	73
●	4 Tottenham	35	17	10	8	50	35	61
●	5 Arsenal	34	17	6	11	57	27	57
●	6 Blackburn	34	16	6	12	45	40	54
↑	7 Newcastle	35	15	6	14	43	42	51
●	8 Bolton	34	13	10	11	43	38	49
...	...	...	...	...	...	...	...	...
●	19 West Brom	35	7	8	20	29	52	29

Statistics	○ West Brom	Bolton ○
Goals	0	0
Shots on Target	1	3
Shots off Target	8	5
Hit Woodwork	0	0
Possession %	48	52
Corners	3	6
Offsides	2	7
Fouls	13	16
Disciplinary Points	0	0

4-1

Bolton Wanderers ○
Charlton Athletic ○

Premiership
22.04.06

▶ Kevin Davies celebrates his second goal of the game

Event Line

14 ○ ⊕	Vaz Te / H / OP / IA	
	Assist: Nakata	
21 ○ ⊕	Davies / RF / IFK / 6Y	
	Assist: Borgetti	
31 ○ ⊕	Borgetti / RF / IFK / IA	
	Assist: Davies	
Half time 3-0		
46 ○ ⇄	Bothroyd > Ambrose	
46 ○ ⇄	Fortune > Rommedahl	
70 ○ ⇄	Okocha > Speed	
70 ○ ⇄	Kishishev > Sankofa	
76 ○ ⊕	Bent D / RF / P / IA	
	Assist: Bothroyd	
80 ○ ⇄	Nolan > Vaz Te	
89 ○ ⊕	Davies / RF / OP / 6Y	
Full time 4-1		

Wanderers got back on track with a comprehensive win again Charlton Athletic at the Reebok Stadium.

Goals from Ricardo Vaz Te, Kevin Davies and Jared Borgetti saw the hosts race into a three-goal lead inside the opening half-an-hour to vindicate Sam Allardyce's surprising team selection.

And although Darren Bent pegged a goal back for the Addicks from the spot, Wanderers extended their lead through another Davies effort to claim a confidence boosting three points and maintain their UEFA Cup charge.

Allardyce kept to his word and made wholesale changes to his side following the scoreless draw against West Brom on Monday which ended the morale-draining run of five successive defeats.

Captain Kevin Nolan was dropped to the bench, where he sat alongside Stelios, Jay Jay Okocha, Bruno N'Gotty and Ian Walker.

Tal Ben Haim, Hidetoshi Nakata, Vaz Te and Ivan Campo, who turned in a man-of-the-match performance, were all recalled.

Quote
❝ Sam Allardyce

Kevin Davies was once again our main man and deserved his two goals.

Premiership Milestone
▶ First Goal

Ricardo Vaz Te netted his first Premiership goal.

Form Coming into Fixture

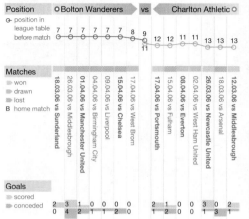

Position

Bolton Wanderers vs **Charlton Athletic**

position in league table before match: 7 7 7 7 7 7 8 9 11 / 12 12 11 11 13 13 13

Matches
- won
- drawn
- lost
- B home match

Bolton Wanderers matches:
18.03.06 vs Sunderland
26.03.06 vs Middlesbrough
01.04.06 vs Manchester United
04.04.06 vs Birmingham City
09.04.06 vs Liverpool
15.04.06 vs Chelsea
17.04.06 vs West Brom

Charlton Athletic matches:
17.04.06 vs Portsmouth
15.04.06 vs Fulham
08.04.06 vs Everton
02.04.06 vs West Ham United
26.03.06 vs Newcastle United
18.03.06 vs Arsenal
12.03.06 vs Middlesbrough

Goals
- scored
- conceded

scored	2	3	1	0	0	0	0		2	1	0	0	3	0	2
conceded	0	4	2	1	1	2	0		1	2	0	0	1	3	1

Goal Statistics

Bolton Wanderers

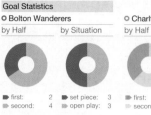

by Half / by Situation

- first: 2
- second: 4
- set piece: 3
- open play: 3

Charlton Athletic

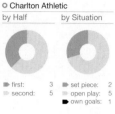

by Half / by Situation

- first: 3
- second: 5
- set piece: 2
- open play: 5
- own goals: 1

Goals by Area

Bolton Wanderers

Scored (Conceded)

3 (3)
3 (6)
0 (1)

Charlton Athletic

Scored (Conceded)

4 (0)
4 (5)
0 (3)

Team Statistics

Starting Line-Ups

Bolton Wanderers:
Jaaskelainen
Gardner, Vaz Te (Nolan), Speed (Okocha), Faye, Campo, Borgetti, Ben Haim, Nakata, Hunt, Davies

4/5/1

Unused Sub: Walker, N'Gotty, Stelios

Charlton Athletic:
Rommedahl (Fortune), Sankofa (Kishishev), Holland, Perry, Bent D, Euell, Myhre, Sorondo, Hughes, Ambrose (Bothroyd), Powell

4/5/1

Unused Sub: Andersen, Youga

Premiership Totals

	Bolton	Charlton
Premiership Appearances	1,650	1,687
Team Appearances	1,108	950
Goals Scored	177	131
Assists	150	74
Clean Sheets (goalkeepers)	49	32
Yellow Cards	234	158
Red Cards	11	8
Full Internationals	9	8

Age/Height

	Bolton Wanderers	Charlton Athletic
Age	28 yrs, 5 mo	28 yrs, 2 mo
Height	6'	6'

Match Statistics

League Table after Fixture

		Played	Won	Drawn	Lost	For	Against	Pts
● 3	Liverpool	35	22	7	6	49	22	73
● 4	Tottenham	36	17	11	8	51	36	62
● 5	Arsenal	35	17	7	11	58	28	58
● 6	Blackburn	35	16	6	13	46	42	54
● 7	Newcastle	36	16	6	14	46	42	54
↑ 8	Bolton	35	14	10	11	47	39	52
↓ 9	Wigan	35	15	6	14	42	45	51
● 10	West Ham	35	14	7	14	48	52	49
● 11	Charlton	36	13	8	15	41	49	47

Statistics

	Bolton	Charlton
Goals	4	1
Shots on Target	11	4
Shots off Target	2	2
Hit Woodwork	1	0
Possession %	61	39
Corners	9	1
Offsides	3	0
Fouls	14	12
Disciplinary Points	0	0

1-0

Tottenham Hotspur ○
Bolton Wanderers ○

▶ Stelios unleashes a venomous effort

Event Line

4 ○ ▪	Ben Haim
31 ○ ▪	Davies

Half time 0-0

46 ○ ⇄	Barnard > Keane
52 ○ ⇄	Vaz Te > Borgetti
60 ○ ⊕	Lennon / RF / OP / IA
	Assist: Carrick
62 ○ ⇄	Okocha > Nakata
72 ○ ▪	Hunt
78 ○ ⇄	Reid > Defoe
82 ○ ⇄	Pedersen > Speed
83 ○ ▪	Gardner
86 ○ ⇄	Davenport > Murphy
88 ○ ▪	Barnard
90 ○ ▪	Campo

Full time 1-0

A glut of wasted golden chances during the first-half came back to haunt Wanderers as they suffered a defeat against Tottenham Hotspur that seriously harmed their chances of qualifying for the UEFA Cup.

Aaron Lennon struck the only goal of the game on the hour mark as Spurs recovered from a first-half battering, which should have seen them go at least two goals down, to keep their Champions League hopes alive.

But Sam Allardyce was left fuming about a penalty decision that failed to go Wanderers' way on 74 minutes when the recalled Stelios was upended by Michael Dawson.

The Greek star was the only change from the side that thumped Charlton Athletic six days earlier. The forward replaced Ricardo Vaz Te, who started from the bench.

Quote

🎔 **Sam Allardyce**

It will be hugely difficult for us to get into Europe now even if we win our last two games.

Venue:	White Hart Lane	Referee:	A.G.Wiley - 05/06
Attendance:	36,179	Matches:	41
Capacity:	36,247	Yellow Cards:	129
Occupancy:	100%	Red Cards:	7

Tottenham Hotspur
Bolton Wanderers

Form Coming into Fixture

Position
position in league table before match

O Tottenham Hotspur vs Bolton Wanderers O

Tottenham: 4 4 4 4 4 4 4 4
Bolton: 9 8 8 7 7 7 7 7

Matches
- won
- drawn
- lost
- B home match

18.03.06 vs Birmingham City
27.03.06 vs West Brom
01.04.06 vs Newcastle United
08.04.06 vs Manchester City
15.04.06 vs Everton
17.04.06 vs Manchester United
22.04.06 vs Arsenal

22.04.06 vs Charlton Athletic
17.04.06 vs West Brom
15.04.06 vs Chelsea
09.04.06 vs Liverpool
04.04.06 vs Birmingham City
01.04.06 vs Manchester United
26.03.06 vs Middlesbrough

Goals
	scored	conceded
Tottenham	2 2 1 2 1 1 1	0 1 3 1 0 2 1
Bolton	4 0 0 0 0 1 3	1 0 2 1 1 2 4

Goal Statistics

O Tottenham Hotspur

by Half
- first: 3
- second: 7

by Situation
- set piece: 4
- open play: 6

O Bolton Wanderers

by Half
- first: 5
- second: 3

by Situation
- set piece: 4
- open play: 4

Goals by Area

O Tottenham Hotspur
Scored (Conceded)

4 (3)
6 (5)
0 (0)

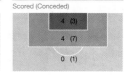

O Bolton Wanderers
Scored (Conceded)

4 (3)
4 (7)
0 (1)

Team Statistics

Starting Line-Ups

Tottenham:
Lee, Murphy (Davenport), Gardner, Carrick, Defoe (Reid), Robinson, Dawson, Tainio, Keane (Barnard), Stalteri, Lennon

Bolton:
Davies, Hunt, Nakata (Okocha), Ben Haim, Borgetti (Vaz Té), Campo, Jaaskelainen, Faye, Speed (Pedersen), Stelios, Gardner

▶ 4/4/2   ▶ 4/5/1

Unused Sub: Cerny, Huddlestone
Unused Sub: Walker, Jaidi

Premiership Totals
	O Tottenham	Bolton O
Premiership Appearances	1,221	1,706
Team Appearances	630	1,164
Goals Scored	170	189
Assists	138	162
Clean Sheets (goalkeepers)	42	49
Yellow Cards	98	219
Red Cards	6	11
Full Internationals	10	11

Age/Height
Tottenham Hotspur Age
▶ **25 yrs**

Bolton Wanderers Age
▶ **29 yrs, 2 mo**

Tottenham Hotspur Height
▶ **5'11"**

Bolton Wanderers Height
▶ **6'**

Match Statistics

League Table after Fixture
		Played	Won	Drawn	Lost	For	Against	Pts
● 4	Tottenham	37	18	11	8	52	36	65
● 5	Arsenal	35	17	7	11	58	28	58
● 6	Blackburn	36	17	6	13	48	42	57
● 7	Newcastle	37	16	7	14	46	42	55
● 8	Bolton	36	14	10	12	47	40	52
● 9	Wigan	37	15	6	16	43	48	51
● 10	West Ham	36	14	7	15	49	54	49
● 11	Everton	37	14	7	16	32	47	49
● 12	Charlton	37	13	8	16	41	51	47

Statistics
	O Tottenham	Bolton O
Goals	1	0
Shots on Target	4	6
Shots off Target	5	8
Hit Woodwork	0	1
Possession %	46	54
Corners	6	8
Offsides	1	1
Fouls	11	12
Disciplinary Points	4	20

1-1

Bolton Wanderers ○
Middlesbrough ○

▶ Referee Howard Webb has a word with Abdoulaye Faye

Event Line	
14 ○ ▢ Vaz Te	
45 ○ ▢ Cattermole	
Half time 0-0	
47 ○ ⊕ Johnson / RF / OP / IA	
Assist: Wheater	
51 ○ ⊕ Vaz Te / H / OP / IA	
Assist: Okocha	
59 ○ ⇄ Davies > McMahon	
64 ○ ⇄ Maccarone > Christie	
66 ○ ⇄ Giannakopoulos > Nolan	
73 ○ ⇄ Taylor > Johnson	
75 ○ ⇄ Speed > Nakata	
86 ○ ⇄ Borgetti > Campo	
Full time 1-1	

Wanderers must beat Birmingham City on the final day of the season and hope that champions Chelsea avoid defeat away to Newcastle United if they are to qualify for the InterToto Cup after coming from behind to grab a point against Middlesbrough.

The chance of taking the backdoor route into the UEFA Cup was taken out of their own hands when they failed to secure a victory against Steve McClaren's UEFA Cup finalists.

Boro scored the opening goal of the game two minutes into the second half with a well taken effort from the highly impressive Adam Johnson.

Wanderers fought back in fine style and Portuguese starlet Ricardo Vaz Te hammered home the equalizer from close range on 51 minutes. Sam Allardyce's men finished the stronger but failed to capitalise on their advantage.

Quote

 Sam Allardyce

Yet again we have not converted our chances. We should have been two or three in front by half-time.

Venue:	Reebok Stadium	Referee:	H.M.Webb - 05/06		**Bolton Wanderers**
Attendance:	22,733	Matches:	42		**Middlesbrough**
Capacity:	28,101	Yellow Cards:	106		
Occupancy:	81%	Red Cards:	6		

Form Coming into Fixture

Position

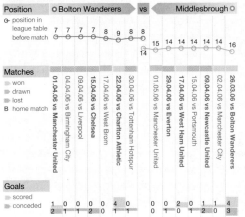

Bolton Wanderers: 7 7 7 7 8 9 8 8 · 14

Middlesbrough: 15 14 14 14 14 14 16

Matches
- won
- drawn
- lost
- B home match

Bolton matches:
- 01.04.06 vs Manchester United
- 04.04.06 vs Birmingham City
- 09.04.06 vs Liverpool
- 15.04.06 vs Chelsea
- 17.04.06 vs West Brom
- 22.04.06 vs Charlton Athletic
- 30.04.06 vs Tottenham Hotspur

Middlesbrough matches:
- 01.05.06 vs Manchester United
- 29.04.06 vs Everton
- 17.04.06 vs West Ham United
- 15.04.06 vs Portsmouth
- 09.04.06 vs Newcastle United
- 02.04.06 vs Manchester City
- 26.03.06 vs Bolton Wanderers

Goals
	scored	1	0	0	0	0	4	0		0	0	2	0	1	1	4
	conceded	2	1	1	2	0	1	1		0	1	0	1	2	0	3

Goal Statistics

Bolton Wanderers

by Half	by Situation
first: 4	set piece: 2
second: 1	open play: 3

Middlesbrough

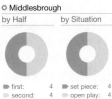

by Half	by Situation
first: 4	set piece: 4
second: 4	open play: 4

Goals by Area

Bolton Wanderers

Scored (Conceded)

2 (2)
3 (5)
0 (1)

Middlesbrough

Scored (Conceded)

1 (3)
6 (3)
1 (1)

Team Statistics

Starting Line-Ups

Bolton Wanderers
- Jaaskelainen
- Pedersen
- Vaz Te
- Nakata / Speed
- Faye
- Campo / Borgetti
- Davies
- Ben Haim
- Okocha
- Hunt
- Nolan / Stelios

▶ 4/5/1

Unused Sub: Walker, Jaidi

Middlesbrough
- Christie / Maccarone
- McMahon / Davies
- Parlour
- Ehiogu
- Yakubu
- Doriva
- Turnbull
- Wheater
- Cattermole
- Johnson / Taylor
- Queudrue

▶ 4/5/1

Unused Sub: Knight, Kennedy

Premiership Totals

	○ Bolton	Boro ○
Premiership Appearances	1,747	1,329
Team Appearances	1,205	608
Goals Scored	215	139
Assists	161	104
Clean Sheets (goalkeepers)	49	0
Yellow Cards	236	174
Red Cards	8	14
Full Internationals	10	5

Age/Height

Bolton Wanderers Age	Middlesbrough Age
▶ **28 yrs, 11 mo**	▶ **24 yrs, 7 mo**
Bolton Wanderers Height	Middlesbrough Height
▶ **6'**	▶ **6'**

Match Statistics

League Table after Fixture

		Played	Won	Drawn	Lost	For	Against	Pts
● 5	Arsenal	36	18	7	11	61	28	61
● 6	Blackburn	37	18	6	13	49	42	60
● 7	Newcastle	37	16	7	14	46	42	55
● 8	Bolton	37	14	11	12	48	41	53
● 9	West Ham	37	15	7	15	50	54	52
● 10	Wigan	37	15	6	16	43	48	51
● 11	Everton	37	14	7	16	32	47	49
● 12	Charlton	37	13	8	16	41	51	47
↑ 13	Middlesbrough	37	12	9	16	48	57	45

Statistics

	○ Bolton	Boro ○
Goals	1	1
Shots on Target	9	3
Shots off Target	8	2
Hit Woodwork	0	0
Possession %	50	50
Corners	6	1
Offsides	1	5
Fouls	9	10
Disciplinary Points	4	4

1-0

Bolton Wanderers ○
Birmingham City ○

► Gary Speed outjumps Mehdi Nafti

Event Line

Half time 0-0

53 ○ ⇄	Okocha > Nakata	
54 ○ ⇄	Vaz Te > Campo	
65 ○ ⊕	Vaz Te / RF / OP / 6Y	
	Assist: Nolan	
71 ○ ⇄	Kilkenny > Nafti	
72 ○ ▢	Taylor Martin	
86 ○ ⇄	Borgetti > Giannakopoulos	

Full time 1-0

Ricardo Vaz Te's sixth goal of the season ensured that Wanderers finished the campaign on a winning note, but the victory wasn't enough to see them qualify for the InterToto Cup as Newcastle United beat champions Chelsea to finish in seventh spot.

The Portuguese starlet came off the bench to net the only goal of the game in the second-half to give Wanderers a glimmer of hope, but Newcastle held on to Titus Bramble's winner to seal their place in Europe for next season.

Quote

 Sam Allardyce

The season caught up with us in the end. We have played a lot of games, but at least we finished with a flourish.

Venue:	Reebok Stadium	Referee:	S.G.Bennett - 05/06
Attendance:	26,275	Matches:	40
Capacity:	28,101	Yellow Cards:	135
Occupancy:	94%	Red Cards:	12

Bolton Wanderers
Birmingham City

Form Coming into Fixture

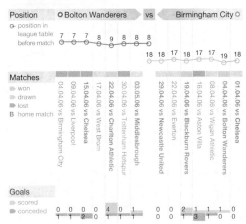

Position ○ Bolton Wanderers vs Birmingham City ○

position in league table before match

Bolton: 7 7 7 8 9 8 8 8
Birmingham: 18 18 17 18 17 17 19 18

Matches
- won
- drawn
- lost
- B home match

04.04.06 vs Birmingham City
09.04.06 vs Liverpool
15.04.06 vs Chelsea
17.04.06 vs West Brom
22.04.06 vs Charlton Athletic
30.04.06 vs Tottenham Hotspur
03.05.06 vs Middlesbrough

29.04.06 vs Newcastle United
22.04.06 vs Everton
19.04.06 vs Blackburn Rovers
16.04.06 vs Aston Villa
08.04.06 vs Wigan Athletic
04.04.06 vs Bolton Wanderers
01.04.06 vs Chelsea

Goals
- scored: 0 0 0 0 4 0 1 | 0 0 2 1 1 1 0
- conceded: 1 1 2 0 1 1 | 0 0 1 3 1 0 0

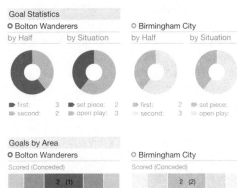

Goal Statistics

○ Bolton Wanderers
by Half / by Situation
- first: 3 / set piece: 2
- second: 2 / open play: 3

○ Birmingham City
by Half / by Situation
- first: 2 / set piece: 2
- second: 3 / open play: 3

Goals by Area

○ Bolton Wanderers
Scored (Conceded)
2 (1)
3 (5)
0 (1)

○ Birmingham City
Scored (Conceded)
2 (2)
2 (3)
1 (0)

Team Statistics

Starting Line-Ups

Bolton Wanderers:
Pedersen, Stelios (Borgetti), Nakata (Okocha), Faye, Jaaskelainen, Campo (Vaz Te), Davies, Ben Haim, Speed, O'Brien, Nolan

Birmingham City:
Pennant, Melchiot, Butt, Bruce, Heskey, Nafti (Kilkenny), Taylor Maik, Taylor Martin, Johnson, Campbell, Sadler

▶ 4/5/1 ▶ 4/5/1

Unused Sub: Al Habsi, Jaidi

Unused Sub: Vaesen, Latka, Painter, Clemence

Premiership Totals	○ Bolton	Birmingham ○
Premiership Appearances	1,704	1,394
Team Appearances	1,162	521
Goals Scored	215	131
Assists	156	130
Clean Sheets (goalkeepers)	49	43
Yellow Cards	227	162
Red Cards	8	14
Full Internationals	11	6

Age/Height

Bolton Wanderers Age
▶ **28 yrs, 9 mo**

Birmingham City Age
▶ 26 yrs, 5 mo

Bolton Wanderers Height
▶ **6'**

Birmingham City Height
▶ 6'

Match Statistics

League Table after Fixture

		Played	Won	Drawn	Lost	For	Against	Pts
●	2 Man Utd	38	25	8	5	72	34	83
●	3 Liverpool	38	25	7	6	57	25	82
↑	4 Arsenal	38	20	7	11	68	31	67
↓	5 Tottenham	38	18	11	9	53	38	65
●	6 Blackburn	38	19	6	13	51	42	63
●	7 Newcastle	38	17	7	14	47	42	58
●	8 Bolton	38	15	11	12	49	41	56
...	...	...	...	...	...	...	...	...
●	18 Birmingham	38	8	10	20	28	50	34

Statistics	○ Bolton	Birmingham ○
Goals	1	0
Shots on Target	6	2
Shots off Target	10	3
Hit Woodwork	0	0
Possession %	49	51
Corners	5	2
Offsides	2	3
Fouls	7	14
Disciplinary Points	0	4

► Stade Velodrome in Marseille welcomes Wanderers

► Kevin Davies extends a hand to Lokomotiv Plovdiv

► Stelios fighting to the end in Marseille

We can look upon last season as being very successful and even though we failed in our ultimate goal of clinching a UEFA Cup spot, it cannot be denied just how far Bolton Wanderers has come. After those couple of edge-of-the-seat seasons, we have now established ourselves in the top-half of the Premier League on a regular basis. In the past three seasons we have finished eighth, sixth and eighth, which is a gargantuan achievement for a club of our size. You have to go back to those heady days of the 1920s to share comparative league seasons.

That said, we are aware of our limitations, but we also know, with the quality we have at our disposal, that we can be in this position for many years to come.

Many people in the game cannot believe we can continue to achieve what we are doing, but I like to prove people wrong and I will continue to do so.

The players will come back fitter and fresher for this coming season and our objective is to maintain and improve on the season just gone. Europe is not beyond us and with the right blend we can get back into the top six and hopefully back in to the UEFA Cup.

European football – for the first time in the Club's history – was a fantastic achievement. We enjoyed the experience and feel disappointed that we won't be involved this season.

Reflecting on the games we played gives me some great satisfaction. From the nailbiting encounters against Lokomotiv Plovdiv, when we had to come back from behind in both matches to progress into the next stage, to what was ultimately our final game against Marseille at the Stade Velodrome, we can all look back at what we achieved with some great pride.

The Intertoto Cup would have been a positive move for us but we just missed out. Many clubs would have loved to have been in the same position as ourselves. The majority of those clubs are a lot bigger than us and even with more resources and playing less matches than ourselves they still could not match what we achieved and that is something that we should all take heart from.

The Premier League is now stronger than it has ever been and as we improve at pace so does every other team we face. Therefore, we cannot afford to standstill and we have noticed that, in particular, last season.

The overall extra demand we faced took its toll on the squad. We played 53 competitive matches, which is unprecedented for Bolton Wanderers. Added to that was the international matches and the African Cup of Nations tournament. The players coped admirably and it was a steep learning curve for myself and the backroom staff.

On reflection, we have never faced such a demanding season, but we came through it with a great deal of success and will learn from the experience.

Sam Allardyce
Manager

▶ Okocha grapples with the conditions and an opponent at the Reebok Stadium

Premiership Results Table 2005/06

Legend:
- ▦ Won / ▦ Drawn / ▦ Lost
- ▦ Yellow Card / ▦ Red Card / ▦ Goal
- 45 Time of 1st Sub
- 45 Time of 2nd Sub
- 45 Time of 3rd Sub
- 45 Time of Goal
- 45 Time of Assist

Match: / Players: / Substitutes:

Date	H/A	Opponent	H/T	F/T	Pos	First String (GK)
13-08	A	Aston Villa	2-2	2-2	06	Jaaskelainen
21-08	H	Everton	1-0	0-1	13	Jaaskelainen
24-08	H	Newcastle	1-0	2-0	08	Jaaskelainen
27-08	A	West Ham	0-0	0-2	05	Jaaskelainen
11-09	H	Blackburn	0-0	0-0	05	Jaaskelainen
18-09	A	Man City	0-0	1-0	04	Jaaskelainen
24-09	H	Portsmouth	1-0	1-0	03	Jaaskelainen
01-10	A	Wigan	0-1	0-2	05	Jaaskelainen
15-10	A	Chelsea	1-0	1-5	07	Jaaskelainen
23-10	H	West Brom	0-0	2-0	07	Jaaskelainen
29-10	H	Charlton	0-0	1-0	04	Jaaskelainen
07-11	H	Tottenham	1-0	1-0	03	Jaaskelainen
27-11	A	Fulham	0-2	1-2	06	Jaaskelainen
03-12	H	Arsenal	2-0	2-0	06	Jaaskelainen
12-12	A	Aston Villa	0-0	1-1	05	Jaaskelainen
17-12	H	Everton	1-0	4-0	05	Jaaskelainen
26-12	A	Sunderland	0-0	0-0	05	Jaaskelainen
31-12	A	Man Utd	1-2	1-4	07	Jaaskelainen
02-01	H	Liverpool	1-0	2-2	07	Jaaskelainen
14-01	A	Blackburn	1-0	2-0	07	Jaaskelainen
21-01	H	Man City	2-0	2-0	07	Jaaskelainen
01-02	A	Portsmouth	0-0	0-1	07	Jaaskelainen
11-02	A	Arsenal	1-0	1-1	06	Jaaskelainen
26-02	H	Fulham	1-1	2-1	06	Jaaskelainen
04-03	H	Newcastle	0-2	1-3	07	Jaaskelainen
11-03	H	West Ham	3-0	4-1	06	Jaaskelainen
18-03	H	Sunderland	0-0	2-0	07	Jaaskelainen
26-03	A	Middlesbrough	1-2	3-4	07	Jaaskelainen
01-04	H	Man Utd	1-1	1-2	07	Jaaskelainen
04-04	A	Birmingham	1-1	1-2	07	Jaaskelainen
09-04	H	Liverpool	0-1	0-1	07	Jaaskelainen
15-04	H	Chelsea	0-1	0-2	08	Jaaskelainen
17-04	A	West Brom	0-0	0-0	08	Jaaskelainen
22-04	A	Charlton	3-0	4-1	08	Jaaskelainen
30-04	A	Tottenham	0-0	1-1	08	Jaaskelainen
03-05	H	Middlesbrough	0-0	1-1	08	Jaaskelainen
07-05	H	Birmingham	1-0	1-0	08	Jaaskelainen

Sam Allardyce
Manager

Date of Birth:	19.10.1954
Place of Birth:	Dudley, England
Nationality:	English
Date appointed:	19.10.1999
Other clubs coached:	Notts County, Blackpool, Limerick (Ire)

Managerial Career

Last season, Sam Allardyce enjoyed the distinction of becoming the first manager in the Club's history to lead out a Bolton Wanderers side in a competitive European fixture. That game, against Lokomotiv Plovdiv at the Reebok Stadium, ended in a victory to his Wanderers side. The Club advanced past the group stage but fell in a closely-fought two-legged encounter against Marseille in the UEFA Cup's last-32 stage. Such is the reputation that Allardyce has acquired during his tenure at the Reebok Stadium, the Football Association interviewed him for the England Head Coach's job. Although he lost out to Steve McClaren, Allardyce will commence his sixth season in charge with the hope of qualifying for European football once again.

Big Sam returned 'home' on his birthday in October 1999, after leaving Notts County, to manage the club he signed for as a 15 year-old in 1969. In his first season at the Reebok Stadium, he guided Wanderers to the semi-finals of the FA Cup, League Cup and the First Division Play-Offs.

The following season, Wanderers put the abject disappointment of the previous season's play-off defeat behind them to record an emphatic 3-0 victory over Preston North End in the First Division Play-Off Final at Cardiff's Millennium Stadium. That result earned Wanderers promotion to the Premiership for the first time since 1997 and enabled Big Sam to realise his lifelong ambition of managing the Wanderers in the Premiership.

He commenced his coaching career in football in his native West Midlands with West Bromwich Albion whilst still playing for The Baggies. He then became Assistant Manager at Preston North End and Sunderland.

He became manager of Limerick in Ireland before taking charge at Blackpool. Whilst at Bloomfield Road he took The Tangerines to the 1996 Second Division play-off final. In 1997 he took charge of Notts County and won the Third Division Championship in 1998.

Playing Career

15 year-old Sam Allardyce arrived at Burnden Park in 1969 and turned professional with the Wanderers in November 1973. He made his league debut in November 1973 and was a regular member of the successful Wanderers sides in the mid 1970s who twice narrowly missed out on promotion to the old First Division. In 1978 he won a Second Division Championship medal with Bolton.

After a total of 214 first class games he left the Wanderers to join Sunderland in 1980 for a fee of £150,000.

When his spell at Roker Park came to an end he then played for Millwall, Tampa Bay Rowdies, Coventry City and Huddersfield Town before returning to Burnden Park for another spell in 1985. He only managed 17 appearances in his one season back in Bolton and then joined neighbours Preston North End where he helped them to win promotion from the old Fourth Division in 1987.

Sammy Lee
Assistant Manager

Date of Birth:	07.02.1959
Place of Birth:	Liverpool
Nationality:	English
Date appointed:	30.06.2005
Other clubs coached:	Liverpool

Coaching Career

It was a memorable season for Assistant Manager Sammy Lee, who enjoyed the honour of being involved in Wanderers' first-ever season of competitive European football.

Lee was also involved in England's World Cup challenge in Germany during the summer where he was a vital member of Sven-Goran Eriksson's backroom staff.

Sammy began his coaching career by taking charge of Liverpool's reserve team, initially under Roy Evans. After Gerard Houllier had been appointed sole manager at the end of 1998, the reserves put together a late run that almost snatched the Pontins League title.

Sammy was promoted to share both First and Reserve Team duties with Jacques Crevoisier.

In the summer of 1999 he was linked with a move to Sheffield United but decided to concentrate on furthering his coaching credentials at Anfield.

Regarded as one of the most talented coaches in the English game, Sammy was a regular member of the coaching staff with the England Under-21 side before moving on to become a regular member of the Senior Team's coaching set-up under former head coach Sven-Goran Eriksson.

Playing Career

Sammy, 45, was an England international as a player, winning 14 caps as a midfielder in the early 1980s. He scored on his debut against Greece in a European Championship qualifier in 1982.

Liverpool-born, he came to Anfield as a 16-year-old midfielder and made a scoring debut against Leicester City three years later. Always popular with the fans, he was devoted to Liverpool and as passionate about the club as any player who has worn the red shirt.

Sammy went on to make almost 200 League appearances and won two European Cups, three League Championships and four League Cups.

He later played for QPR, Real Osasuna (Spain), Southampton and Bolton.

Jussi Jaaskelainen
Goalkeeper

An ever-present in Wanderers' 2005/2006 Barclays Premiership campaign, the Finland international maintained his reputation as one of the best goalkeepers in England's top-flight.

Now starting his ninth season as a Wanderer, Jaaskelainen will be hoping to keep his position as first-choice goalkeeper despite facing quality competition from Ian Walker and Ali Al Habsi.

Player Details:

Date of Birth:	19.04.1975
Place of Birth:	Mikkeli
Nationality:	Finnish
Height:	6'3"
Weight:	12st 10lb
Foot:	Right

Player Performance 05/06

League Performance

Percentage of total possible time player was on pitch   ⊙ position in league table at end of month

Month:	Aug	Sep	Oct	Nov	Dec	Jan	Feb	Mar	Apr	May	Total
	100%	100%	100%	100%	100%	100%	100%	100%	100%	100%	100%
	5	3	5	7	7	7	6	7	8	8	
Team Pts:	7/12	7/9	6/12	3/6	8/15	5/9	6/12	6/12	4/21	4/6	56/114
Team Gls F:	6	2	5	2	8	4	5	10	5	2	49
Team Gls A:	4	0	7	2	5	2	4	8	8	1	41
Total mins:	360	270	360	180	450	270	360	360	630	180	3,420
Starts (sub):	4	3	4	2	5	3	4	4	7	2	38
Goals:	0	0	0	0	0	0	0	0	0	0	0
Assists:	0	0	0	0	0	0	0	0	0	0	0
Clean sheets:	1	3	2	1	3	2	0	1	1	1	15
Cards (Y/R):	0	0	0	0	0	1	0	1	0	0	2

League Performance Totals

Clean Sheets
- Jaaskelainen: 15
- Team-mates: 0
- **Total: 15**

Assists
- Jaaskelainen: 0
- Team-mates: 44
- **Total: 44**

Cards
- Jaaskelainen: 2
- Team-mates: 63
- **Total: 65**

Cup Games

	Apps	CS	Cards
UEFA Cup	5	2	1
FA Cup	3	2	0
Carling Cup	2	0	0
Total	**10**	**4**	**1**

Career History

Career Milestones

Club Debut:
vs Crystal Palace (A), D 2-2, Champ.

 **08.08.98**

First Goal Scored for the Club:
—

 —

Time Spent at the Club:

8.5 Seasons

Full International:

Finland

Premiership Totals

92-06

Appearances	184
Clean Sheets	50
Assists	1
Yellow Cards	8
Red Cards	3

Clubs

Year	Club	Apps	CS
97-06	Bolton	313	99
	VPS Vaasa		
	MP Mikkelin		

Off the Pitch

Age:
- Jaaskelainen: 31 years, 1 month
- Team: 28 years, 5 months
- League: 26 years, 11 months

Height:
- Jaaskelainen: 6'3"
- Team: 5'11"
- League: 5'11"

Weight:
- Jaaskelainen: 12st 10lb
- Team: 12st 1lb
- League: 12st

Ian Walker
Goalkeeper

The former England international signed a new two-year deal during the summer despite only making a handful of appearances for the Club.

The goalkeeper couldn't oust Jussi Jaaskelainen from in between the sticks during the Premier League campaign, but proved to be a more than able deputy during the cup competitions, where he made a total of five appearances in the FA Cup, League Cup and UEFA Cup.

Player Details:

Date of Birth:	31.10.1971
Place of Birth:	Watford
Nationality:	English
Height:	6'2"
Weight:	13st 1lb
Foot:	Right

Player Performance 05/06

League Performance

Percentage of total possible time player was on pitch   ⊙ position in league table at end of month

Month:	Aug	Sep	Oct	Nov	Dec	Jan	Feb	Mar	Apr	May	Total
	5	3	5	7	7	7	6	7	8	8	
	0%	0%	0%	0%	0%	0%	0%	0%	0%	0%	0%
Team Pts:	7/12	7/9	6/12	3/6	8/15	5/9	6/12	6/12	4/21	4/6	56/114
Team Gls F:	6	2	5	2	8	4	5	10	5	2	49
Team Gls A:	4	0	7	2	5	2	4	8	8	1	41
Total mins:	0	0	0	0	0	0	0	0	0	0	0
Starts (sub):	0	0	0	0	0	0	0	0	0	0	0
Goals:	0	0	0	0	0	0	0	0	0	0	0
Assists:	0	0	0	0	0	0	0	0	0	0	0
Clean sheets:	0	0	0	0	0	0	0	0	0	0	0
Cards (Y/R):	0	0	0	0	0	0	0	0	0	0	0

League Performance Totals

Clean Sheets
- Walker: 0
- Team-mates: 15

Total: 15

Assists
- Walker: 0
- Team-mates: 44

Total: 44

Cards
- Walker: 0
- Team-mates: 65

Total: 65

Cup Games

	Apps	CS	Cards
UEFA Cup	3	0	0
FA Cup	1	1	0
Carling Cup	1	1	0
Total	**5**	**2**	**0**

Career History

Career Milestones

Club Debut:
vs Loko Plovdiv (A), W 1-2, UEFA Cup

 **29.09.05**

Time Spent at the Club:

▶ **1 Season**

First Goal Scored for the Club:
—

▶ —

Full International:

▶ **England**

Premiership Totals

92-06

Appearances	312
Clean Sheets	77
Assists	7
Yellow Cards	3
Red Cards	1

Clubs

Year	Club	Apps	CS
05-06	Bolton	5	2
01-05	Leicester	156	44
90-90	Ipswich	0	0
90-90	Oxford Utd	3	
89-01	Tottenham	314	

Off the Pitch

Age:

- Walker: 34 years, 7 months
- Team: 28 years, 5 months
- League: 26 years, 11 months

Height:

- Walker: 6'2"
- Team: 5'11"
- League: 5'11"

Weight:

- Walker: 13st 1lb
- Team: 12st 1lb
- League: 12st

Ali Al Habsi
Goalkeeper

The goalkeeper had the distinction of being the first Omani footballer to sign for a Barclays Premiership football club when he arrived at the Reebok Stadium in January 2006, having signed a pre-contract agreement with the Club in the summer of 2005. The 6ft 4ins tall goalkeeper was recruited from Norwegian outfit FC Lyn Oslo having earned rave reviews in the Scandinavian country.

The 24 year-old has yet to make his first-team debut for his new club, but was named as a substitute in several games last term.

Player Details:

Date of Birth:	30.12.1981
Place of Birth:	Sinaw, Oman
Nationality:	Omani
Height:	6'4"
Weight:	12st 6lb
Foot:	Right

Player Performance 05/06

League Performance

Percentage of total possible time player was on pitch   ○ position in league table at end of month

Month:	Aug	Sep	Oct	Nov	Dec	Jan	Feb	Mar	Apr	May	Total
	0%	0%	0%	0%	0%	0%	0%	0%	0%	0%	0%
Team Pts:	7/12	7/9	6/12	3/6	8/15	5/9	6/12	6/12	4/21	4/6	56/114
Team Gls F:	6	2	5	2	8	4	5	10	5	2	49
Team Gls A:	4	0	7	2	5	2	4	8	8	1	41
Total mins:	0	0	0	0	0	0	0	0	0	0	0
Starts (sub):	0	0	0	0	0	0	0	0	0	0	0
Goals:	0	0	0	0	0	0	0	0	0	0	0
Assists:	0	0	0	0	0	0	0	0	0	0	0
Clean sheets:	0	0	0	0	0	0	0	0	0	0	0
Cards (Y/R):	0	0	0	0	0	0	0	0	0	0	0

League Performance Totals

Clean Sheets
- Al Habsi: 0
- Team-mates: 15
- **Total: 15**

Assists
- Al Habsi: 0
- Team-mates: 44
- **Total: 44**

Cards
- Al Habsi: 0
- Team-mates: 65
- **Total: 65**

Cup Games

	Apps	CS	Cards
UEFA Cup	0	0	0
FA Cup	0	0	0
Carling Cup	0	0	0
Total	**0**	**0**	**0**

Career History

Career Milestones

Club Debut:
—

 —

Time Spent at the Club:

▶ **0.5 Seasons**

First Goal Scored for the Club:
—

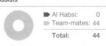 —

Full International:

▶ **Oman**

Premiership Totals
92-06

Appearances	0
Clean Sheets	0
Assists	0
Yellow Cards	0
Red Cards	0

Clubs

Year	Club	Apps	CS
06-06	Bolton	0	0
	Lyn Oslo		

Off the Pitch

Age:

- Al Habsi: 24 years, 5 months
- Team: 28 years, 5 months
- League: 26 years, 11 months

Height:
- Al Habsi: 6'4"
- Team: 5'11"
- League: 5'11"

Weight:
- Al Habsi: 12st 6lb
- Team: 12st 1lb
- League: 12st

Chris Howarth
Goalkeeper

Player Details:

Date of Birth:	23.05.1986
Place of Birth:	Bolton
Nationality:	English
Height:	6'2"
Weight:	12st 2lb
Foot:	Right

Player Performance 05/06

League Performance

Percentage of total possible time player was on pitch   ⊖ position in league table at end of month

Month:	Aug	Sep	Oct	Nov	Dec	Jan	Feb	Mar	Apr	May	Total
	5	3	5	7	7	7	6	7	8	8	
	0%	0%	0%	0%	0%	0%	0%	0%	0%	0%	0%
Team Pts:	7/12	7/9	6/12	3/6	8/15	5/9	6/12	6/12	4/21	4/6	56/114
Team Gls F:	6	2	5	2	8	4	5	10	5	2	49
Team Gls A:	4	0	7	2	5	2	4	8	8	1	41
Total mins:	0	0	0	0	0	0	0	0	0	0	0
Starts (sub):	0	0	0	0	0	0	0	0	0	0	0
Goals:	0	0	0	0	0	0	0	0	0	0	0
Assists:	0	0	0	0	0	0	0	0	0	0	0
Clean sheets:	0	0	0	0	0	0	0	0	0	0	0
Cards (Y/R):	0	0	0	0	0	0	0	0	0	0	0

League Performance Totals

Clean Sheets

- Howarth: 0
- Team-mates: 15

Total: 15

Assists

- Howarth: 0
- Team-mates: 44

Total: 44

Cards

- Howarth: 0
- Team-mates: 65

Total: 65

Cup Games

	Apps	CS	Cards
UEFA Cup	0	0	0
FA Cup	0	0	0
Carling Cup	0	0	0
Total	**0**	**0**	**0**

Career History

Career Milestones

Club Debut:
—

 —

First Goal Scored for the Club:
—

▶ —

Time Spent at the Club:

▶ **1 Season**

Full International:

▶ —

Premiership Totals

92-06

Appearances	0
Clean Sheets	0
Assists	0
Yellow Cards	0
Red Cards	0

Clubs

Year	Club	Apps	CS
06-06	Stockport Cty	0	0
05-06	Bolton	0	0

Off the Pitch

Age:

- Howarth: 20 years
- Team: 28 years, 5 months
- League: 26 years, 11 months

Height:

- Howarth: 6'2"
- Team: 5'11"
- League: 5'11"

Weight:

- Howarth: 12st 2lb
- Team: 12st 1lb
- League: 12st

Joey O'Brien
Defence

Player Details:

Date of Birth:	17.02.1986
Place of Birth:	Dublin
Nationality:	Irish
Height:	5'11"
Weight:	10st 13lb
Foot:	Right/Left

Season Review 05/06

The Dublin-born youngster started the campaign as an Academy graduate and ended it as a fully-fledged Barclays Premiership performer and a full international for the Republic of Ireland.

O'Brien was thrown in at the deep-end when he came on as a tenth minute substitute for the injured Gary Speed during the home game against Portsmouth in September 2005. He then kept his place in the team, although he switched to an unfamiliar position of right-back. It was in that role he excelled and went on to keep out regular right-back Nicky Hunt when the England under 21 international returned to fitness. He made his full RoI debut in a 3-0 victory against Sweden in March 2006.

Player Performance 05/06

League Performance

Percentage of total possible time player was on pitch   position in league table at end of month

Month:	Aug	Sep	Oct	Nov	Dec	Jan	Feb	Mar	Apr	May	Total
	5	3	5	100% / 7	80% / 7	100% / 7	100% / 6	94% / 7	8	8 50%	58%
	0%	30%	50%						19%		
Team Pts:	7/12	7/9	6/12	3/6	8/15	5/9	6/12	6/12	4/21	4/6	56/114
Team Gls F:	6	2	5	2	8	4	5	10	5	2	49
Team Gls A:	4	0	7	2	5	2	4	8	8	1	41
Total mins:	0	80	180	180	360	270	360	337	120	90	1,977
Starts (sub):	0	0 (1)	2	2	4	3	4	4	2	1	22 (1)
Goals:	0	0	0	0	0	0	0	0	0	0	0
Assists:	0	0	0	0	0	0	0	0	0	0	0
Clean sheets:	0	1	2	1	2	2	0	1	0	1	10
Cards (Y/R):	0	0	0	1	0	1	0	0	0	0	2

League Performance Totals

Goals
- O'Brien: 0
- Team-mates: 47
- **Total: 47**
- own goals: 2

Assists
- O'Brien: 0
- Team-mates: 44
- **Total: 44**

Cards
- O'Brien: 2
- Team-mates: 63
- **Total: 65**

Cup Games

	Apps	Goals	Cards
UEFA Cup	6	0	1
FA Cup	3	0	0
Carling Cup	2	0	0
Total	**11**	**0**	**1**

Career History

Career Milestones

Club Debut:
vs Yeovil (A), W 0-2, League Cup
 **21.09.04**

Time Spent at the Club:
▶ **2 Seasons**

First Goal Scored for the Club:
—
▶ —

Full International:
▶ **Rep. Ireland**

Premiership Totals

92-06

Appearances	24
Goals	0
Assists	0
Yellow Cards	2
Red Cards	0

Clubs

Year	Club	Apps	Gls
04-05	Sheff Wed	15	2
04-06	Bolton	36	0

Off the Pitch

Age:
- O'Brien: 20 years, 3 months
- Team: 28 years, 5 months
- League: 26 years, 11 months

Height:
- O'Brien: 5'11"
- Team: 5'11"
- League: 5'11"

Weight:
- O'Brien: 10st 13lb
- Team: 12st 1lb
- League: 12st

Nicky Hunt
Defence

Season Review 05/06

The Westhoughton-born defender endured a season of frustration last campaign. The 22 year-old suffered a fractured leg during the home win against Portsmouth in September and was out of action for two months.

Upon his recuperation, he was forced to witness the emergence of Joey O'Brien in the right-back berth.

Hunt regained his place in the latter part of the campaign and will look to re-establish himself in the first team squad for the coming season.

Player Details:

Date of Birth:	03.09.1983
Place of Birth:	Westhoughton
Nationality:	English
Height:	6'1"
Weight:	10st 6lb
Foot:	Right

Player Performance 05/06

League Performance

Percentage of total possible time player was on pitch   ⊙ position in league table at end of month

Month:	Aug	Sep	Oct	Nov	Dec	Jan	Feb	Mar	Apr	May	Total
	97%	38%	0%	0%	25%	0%	39%	6%	67%	50%	36%
Team Pts:	7/12	7/9	6/12	3/6	8/15	5/9	6/12	6/12	4/21	4/6	56/114
Team Gls F:	6	2	5	2	8	4	5	10	5	2	49
Team Gls A:	4	0	7	2	5	2	4	8	8	1	41
Total mins:	348	102	0	0	113	0	142	23	420	90	1,238
Starts (sub):	4	1 (1)	0	0	1 (1)	0 (1)	1 (2)	0 (1)	4 (2)	1	12 (8)
Goals:	0	0	0	0	0	0	0	0	0	0	0
Assists:	1	0	0	0	0	0	0	0	0	0	1
Clean sheets:	1	1	0	0	1	0	0	0	1	0	4
Cards (Y/R):	0	0	0	0	0	0	0	0	1	0	1

League positions: 5, 3, 5, 7, 7, 7, 6, 7, 8, 8

League Performance Totals

Goals

▶ Hunt:	0
▷ Team-mates:	47
Total:	**47**
▶ own goals:	2

Assists

▶ Hunt:	1
▷ Team-mates:	43
Total:	**44**

Cards

▶ Hunt:	1
▷ Team-mates:	64
Total:	**65**

Cup Games

	Apps	Goals	Cards
UEFA Cup	2	0	0
FA Cup	2	0	0
Carling Cup	1	0	0
Total	**5**	**0**	**0**

Career History

Career Milestones

Club Debut:

vs Sheff Utd (H), D 1-1, Championship

▶ **06.05.01**

Time Spent at the Club:

▶ **6 Seasons**

First Goal Scored for the Club:

vs Liverpool (H), D 2-2, Premiership

▶ **07.02.04**

Full International:

▶ **—**

Premiership Totals

92-06

Appearances	80
Goals	1
Assists	6
Yellow Cards	12
Red Cards	0

Clubs

Year	Club	Apps	Gls
00-06	Bolton	100	1

Off the Pitch

Age:

- ▶ Hunt: 22 years, 8 months
- ▷ Team: 28 years, 5 months
- | League: 26 years, 11 months

Height:

- ▶ Hunt: 6'1"
- ▷ Team: 5'11"
- | League: 5'11"

Weight:

- ▶ Hunt: 10st 6lb
- ▷ Team: 12st 1lb
- | League: 12st

141

Radhi Jaidi
Defence

A star with Tunisia during the World Cup in Germany, the big central defender was unable to command a regular place in the heart of the Wanderers defence, although he managed to net on three occasions.

With the departure of Bruno N'Gotty during the summer, the former Esperance defender will be hoping to force his way back into Sam Allardyce's first-team plans.

Player Details:

Date of Birth:	30.08.1975
Place of Birth:	Tunis
Nationality:	Tunisian
Height:	6'2"
Weight:	14st
Foot:	Right

Player Performance 05/06

League Performance

Percentage of total possible time player was on pitch   G· position in league table at end of month

Month:	Aug	Sep	Oct	Nov	Dec	Jan	Feb	Mar	Apr	May	Total
	56% 5	3 / 33%	75% 5	68% 7 / 21%	7 / 33%	7	6 / 25%	75% 7	8 / 0%	8 / 0%	36%
Team Pts:	7/12	7/9	6/12	3/6	8/15	5/9	6/12	6/12	4/21	4/6	56/114
Team Gls F:	6	2	5	2	8	4	5	10	5	2	49
Team Gls A:	4	0	7	2	5	2	4	8	8	1	41
Total mins:	203	90	270	122	94	90	90	270	0	0	1,229
Starts (sub):	3	1	3	2	1 (1)	1	1	3	0	0	15 (1)
Goals:	0	0	1	0	0	1	0	1	0	0	3
Assists:	1	0	0	0	0	0	0	1	0	0	2
Clean sheets:	0	1	1	1	1	0	0	0	0	0	4
Cards (Y/R):	0	0	1	0	0	0	0	0	0	0	1

League Performance Totals

Goals

Jaidi:	3
Team-mates:	44
Total:	**47**
own goals:	2

Assists

Jaidi:	2
Team-mates:	42
Total:	**44**

Cards

Jaidi:	1
Team-mates:	64
Total:	**65**

Cup Games

	Apps	Goals	Cards
UEFA Cup	3	0	0
FA Cup	2	0	0
Carling Cup	3	0	0
Total	**8**	**0**	**0**

Career History

Career Milestones

Club Debut:
vs Southampton (A), W 1-2, Prem.
 **25.08.04**

Time Spent at the Club:
2 Seasons

First Goal Scored for the Club:
vs Arsenal (A), D 2-2, Prem.
18.09.04

Full International:
Tunisia

Premiership Totals
92-06

Appearances	43
Goals	8
Assists	3
Yellow Cards	3
Red Cards	0

Clubs

Year	Club	Apps	Gls
04-06	Bolton	52	8
	Esperance		

Off the Pitch

Age:

- Jaidi: 30 years, 9 months
- Team: 28 years, 5 months
- League: 26 years, 11 months

Height:

- Jaidi: 6'2"
- Team: 5'11"
- League: 5'11"

Weight:

- Jaidi: 14st
- Team: 12st 1lb
- League: 12st

Ricardo Gardner
Defence

Season Review 05/06

The overwhelming choice for Player of the Year, the Jamaican was simply awesome in his eighth season with the Club. Having converted from being a skilful midfielder several seasons ago, Gardner has now matured in this defensive role and it is difficult to think of a better left-back in the Barclays Premiership.

The experienced campaigner also stood in as captain on occasions last term and has more than 250 appearances for the Club under his belt.

Player Details:

Date of Birth:	25.09.1978
Place of Birth:	St Andrews
Nationality:	Jamaican
Height:	5'9"
Weight:	11st
Foot:	Left

Player Performance 05/06

League Performance

Percentage of total possible time player was on pitch — position in league table at end of month

Month:	Aug	Sep	Oct	Nov	Dec	Jan	Feb	Mar	Apr	May	Total
	50%	55%	45%	100%	80%	100%	100%	83%	71%	0%	70%
	5	3	5	7	7	7	6	7	8	8	
Team Pts:	7/12	7/9	6/12	3/6	8/15	5/9	6/12	6/12	4/21	4/6	56/114
Team Gls F:	6	2	5	2	8	4	5	10	5	2	49
Team Gls A:	4	0	7	2	5	2	4	8	8	1	41
Total mins:	180	148	163	180	360	270	360	300	450	0	2,411
Starts (sub):	2	1 (2)	2 (1)	2	4	3	4	4	5	0	27 (3)
Goals:	0	0	0	0	0	0	0	0	0	0	0
Assists:	0	0	0	0	0	0	0	2	0	0	2
Clean sheets:	0	1	1	1	2	2	0	0	1	0	8
Cards (Y/R):	0	0	0/1	0	1	0	0	0	2	0	3/1

League Performance Totals

Goals

- Gardner: 0
- Team-mates: 47
- **Total: 47**
- own goals: 2

Assists

- Gardner: 2
- Team-mates: 42
- **Total: 44**

Cards

- Gardner: 4
- Team-mates: 61
- **Total: 65**

Cup Games

	Apps	Goals	Cards
UEFA Cup	7	0	1
FA Cup	4	0	0
Carling Cup	3	0	0
Total	**14**	**0**	**1**

Career History

Career Milestones

Club Debut:
vs Hartlepool (A), W 0-3, League Cup

 **25.08.98**

First Goal Scored for the Club:
vs West Brom (A), W 2-3, Champ.

 **08.09.98**

Time Spent at the Club:

 **8 Seasons**

Full International:

 Jamaica

Premiership Totals

92-06

Appearances	148
Goals	5
Assists	15
Yellow Cards	18
Red Cards	3

Clubs

Year	Club	Apps	Gls
98-06	Bolton	290	19
	Harbour View		

Off the Pitch

Age:

- Gardner: 27 years, 8 months
- Team: 28 years, 5 months
- League: 26 years, 11 months

Height:

- Gardner: 5'9"
- Team: 5'11"
- League: 5'11"

Weight:

- Gardner: 11st
- Team: 12st 1lb
- League: 12st

Tal Ben Haim
Defence

If the Israeli international's first season with the Club can be described as outstanding then his second year at the Reebok Stadium must be deemed as awesome.

The composed centre-half's performances were virtually infallible as he made 35 league appearances for the Club.

The defender will be looking for a repeat in the 2006/2007 season.

Player Details:

Date of Birth:	31.03.1982
Place of Birth:	Rishon Letzion
Nationality:	Israeli
Height:	5'11"
Weight:	11st 9lb
Foot:	Right/Left

Player Performance 05/06

League Performance

Percentage of total possible time player was on pitch   ⊖ position in league table at end of month

Month:	Aug	Sep	Oct	Nov	Dec	Jan	Feb	Mar	Apr	May	Total
	98%	100%	76%	100%	70%	69%	75%	75%	86%	100%	83%
	5	3	5	7	7	7	6	7	8	8	
Team Pts:	7/12	7/9	6/12	3/6	8/15	5/9	6/12	6/12	4/21	4/6	56/114
Team Gls F:	6	2	5	2	8	4	5	10	5	2	49
Team Gls A:	4	0	7	2	5	2	4	8	8	1	41
Total mins:	353	270	274	180	316	187	270	270	540	180	2,840
Starts (sub):	4	3	3 (1)	2	4	2 (1)	3 (1)	3	6	2	32 (3)
Goals:	0	0	0	0	0	0	0	0	0	0	0
Assists:	0	0	0	0	0	0	0	0	0	0	0
Clean sheets:	1	3	1	1	2	2	0	1	0	1	12
Cards (Y/R):	1	1	0	1	2	1	0	0	1/1	0	7/1

League Performance Totals

Goals

- Ben Haim: 0
- Team-mates: 47

Total: 47

- own goals: 2

Assists

- Ben Haim: 0
- Team-mates: 44

Total: 44

Cards

- Ben Haim: 8
- Team-mates: 57

Total: 65

Cup Games

	Apps	Goals	Cards
UEFA Cup	7	0	0
FA Cup	4	0	1
Carling Cup	3	0	1
Total	**14**	**0**	**2**

Career History

Career Milestones

Club Debut:

vs Charlton (H), W 4-1, Premiership

▶ **14.08.04**

Time Spent at the Club:

▶ **2 Seasons**

First Goal Scored for the Club:

vs Tottenham (H), W 3-1, Premiership

▶ **01.02.05**

Full International:

▶ **Israel**

Premiership Totals

92-06

Appearances	56
Goals	1
Assists	0
Yellow Cards	12
Red Cards	1

Clubs

Year	Club	Apps	Gls
04-06	Bolton	76	1
	Maccabi Tel-Aviv		

Off the Pitch

Age:

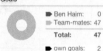

- Ben Haim: 24 years, 2 months
- Team: 28 years, 5 months
- League: 26 years, 11 months

Height:

- Ben Haim: 5'11"
- Team: 5'11"
- League: 5'11"

Weight:

- Ben Haim: 11st 9lb
- Team: 12st 1lb
- League: 12st

Bruno N'Gotty
Defence

(released)

Arrived in 2001 from Marseille, initially on loan, the former France international soon became the mainstay of the Wanderers defence. Over the next five years he proved to be a colossus in the back four.

He made over 150 appearances for the Club before being released by the Club in the summer of 2006.

Player Details:

Date of Birth:	10.06.1971
Place of Birth:	Lyon
Nationality:	French
Height:	6'1"
Weight:	13st 8lb
Foot:	Right/Left

Player Performance 05/06

League Performance

Percentage of total possible time player was on pitch   ⊖ position in league table at end of month

Month:	Aug	Sep	Oct	Nov	Dec	Jan	Feb	Mar	Apr	May	Total
	25%	100%	100%	36%	100%	100%	100%	38%	71%	0%	72%
Team Pts:	7/12	7/9	6/12	3/6	8/15	5/9	6/12	6/12	4/21	4/6	56/114
Team Gls F:	6	2	5	2	8	4	5	10	5	2	49
Team Gls A:	4	0	7	2	5	2	4	8	8	1	41
Total mins:	90	270	360	64	450	270	360	136	450	0	2,450
Starts (sub):	1	3	4	0 (2)	5	3	4	2	5	0	27 (2)
Goals:	0	0	0	0	0	0	0	0	0	0	0
Assists:	0	0	0	0	0	0	1	0	0	0	1
Clean sheets:	0	3	2	0	3	2	0	1	1	0	12
Cards (Y/R):	0	0	1	0	0	1	0	0	0	0	2

League Performance Totals

Goals

▶ N'Gotty:	0
▶ Team-mates:	47
Total:	**47**
▶ own goals:	2

Assists

▶ N'Gotty:	1
▶ Team-mates:	43
Total:	**44**

Cards

▶ N'Gotty:	2
▶ Team-mates:	63
Total:	**65**

Cup Games

	Apps	Goals	Cards
UEFA Cup	7	1	0
FA Cup	2	0	0
Carling Cup	1	0	0
Total	**10**	**1**	**0**

Career History

Career Milestones

Club Debut:
vs Blackburn (A), D 1-1, Premiership
▶ **19.09.01**

Time Spent at the Club:
▶ **5 Seasons**

First Goal Scored for the Club:
vs Everton (A), L 3-1, Premiership
▶ **01.04.02**

Full International:
▶ **France**

Premiership Totals

92-06

Appearances	148
Goals	5
Assists	6
Yellow Cards	12
Red Cards	2

Clubs

Year	Club	Apps	Gls
01-06	Bolton	172	7
	Marseille		
	Venezia		
	AC Milan		
	Paris-SG		
	Olympique Lyonnais		

Off the Pitch

Age:
- ▶ N'Gotty: 34 years, 11 months
- ▶ Team: 28 years, 5 months
- | League: 26 years, 11 months

Height:
- ▶ N'Gotty: 6'1"
- ▶ Team: 5'11"
- | League: 5'11"

Weight:
- ▶ N'Gotty: 13st 8lb
- ▶ Team: 12st 1lb
- | League: 12st

Jay-Jay Okocha
Midfield
(released)

Season Review 05/06

The Nigerian's four-year tenure at the Reebok Stadium came to an end in the summer of 2006, but the legacy left by the superstar midfielder will continue for years to come.

When he arrived at the Club, Wanderers were a side that were fighting in the lower reaches of the league. During his stay in the North West, he transformed Wanderers into a top-ten outfit. A midfielder with a venomous shot, the former Paris Saint Germain star was a sublime footballer with a vast array of tricks and an immense passing ability.

Player Details:

Date of Birth:	14.08.1973
Place of Birth:	Enugu
Nationality:	Nigerian
Height:	5'8"
Weight:	11st
Foot:	Right/Left

Player Performance 05/06

League Performance

Percentage of total possible time player was on pitch   ⊙ position in league table at end of month

Month:	Aug	Sep	Oct	Nov	Dec	Jan	Feb	Mar	Apr	May	Total
	84%	57% 3	17% 5	21% 7	42% 7	0% 7	25% 6	77% 7	60% 8	71% 8	47%
Team Pts:	7/12	7/9	6/12	3/6	8/15	5/9	6/12	6/12	4/21	4/6	56/114
Team Gls F:	6	2	5	2	8	4	5	10	5	2	49
Team Gls A:	4	0	7	2	5	2	4	8	8	1	41
Total mins:	303	153	61	37	190	0	90	278	379	127	1,618
Starts (sub):	3 (1)	2	1 (1)	0 (1)	2 (2)	0	1 (1)	4	4 (2)	1 (1)	18 (9)
Goals:	0	0	0	0	0	0	0	1	0	0	1
Assists:	1	0	0	0	0	0	0	0	0	1	2
Clean sheets:	1	2	0	0	0	0	1	1	1	0	5
Cards (Y/R):	0	0	0	1	0	0	0	0	0	0	1

League Performance Totals

Goals

▶ Okocha: 1
▷ Team-mates: 46
Total: 47
■ own goals: 2

Assists

▶ Okocha: 2
▷ Team-mates: 42
Total: 44

Cards

▶ Okocha: 1
▷ Team-mates: 64
Total: 65

Cup Games

	Apps	Goals	Cards
UEFA Cup	7	0	0
FA Cup	3	0	0
Carling Cup	2	0	0
Total	**12**	**0**	**0**

Career History

Career Milestones

Club Debut:
vs Fulham (A), L 4-1, Premiership
 **17.08.02**

Time Spent at the Club:
 4 Seasons

First Goal Scored for the Club:
vs Birmingham (A), L 3-1, Premiership
 **02.11.02**

Full International:
 Nigeria

Premiership Totals
92-06

Appearances	124
Goals	14
Assists	19
Yellow Cards	7
Red Cards	0

Clubs

Year	Club	Apps	Gls
02-06	Bolton	145	18
	Paris-SG		
	Fenerbahce		
	Eintracht Frankfurt		

Off the Pitch

Age:

▶ Okocha: 32 years, 9 months
▷ Team: 28 years, 5 months
| League: 26 years, 11 months

Height:

▶ Okocha: 5'8"
▷ Team: 5'11"
| League: 5'11"

Weight:
▶ Okocha: 11st
▷ Team: 12st 1lb
| League: 12st

Abdoulaye Faye
Midfield

This midfield enforcer initially joined the Club on a season-long loan from French outfit Lens during the summer of 2005.

His immediate acclimatisation of the Barclays Premiership was rewarded when he turned his loan spell into a permanent arrangement in January 2006.

His fierce and well-timed tackling plus his outstanding aerial abilities saw him move to the centre of defence during the final phase of the campaign where he adeptly slotted alongside Tal Ben Haim.

Player Details:

Date of Birth:	26.02.1978
Place of Birth:	Dakar
Nationality:	Senegalese
Height:	6'2"
Weight:	13st 3lb
Foot:	Right

Player Performance 05/06

League Performance

Percentage of total possible time player was on pitch   ⊕ position in league table at end of month

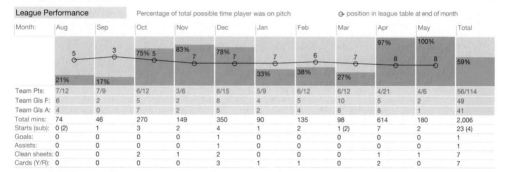

Month:	Aug	Sep	Oct	Nov	Dec	Jan	Feb	Mar	Apr	May	Total
	21%	17%	75% 5	83% 7	78% 7	33% 7	38% 6	27% 7	97% 8	100% 8	59%
	5	3									
Team Pts:	7/12	7/9	6/12	3/6	8/15	5/9	6/12	6/12	4/21	4/6	56/114
Team Gls F:	6	2	5	2	8	4	5	10	5	2	49
Team Gls A:	4	0	7	2	5	2	4	8	8	1	41
Total mins:	74	46	270	149	350	90	135	98	614	180	2,006
Starts (sub):	0 (2)	1	3	2	4	1	2	1 (2)	7	2	23 (4)
Goals:	0	0	0	0	1	0	0	0	0	0	1
Assists:	0	0	0	0	1	0	0	0	0	0	1
Clean sheets:	0	0	2	1	2	0	0	0	1	1	7
Cards (Y/R):	0	0	0	0	3	1	1	0	2	0	7

League Performance Totals

Goals

▶ Faye:	1
▷ Team-mates:	46
Total:	**47**
▶ own goals:	2

Assists

▶ Faye:	1
▷ Team-mates:	43
Total:	**44**

Cards

▶ Faye:	7
▷ Team-mates:	58
Total:	**65**

Cup Games

	Apps	Goals	Cards
European	0	0	0
FA Cup	1	0	0
Carling Cup	2	0	1
Total	**3**	**0**	**1**

Career History

Career Milestones

Club Debut:
vs Newcastle (H), W 2-0, Premiership

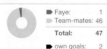 **24.08.05**

Time Spent at the Club:

 1 Season

First Goal Scored for the Club:
vs Arsenal (H), W 2-0, Premiership

▶ **03.12.05**

Full International:

▶ **Senegal**

Premiership Totals

92-06

Appearances	27
Goals	1
Assists	1
Yellow Cards	7
Red Cards	0

Clubs

Year	Club	Apps	Gls
05-06	Bolton	37	1
	Istres		
	RC Lens		
	Guingamp		

Off the Pitch

Age:

- ▶ Diagne-Faye: 28 years, 3 months
- ▷ Team: 28 years, 5 months
- | League: 26 years, 11 months

Height:

- ▶ Faye: 6'2"
- ▷ Team: 5'11"
- | League: 5'11"

Weight:

- ▶ Faye: 13st 3lb
- ▷ Team: 12st 1lb
- | League: 12st

Gary Speed
Midfield

Season Review 05/06

The veteran former Wales midfielder chipped in with four vital goals last season, including a spectacular overhead effort in the 4-1 home victory against West Ham United in March 2006.

Now, in his third season with the Club, Speed will be hoping to help Wanderers maintain their status as an established top ten club.

Player Details:

Date of Birth:	08.09.1969
Place of Birth:	Mancot
Nationality:	Welsh
Height:	5'10"
Weight:	10st 12lb
Foot:	Left

Player Performance 05/06

League Performance

Percentage of total possible time player was on pitch   ⊖ position in league table at end of month

Month:	Aug	Sep	Oct	Nov	Dec	Jan	Feb	Mar	Apr	May	Total
	100%	70%	63%	100%	100%	33%	8%	99%	78%	58%	72%
Team Pts:	7/12	7/9	6/12	3/6	8/15	5/9	6/12	6/12	4/21	4/6	56/114
Team Gls F:	6	2	5	2	8	4	5	10	5	2	49
Team Gls A:	4	0	7	2	5	2	4	8	8	1	41
Total mins:	360	190	226	180	450	90	30	355	489	105	2,475
Starts (sub):	4	3	3	2	5	1	0 (1)	4	6	1 (1)	29 (2)
Goals:	0	1	0	0	2	0	0	1	0	0	4
Assists:	2	0	0	0	1	0	0	1	0	0	4
Clean sheets:	1	2	1	1	3	0	0	1	1	1	11
Cards (Y/R):	1	0	0	1	0	0	0	0	0	0	2

League Performance Totals

Goals

▶ Speed:	4
▷ Team-mates:	43
Total:	**47**
● own goals:	2

Assists

▶ Speed:	4
▷ Team-mates:	40
Total:	**44**

Cards

▶ Speed:	2
▷ Team-mates:	63
Total:	**65**

Cup Games

	Apps	Goals	Cards
UEFA Cup	5	0	0
FA Cup	2	0	0
Carling Cup	2	0	0
Total	**9**	**0**	**0**

Career History

Career Milestones

Club Debut:
vs Charlton (H), W 4-1, Premiership

▶ **14.08.04**

Time Spent at the Club:

▶ **2 Seasons**

First Goal Scored for the Club:
vs Aston Villa (A), D 1-1, Premiership

▶ **23.04.05**

Full International:

▶ **Wales**

Premiership Totals

92-06

Appearances	483
Goals	72
Assists	49
Yellow Cards	62
Red Cards	1

Clubs

Year	Club	Apps	Gls
04-06	Bolton	80	5
98-04	Newcastle	284	40
96-98	Everton	65	17
88-96	Leeds	312	57

Off the Pitch

Age:

▶ Speed: 36 years, 8 months
▷ Team: 28 years, 5 months
| League: 26 years, 11 months

Height:

▶ Speed: 5'10"
▷ Team: 5'11"
| League: 5'11"

Weight:

▶ Speed: 10st 12lb
▷ Team: 12st 1lb
| League: 12st

Hidetoshi Nakata
Midfield

(retired)

Season Review 05/06

The Japan international featured sporadically for Wanderers during the campaign and at times displayed the kind of form that propelled him into international stardom earlier in his career. Following his country's exit from the World Cup, Hide decided to call time on his football career at the tender age of 29.

Player Details:

Date of Birth:	22.01.1977
Place of Birth:	Yamanashi
Nationality:	Japanese
Height:	5'9"
Weight:	11st
Foot:	Right/Left

Player Performance 05/06

League Performance

Percentage of total possible time player was on pitch   ⚲ position in league table at end of month

Month:	Aug	Sep	Oct	Nov	Dec	Jan	Feb	Mar	Apr	May	Total
	0%	46%	84%	47%	0%	12%	73%	27%	42%	71%	38%
Team Pts:	7/12	7/9	6/12	3/6	8/15	5/9	6/12	6/12	4/21	4/6	56/114
Team Gls F:	6	2	5	2	8	4	5	10	5	2	49
Team Gls A:	4	0	7	2	5	2	4	8	8	1	41
Total mins:	0	124	304	84	0	33	262	97	262	128	1,294
Starts (sub):	0	1 (1)	3 (1)	1 (1)	0	1	3	0 (3)	3 (1)	2	14 (7)
Goals:	0	0	1	0	0	0	0	0	0	0	1
Assists:	0	0	2	0	0	0	0	0	1	0	3
Clean sheets:	0	1	2	0	0	1	0	0	1	0	5
Cards (Y/R):	0	0	1	0	0	0/1	0	0	0	0	1/1

League Performance Totals

Goals
- Nakata: 1
- Team-mates: 46
- **Total:** 47
- own goals: 2

Assists
- Nakata: 3
- Team-mates: 41
- **Total:** 44

Cards
- Nakata: 2
- Team-mates: 63
- **Total:** 65

Cup Games

	Apps	Goals	Cards
UEFA Cup	6	0	3
FA Cup	3	0	0
Carling Cup	2	0	0
Total	**11**	**0**	**3**

Career History

Career Milestones

Club Debut:
vs Loko Plovdiv (H), W 2-1, UEFA Cup
▶ **15.09.05**

Time Spent at the Club:
▶ **1 Season**

First Goal Scored for the Club:
vs West Brom (H), W 2-0, Premiership
▶ **23.10.05**

Full International:
▶ **Japan**

Premiership Totals

92-06

Appearances	21
Goals	1
Assists	3
Yellow Cards	1
Red Cards	1

Clubs

Year	Club	Apps	Gls
05-06	Bolton	32	1
	Fiorentina		
	Bologna		
	Parma		
	AS Roma		
	Perugia		
	Bellmare Hiratsuka		

Off the Pitch

Age:

- Nakata: 29 years, 4 months
- Team: 28 years, 5 months
- League: 26 years, 11 months

Height:

- Nakata: 5'9"
- Team: 5'11"
- League: 5'11"

Weight:

- Nakata: 11st
- Team: 12st 1lb
- League: 12st

Ivan Campo
Midfield

Season Review 05/06

Started the season off in fine style with a goal on the opening day against Aston Villa but suffered a broken foot on two separate occasions as the campaign went on. However, the classy midfielder forced his way back into the reckoning towards to the end of the season and showed the form that persuaded manager Sam Allardyce to offer him a new contract.

Player Details:

Date of Birth:	21.02.1974
Place of Birth:	San Sebastian
Nationality:	Spanish
Height:	6'1"
Weight:	12st 11lb
Foot:	Right

Player Performance 05/06

League Performance

Percentage of total possible time player was on pitch   ⊙ position in league table at end of month

Month:	Aug	Sep	Oct	Nov	Dec	Jan	Feb	Mar	Apr	May	Total
Position	5	3	5	7	7	7	6	7	8	8	
Percentage	34%	50%	0%	0%	7%	53%	0%	0%	45%	78%	25%
Team Pts:	7/12	7/9	6/12	3/6	8/15	5/9	6/12	6/12	4/21	4/6	56/114
Team Gls F:	6	2	5	2	8	4	5	10	5	2	49
Team Gls A:	4	0	7	2	5	2	4	8	8	1	41
Total mins:	124	134	0	0	33	144	0	0	286	140	861
Starts (sub):	1 (3)	1 (1)	0	0	0 (1)	1 (1)	0	0	3 (1)	2	8 (7)
Goals:	2	0	0	0	0	0	0	0	0	0	2
Assists:	0	0	0	0	0	0	0	0	0	0	0
Clean sheets:	0	1	0	0	0	1	0	0	0	0	2
Cards (Y/R):	0	1	0	0	0	0	0	0	1	0	2

League Performance Totals

Goals

▶ Campo:	2
▦ Team-mates:	45
Total	**47**
▶ own goals:	2

Assists

▶ Campo:	0
▦ Team-mates:	44
Total	**44**

Cards

▶ Campo:	2
▦ Team-mates:	63
Total	**65**

Cup Games

	Apps	Goals	Cards
UEFA Cup	1	0	0
FA Cup	1	0	0
Carling Cup	1	0	0
Total	**3**	**0**	**0**

Career History

Career Milestones

Club Debut:
vs Man Utd (A), W 0-1, Premiership

▶ **11.09.02**

Time Spent at the Club:

▶ **4 Seasons**

First Goal Scored for the Club:
vs Liverpool (H), L 2-3, Premiership

▶ **14.09.02**

Full International:

▶ **Spain**

Premiership Totals

92-06

Appearances	111
Goals	8
Assists	3
Yellow Cards	27
Red Cards	1

Clubs

Year	Club	Apps	Gls
02-06	Bolton	125	8
	Real Madrid		
	RCD Mallorca		
	Valencia		
	Real Valladolid		
	Alaves		

Off the Pitch

Age:

▶ Campo: 32 years, 3 months
▦ Team: 28 years, 5 months
| League: 26 years, 11 months

Height:

▶ Campo: 6'1"
▦ Team: 5'11"
| League: 5'11"

Weight:

▶ Campo: 12st 11lb
▦ Team: 12st 1lb
| League: 12st

Idan Tal
Midfield

(new signing)

Season Review 05/06

Sam Allardyce completed his first signing of the 2006/2007 season in January 2006 when the Israeli international signed a pre-contract agreement with the Club.

The creative midfielder, who plied his trade with Maccabi Haifa, has Premier League experience after spending a short period with Everton earlier in his career.

Player Details:

Date of Birth:	13.10.1975
Place of Birth:	Petah Tikva
Nationality:	Israeli
Height:	5'11"
Weight:	11st 7lb
Foot:	Left

Player Performance 05/06

League Performance

Percentage of total possible time player was on pitch   ⊙ position in league table at end of month

Month:	Aug	Sep	Oct	Nov	Dec	Jan	Feb	Mar	Apr	May	Total
position	5	3	5	7	7	7	6	7	8	8	
	0%	0%	0%	0%	0%	0%	0%	0%	0%	0%	0%
Team Pts:	7/12	7/9	6/12	3/6	8/15	5/9	6/12	6/12	4/21	4/6	56/114
Team Gls F:	6	2	5	2	8	4	5	10	5	2	49
Team Gls A:	4	0	7	2	5	2	4	8	8	1	41
Total mins:	0	0	0	0	0	0	0	0	0	0	0
Starts (sub):	0	0	0	0	0	0	0	0	0	0	0
Goals:	0	0	0	0	0	0	0	0	0	0	0
Assists:	0	0	0	0	0	0	0	0	0	0	0
Clean sheets:	0	0	0	0	0	0	0	0	0	0	0
Cards (Y/R):	0	0	0	0	0	0	0	0	0	0	0

League Performance Totals

Goals
- Tal: 0
- Team-mates: 47
- **Total: 47**
- own goals: 2

Assists
- Tal: 0
- Team-mates: 44
- **Total: 44**

Cards
- Tal: 0
- Team-mates: 65
- **Total: 65**

Cup Games

	Apps	Goals	Cards
UEFA Cup	0	0	0
FA Cup	0	0	0
Carling Cup	0	0	0
Total	**0**	**0**	**0**

Career History

Career Milestones

Club Debut:
—

First Goal Scored for the Club:
—

Time Spent at the Club:
—

Full International:

 **Israel**

Premiership Totals

92-06

Appearances	29
Goals	2
Assists	4
Yellow Cards	3
Red Cards	0

Clubs

Year	Club	Apps	Gls
06-06	Bolton	0	0
	Maccabi Haifa		
	Rayo Vallecano		
00-02	Everton	33	2
	Hapoel Petah Tikva		

Off the Pitch

Age:

- Tal: 30 years, 7 months
- Team: 28 years, 5 months
- League: 26 years, 11 months

Height:
- Tal: 5'11"
- Team: 5'11"
- League: 5'11"

Weight:
- Tal: 11st 7lb
- Team: 12st 1lb
- League: 12st

Kevin Nolan
Midfield

Season Review 05/06

The career of this dynamic and versatile midfielder continues to go from strength to strength.

Aside from netting 11 goals in all competitions, including two during the Club's inaugural UEFA Cup campaign, Nolan took over the captain's armband from Jay Jay Okocha midway through the season.

As he starts his seventh season as a professional with the club, Nolan will be looking to not only lead his side to some sort of glory, but also to win some much-deserved international recognition after being overlooked by England for the World Cup.

Player Details:

Date of Birth:	24.06.1982
Place of Birth:	Liverpool
Nationality:	English
Height:	6'
Weight:	14st
Foot:	Right

Player Performance 05/06

League Performance

Percentage of total possible time player was on pitch   ⟲ position in league table at end of month

Month:	Aug	Sep	Oct	Nov	Dec	Jan	Feb	Mar	Apr	May	Total
	100%	100%	100%	100%	80%	100%	100%	95%	72%	87%	91%
	5	3	5	7	7	7	6	7	8	8	
Team Pts:	7/12	7/9	6/12	3/6	8/15	5/9	6/12	6/12	4/21	4/6	56/114
Team Gls F:	6	2	5	2	8	4	5	10	5	2	49
Team Gls A:	4	0	7	2	5	2	4	8	8	1	41
Total mins:	360	270	360	180	360	270	360	342	456	156	3,114
Starts (sub):	4	3	4	2	4	3	4	4	5 (1)	2	35 (1)
Goals:	1	1	2	1	0	1	2	1	0	0	9
Assists:	0	0	0	1	1	0	0	1	1	1	5
Clean sheets:	1	3	2	1	2	2	0	1	1	1	14
Cards (Y/R):	0	0	2	1	1	1	1	1	0	0	7

League Performance Totals

Goals

▶ Nolan:	9
▧ Team-mates:	38
Total:	**47**
◆ own goals:	2

Assists

▶ Nolan:	5
▧ Team-mates:	39
Total:	**44**

Cards

▶ Nolan:	7
▧ Team-mates:	58
Total:	**65**

Cup Games

	Apps	Goals	Cards
UEFA Cup	7	2	1
FA Cup	3	0	1
Carling Cup	2	0	1
Total	**12**	**2**	**3**

Career History

Career Milestones

Club Debut:

vs Charlton Ath (H), L 0-2, Champ.

 **04.03.00**

Time Spent at the Club:

▶ **7 Seasons**

First Goal Scored for the Club:

vs Crewe Alx (H), W 4-1, Champ.

▶ **09.12.00**

Full International:

▶ —

Premiership Totals

92-06

Appearances	177
Goals	31
Assists	15
Yellow Cards	30
Red Cards	0

Clubs

Year	Club	Apps	Gls
99-06	Bolton	250	39

Off the Pitch

Age:

- ▶ Nolan: 23 years, 11 months
- ▧ Team: 28 years, 5 months
- ▎ League: 26 years, 11 months

Height:

- ▶ Nolan: 6'
- ▧ Team: 5'11"
- ▎ League: 5'11"

Weight:

- ▶ Nolan: 14st
- ▧ Team: 12st 1lb
- ▎ League: 12st

Stelios
Midfield

The Greek international ended his third season with Bolton Wanderers as the Club's top goalscorer.

The European Championship winner struck 12 goals, which played a significant role in him being named as the runner-up to Ricardo Gardner at the Player of the Year awards night.

Player Details:

Date of Birth:	12.07.1974
Place of Birth:	Athens
Nationality:	Greek
Height:	5'8"
Weight:	11st
Foot:	Right/Left

Player Performance 05/06

League Performance

Percentage of total possible time player was on pitch   ⊖ position in league table at end of month

Month:	Aug	Sep	Oct	Nov	Dec	Jan	Feb	Mar	Apr	May	Total
	56%	51%	60%	33%	93%	90%	100%	96%	71%	61%	74%
position	5	3	5	7	7	7	6	7	8	8	
Team Pts:	7/12	7/9	6/12	3/6	8/15	5/9	6/12	6/12	4/21	4/6	56/114
Team Gls F:	6	2	5	2	8	4	5	10	5	2	49
Team Gls A:	4	0	7	2	5	2	4	8	8	1	41
Total mins:	203	137	216	59	417	242	360	345	450	110	2,539
Starts (sub):	2 (1)	2 (1)	2 (1)	1	5	3	4	4	5 (1)	1 (1)	29 (5)
Goals:	1	0	1	0	3	0	1	3	0	0	9
Assists:	0	0	1	0	1	1	1	1	0	0	5
Clean sheets:	1	0	1	0	3	1	0	1	1	1	9
Cards (Y/R):	1	1	0	0	1	0	0	1	0	0	4

League Performance Totals

Goals
- Stelios: 9
- Team-mates: 38
- **Total: 47**
- own goals: 2

Assists
- Stelios: 5
- Team-mates: 39
- **Total: 44**

Cards
- Stelios: 4
- Team-mates: 61
- **Total: 65**

Cup Games

	Apps	Goals	Cards
European	0	0	0
FA Cup	4	2	0
Carling Cup	2	0	0
Total	**6**	**2**	**0**

Career History

Career Milestones

Club Debut:
vs Man Utd (A), L 4-0, Premiership
▶ **16.08.03**

Time Spent at the Club:
▶ **3 Seasons**

First Goal Scored for the Club:
vs Gillingham (H), W 2-0, League Cup
▶ **28.10.03**

Full International:
▶ **Greece**

Premiership Totals

92-06
Appearances	99
Goals	18
Assists	15
Yellow Cards	13
Red Cards	0

Clubs

Year	Club	Apps	Gls
03-06	Bolton	123	24
	Olympiakos		

Off the Pitch

Age:

- Stelios: 31 years, 10 months
- Team: 28 years, 5 months
- League: 26 years, 11 months

Height:

- Stelios: 5'8"
- Team: 5'11"
- League: 5'11"

Weight:

- Stelios: 11st
- Team: 12st 1lb
- League: 12st

Khalilou Fadiga
Midfield

Season Review 05/06

There was no doubting the Senegalese's talent with a football. His reputation and play earned him a multimillion pounds move to Inter Milan. After being released by the Italian giants after only a season, he linked up with compatriot El-Hadji Diouf at the Reebok Stadium.

He only showed flashes of his skill whilst with Wanderers and his career in Lancashire was blighted by a succession of injuries.

Player Details:

Date of Birth:	30.12.1974
Place of Birth:	Dakar
Nationality:	Senegalese
Height:	6'
Weight:	12st 2lb
Foot:	Left

Player Performance 05/06

League Performance

Percentage of total possible time player was on pitch   ⊕ position in league table at end of month

Month:	Aug	Sep	Oct	Nov	Dec	Jan	Feb	Mar	Apr	May	Total
	0%	0%	2%	0%	21%	37%	30%	0%	0%	0%	9%
Team Pts:	7/12	7/9	6/12	3/6	8/15	5/9	6/12	6/12	4/21	4/6	56/114
Team Gls F:	6	2	5	2	8	4	5	10	5	2	49
Team Gls A:	4	0	7	2	5	2	4	8	8	1	41
Total mins:	0	0	6	0	95	100	109	0	0	0	310
Starts (sub):	0	0	0 (1)	0	1 (1)	2 (1)	2	0	0	0	5 (3)
Goals:	0	0	0	0	0	0	1	0	0	0	1
Assists:	0	0	0	0	0	0	0	0	0	0	0
Clean sheets:	0	0	0	0	1	1	0	0	0	0	2
Cards (Y/R):	0	0	0	0	1	1	0	0	0	0	2

League positions: 5, 3, 5, 7, 7, 7, 6, 7, 8, 8

League Performance Totals

Goals
- Fadiga: 1
- Team-mates: 46
- **Total: 47**
- own goals: 2

Assists
- Fadiga: 0
- Team-mates: 44
- **Total: 44**

Cards
- Fadiga: 2
- Team-mates: 63
- **Total: 65**

Cup Games

	Apps	Goals	Cards
UEFA Cup	2	0	0
FA Cup	1	0	0
Carling Cup	2	0	0
Total	**5**	**0**	**0**

Career History

Career Milestones

Club Debut:
vs Crystal Palace (H), W 1-0, Prem.
▶ **16.10.04**

Time Spent at the Club:
▶ **2 Seasons**

First Goal Scored for the Club:
vs Portsmouth (A), D 1-1, Prem.
▶ **01.02.06**

Full International:
▶ **Senegal**

Premiership Totals
92-06

Appearances	13
Goals	1
Assists	0
Yellow Cards	2
Red Cards	0

Clubs

Year	Club	Apps	Gls
05-05	Derby	4	0
04-06	Bolton	21	1
	Internazionale		
	AJ Auxerre		

Off the Pitch

Age:
- Fadiga: 31 years, 5 months
- Team: 28 years, 5 months
- League: 26 years, 11 months

Height:
- Fadiga: 6'
- Team: 5'11"
- League: 5'11"

Weight:
- Fadiga: 12st 2lb
- Team: 12st 1lb
- League: 12st

Henrik Pedersen
Forward

Season Review 05/06

The vast majority of the Dane's appearances in the 2005/2006 season came in the unfamiliar role of left-back.

As cover for Ricardo Gardner, who was absent during the early part of the season, Pedersen, normally a striker, performed admirably in his new defensive role and earned high acclaim from his manager Sam Allardyce.

Pedersen, though, much prefers his advanced role on the pitch and will be hoping the forthcoming campaign sees him in a position to add to the solitary goal he scored last season.

Player Details:

Date of Birth:	10.06.1975
Place of Birth:	Copenhagen
Nationality:	Danish
Height:	6'1"
Weight:	13st 8lb
Foot:	Right/Left

Player Performance 05/06

League Performance

Percentage of total possible time player was on pitch   ⊖ position in league table at end of month

Month:	Aug	Sep	Oct	Nov	Dec	Jan	Feb	Mar	Apr	May	Total
	94%	100%	62%	7	7	7	6	7	8	100% 8	42%
	5	3	5	0%	0%	0%	0%	48%	43%		
Team Pts:	7/12	7/9	6/12	3/6	8/15	5/9	6/12	6/12	4/21	4/6	56/114
Team Gls F:	6	2	5	2	8	4	5	10	5	2	49
Team Gls A:	4	0	7	2	5	2	4	8	8	1	41
Total mins:	337	270	222	0	0	0	0	172	269	180	1,450
Starts (sub):	4	3	3	0	0	0	0	1 (3)	2 (3)	2	15 (6)
Goals:	0	0	0	0	0	0	0	1	0	0	1
Assists:	0	1	0	0	0	0	0	0	0	0	1
Clean sheets:	1	3	1	0	0	0	0	0	0	1	6
Cards (Y/R):	0	0	0	0	0	0	0	0	0	0	0

League Performance Totals

Goals

► Pedersen:	1
► Team-mates:	46
Total:	**47**
► own goals:	2

Assists

► Pedersen:	1
► Team-mates:	43
Total:	**44**

Cards

► Pedersen:	0
► Team-mates:	65
Total:	**65**

Cup Games

	Apps	Goals	Cards
UEFA Cup	3	0	0
FA Cup	1	0	1
Carling Cup	1	0	0
Total	**5**	**0**	**1**

Career History

Career Milestones

Club Debut:
vs Leicester (A), W 0-5, Premiership

► **18.08.01**

Time Spent at the Club:
► **5 Seasons**

First Goal Scored for the Club:
vs Walsall (H), W 4-3, League Cup

► **11.09.01**

Full International:
► **Denmark**

Premiership Totals
92-06

Appearances	125
Goals	21
Assists	8
Yellow Cards	2
Red Cards	0

Clubs

Year	Club	Apps	Gls
02-02	Silkeborg		
01-06	Bolton	150	28
	Silkeborg		

Off the Pitch

Age:

► Pedersen: 30 years, 11 months
► Team: 28 years, 5 months
| League: 26 years, 11 months

Height:

► Pedersen: 6'1"
► Team: 5'11"
| League: 5'11"

Weight:

► Pedersen: 13st 8lb
► Team: 12st 1lb
| League: 12st

Jared Borgetti
Forward

Season Review 05/06

Although he wasn't able to sustain a regular berth in the starting XI, the Mexican World Cup star netted eight goals from 12 starts. His goals in the UEFA Cup, including a great finish at Besiktas, helped Wanderers to reach the round of 32, where they ultimately fell to French greats, Olympique de Marseille.

Having taken time to adjust to the intensities of the Barclays Premiership, much will be expected from the goalgetter in his second season with the Club.

Player Details:

Date of Birth:	14.08.1973
Place of Birth:	Culiacan
Nationality:	Mexican
Height:	6'
Weight:	11st 5lb
Foot:	Right/Left

Player Performance 05/06

League Performance

Percentage of total possible time player was on pitch   ⊕ position in league table at end of month

Month:	Aug	Sep	Oct	Nov	Dec	Jan	Feb	Mar	Apr	May	Total
	2%	7%	8%	23%	3%	43%	10%	17%	34%	4%	16%
Team Pts:	7/12	7/9	6/12	3/6	8/15	5/9	6/12	6/12	4/21	4/6	56/114
Team Gls F:	6	2	5	2	8	4	5	10	5	2	49
Team Gls A:	4	0	7	2	5	2	4	8	8	1	41
Total mins:	6	20	28	41	14	115	37	62	213	8	544
Starts (sub):	0 (2)	0 (1)	0 (2)	0 (1)	0 (1)	2	0 (1)	0 (2)	3 (2)	0 (2)	5 (14)
Goals:	0	0	0	0	0	1	0	0	1	0	2
Assists:	0	0	0	0	0	0	0	1	1	0	2
Clean sheets:	0	0	0	0	0	1	0	0	0	0	1
Cards (Y/R):	0	0	0	0	0	0	0	0	0	0	0

League Performance Totals

Goals

- ▶ Borgetti: 2
- ▷ Team-mates: 45
- **Total: 47**
- ▶ own goals: 2

Assists

- ▶ Borgetti: 2
- ▷ Team-mates: 42
- **Total: 44**

Cards

- ▶ Borgetti: 0
- ▷ Team-mates: 65
- **Total: 65**

Cup Games

	Apps	Goals	Cards
UEFA Cup	7	2	0
FA Cup	4	1	0
Carling Cup	2	2	0
Total	**13**	**5**	**0**

Career History

Career Milestones

Club Debut:
vs Newcastle (H), W 2-0, Premiership
▶ **24.08.05**

First Goal Scored for the Club:
vs Loko Plovdiv (H), W 2-1, UEFA Cup
▶ **15.09.05**

Time Spent at the Club:
▶ **1 Season**

Full International:
▶ **Mexico**

Premiership Totals

92-06

Appearances	19
Goals	2
Assists	2
Yellow Cards	0
Red Cards	0

Clubs

Year	Club	Apps	Gls
05-06	Bolton	32	7
	Pachuca		
	Santos Laguna		

Off the Pitch

Age:

- ▶ Borgetti: 32 years, 9 months
- ▷ Team: 28 years, 5 months
- | League: 26 years, 11 months

Height:

- ▶ Borgetti: 6'
- ▷ Team: 5'11"
- | League: 5'11"

Weight:

- ▶ Borgetti: 11st 5lb
- ▷ Team: 12st 1lb
- | League: 12st

Matt Jansen
Forward

(released)

Season Review 05/06

He joined Wanderers for a short-spell in January 2006 after being released by neighbours Blackburn Rovers. Ironically, he made his debut against the Lancastrians just several days after being shown the door at Ewood Park.

He failed to make any real headway into the Wanderers first team, although he made seven appearances.

Player Details:

Date of Birth:	20.10.1977
Place of Birth:	Carlisle
Nationality:	English
Height:	5'11"
Weight:	11st 3lb
Foot:	Left/Right

Player Performance 05/06

League Performance

Percentage of total possible time player was on pitch   ⊕ position in league table at end of month

Month:	Aug	Sep	Oct	Nov	Dec	Jan	Feb	Mar	Apr	May	Total
	5	3	5	7	7	7	6 / 61%	7	8	8	
	0%	0%	0%	0%	0%	9%		0%	5%	0%	8%
Team Pts:	7/12	7/9	6/12	3/6	8/15	5/9	6/12	6/12	4/21	4/6	56/114
Team Gls F:	6	2	5	2	8	4	5	10	5	2	49
Team Gls A:	4	0	7	2	5	2	4	8	8	1	41
Total mins:	0	0	0	0	0	23	218	0	29	0	270
Starts (sub):	0	0	0	0	0	0 (2)	3	0	0 (1)	0	3 (3)
Goals:	0	0	0	0	0	0	0	0	0	0	0
Assists:	0	0	0	0	0	1	0	0	0	0	1
Clean sheets:	0	0	0	0	0	0	0	0	0	0	0
Cards (Y/R):	0	0	0	0	0	0	0	0	0	0	0

League Performance Totals

Goals

▶ Jansen:	0
▦ Team-mates:	47
Total:	**47**
▶ own goals:	2

Assists

▶ Jansen:	1
▦ Team-mates:	43
Total:	**44**

Cards

▶ Jansen:	0
▦ Team-mates:	65
Total:	**65**

Cup Games

	Apps	Goals	Cards
UEFA Cup	0	0	0
FA Cup	1	0	0
Carling Cup	0	0	0
Total	**1**	**0**	**0**

Career History

Career Milestones

Club Debut:
vs Blackburn (A), D 0-0, Premiership
▶ **14.01.06**

First Goal Scored for the Club:
—
▶ **—**

Time Spent at the Club:
▶ **0.5 Seasons**

Full International:
▶ **—**

Premiership Totals
92-06

Appearances	97
Goals	20
Assists	10
Yellow Cards	2
Red Cards	0

Clubs

Year	Club	Apps	Gls
06-06	Bolton	7	0
03-03	Coventry	9	2
99-06	Blackburn	182	57
98-99	Crystal Palace	31	10
95-98	Carlisle	57	13

Off the Pitch

Age:

- ▶ Jansen: 28 years, 7 months
- ▦ Team: 28 years, 5 months
- | League: 26 years, 11 months

Height:

- ▶ Jansen: 5'11"
- ▦ Team: 5'11"
- | League: 5'11"

Weight:

- ▶ Jansen: 11st 3lb
- ▦ Team: 12st 1lb
- | League: 12st

Kevin Davies
Forward

Another solid season from the Wanderers striker, who managed to net eight goals during the campaign.

A vital member of Sam Allardyce's team, Davies is the ideal target man, whose work-rate is second-to-none and whose skill often creates openings for his team-mates.

The Sheffield-born star is fast approaching his 150th appearance in all competitions for the Club.

Player Details:

Date of Birth:	26.03.1977
Place of Birth:	Sheffield
Nationality:	English
Height:	6'
Weight:	13st 11lb
Foot:	Right

Player Performance 05/06

League Performance

Percentage of total possible time player was on pitch   ⊖ position in league table at end of month

Month:	Aug	Sep	Oct	Nov	Dec	Jan	Feb	Mar	Apr	May	Total
	93%	93%	90%	77%	75%	100%	90%	100%	100%	100%	92%
	5	3	5	7	7	7	6	7	8	8	
Team Pts:	7/12	7/9	6/12	3/6	8/15	5/9	6/12	6/12	4/21	4/6	56/114
Team Gls F:	6	2	5	2	8	4	5	10	5	2	49
Team Gls A:	4	0	7	2	5	2	4	8	8	1	41
Total mins:	333	250	323	139	336	270	323	360	627	180	3,141
Starts (sub):	4	3	4	2	4	3	4	4	7	2	37
Goals:	1	0	0	0	1	0	0	2	3	0	7
Assists:	1	1	0	1	2	1	1	0	1	0	8
Clean sheets:	0	2	1	0	2	2	0	1	1	1	10
Cards (Y/R):	1	1	0	1	2	1	1	1	2	0	10

League Performance Totals

Goals

◼ Davies:	7
◻ Team-mates:	40
Total:	**47**
◼ own goals:	2

Assists

◼ Davies:	8
◻ Team-mates:	36
Total:	**44**

Cards

◼ Davies:	10
◻ Team-mates:	55
Total:	**65**

Cup Games

	Apps	Goals	Cards
UEFA Cup	5	0	0
FA Cup	3	1	1
Carling Cup	2	0	1
Total	**10**	**1**	**2**

Career History

Career Milestones

Club Debut:
vs Man Utd (A), L 4-0, Premiership

 **16.08.03**

Time Spent at the Club:

 3 Seasons

First Goal Scored for the Club:
vs Blackburn (H), D 2-2, Premiership

 **23.08.03**

Full International:

▶ —

Premiership Totals

92-06

Appearances	238
Goals	44
Assists	36
Yellow Cards	52
Red Cards	1

Clubs

Year	Club	Apps	Gls
03-06	Bolton	131	27
02-02	Millwall	9	3
99-03	Southampton	95	13
98-99	Blackburn	30	2
97-98	Southampton	30	12
94-97	Chesterfield	159	30

Off the Pitch

Age:

▶ Davies: 29 years, 2 months
▷ Team: 28 years, 5 months
| League: 26 years, 11 months

Height:

▶ Davies: 6'
▷ Team: 5'11"
| League: 5'11"

Weight:

▶ Davies: 13st 11lb
▷ Team: 12st 1lb
| League: 12st

Ricardo Vaz Te
Forward

Season Review 05/06

This prodigious Portuguese talent came of age towards the end of the campaign when he netted three goals in the final four games of the campaign.

He burst onto the scene in spectacular fashion by netting a sublime late, late equaliser in the UEFA Cup group game against Guimaraes.

He ended the campaign with six goals to his credit from eight starts and 24 appearances from the bench.

Player Details:

Date of Birth:	01.10.1986
Place of Birth:	Lisbon
Nationality:	Portuguese
Height:	6'2"
Weight:	12st 7lb
Foot:	Right

Player Performance 05/06

League Performance

Percentage of total possible time player was on pitch   ⟲ position in league table at end of month

Month:	Aug	Sep	Oct	Nov	Dec	Jan	Feb	Mar	Apr	May	Total
	5	3	5	7	7	7	6	7	8	70% 8	
	2%	0%	0%	0%	38%	36%	25%	47%	28%		24%
Team Pts:	7/12	7/9	6/12	3/6	8/15	5/9	6/12	6/12	4/21	4/6	56/114
Team Gls F:	6	2	5	2	8	4	5	10	5	2	49
Team Gls A:	4	0	7	2	5	2	4	8	8	1	41
Total mins:	7	0	0	0	170	96	90	170	175	126	834
Starts (sub):	0 (1)	0	0	0	1 (4)	0 (2)	0 (4)	2 (1)	2 (3)	1 (1)	6 (16)
Goals:	0	0	0	0	0	0	0	0	1	2	3
Assists:	0	0	0	0	2	0	1	2	0	0	5
Clean sheets:	0	0	0	0	1	0	0	0	0	0	1
Cards (Y/R):	0	0	0	0	1	0	0	1	0	1	3

League Performance Totals

Goals

- ▶ Vaz Te: 3
- ▷ Team-mates: 44
- **Total: 47**
- ▶ own goals: 2

Assists

- ▶ Vaz Te: 5
- ▷ Team-mates: 39
- **Total: 44**

Cards

- ▶ Vaz Te: 3
- ▷ Team-mates: 62
- **Total: 65**

Cup Games

	Apps	Goals	Cards
UEFA Cup	4	1	0
FA Cup	4	1	0
Carling Cup	2	1	0
Total	**10**	**3**	**0**

Career History

Career Milestones

Club Debut:
vs Tranmere (A), D 1-1, FA Cup

▶ **03.01.04**

First Goal Scored for the Club:
vs Oldham (A), W 0-1, FA Cup

▶ **30.01.05**

Time Spent at the Club:

▶ **3 Seasons**

Full International:

▶ —

Premiership Totals

92-06

Appearances	30
Goals	3
Assists	5
Yellow Cards	4
Red Cards	0

Clubs

Year	Club	Apps	Gls
03-06	Bolton	44	7
	Farense		

Off the Pitch

Age:

- ▶ Vaz Te: 19 years, 7 months
- ▷ Team: 28 years, 5 months
- | League: 26 years, 11 months

Height:

- ▶ Vaz Te: 6'2"
- ▷ Team: 5'11"
- | League: 5'11"

Weight:

- ▶ Vaz Te: 12st 7lb
- ▷ Team: 12st 1lb
- | League: 12st

El-Hadji Diouf
Forward

The Senegal international made his move to the Reebok Stadium a permanent one during the summer prior to 2005/2006 season.

However, he endured a frustrating second-half to the campaign, spending a large part of it on the sidelines with a troublesome double hernia.

He netted four goals in all competitions to add to the nine he scored during his first season at the Club.

Player Details:

Date of Birth:	15.01.1981
Place of Birth:	Dakar
Nationality:	Senegalese
Height:	5'11"
Weight:	11st 11lb
Foot:	Right/Left

Player Performance 05/06

League Performance

Percentage of total possible time player was on pitch   position in league table at end of month

Month:	Aug	Sep	Oct	Nov	Dec	Jan	Feb	Mar	Apr	May	Total
	89%	54%	81%	97%	73%	31%	0%	0%	11%	0%	41%
Team Pts:	7/12	7/9	6/12	3/6	8/15	5/9	6/12	6/12	4/21	4/6	56/114
Team Gls F:	6	2	5	2	8	4	5	10	5	2	49
Team Gls A:	4	0	7	2	5	2	4	8	8	1	41
Total mins:	319	146	290	174	329	83	0	0	71	0	1,412
Starts (sub):	4	2 (1)	3 (1)	2	4	1	0	0	1 (1)	0	17 (3)
Goals:	1	0	0	0	1	1	0	0	0	0	3
Assists:	0	0	1	0	0	0	0	0	0	0	1
Clean sheets:	1	1	2	1	2	0	0	0	0	0	7
Cards (Y/R):	2	0	1	0/1	1	0	0	0	0	0	4/1

League Performance Totals

Goals
- Diouf: 3
- Team-mates: 44
- **Total: 47**
- own goals: 2

Assists
- Diouf: 1
- Team-mates: 43
- **Total: 44**

Cards
- Diouf: 5
- Team-mates: 60
- **Total: 65**

Cup Games

	Apps	Goals	Cards
UEFA Cup	6	1	0
FA Cup	0	0	0
Carling Cup	1	0	1
Total	**7**	**1**	**1**

Career History

Career Milestones

Club Debut:
vs Man Utd (H), D 2-2, Premiership

 11.09.04

First Goal Scored for the Club:
vs Newcastle (H), W 2-1, Premiership

31.10.04

Time Spent at the Club:

 **2 Seasons**

Full International:

Senegal

Premiership Totals

92-06

Appearances	102
Goals	15
Assists	19
Yellow Cards	26
Red Cards	2

Clubs

Year	Club	Apps	Gls
04-06	Bolton	59	13
02-05	Liverpool	80	6
	RC Lens		
	Rennes		
	Sochaux		

Off the Pitch

Age:
- Diouf: 25 years, 4 months
- Team: 28 years, 5 months
- League: 26 years, 11 months

Height:
- Diouf: 5'11"
- Team: 5'11"
- League: 5'11"

Weight:
- Diouf: 11st 11lb
- Team: 12st 1lb
- League: 12st

Academy & Reserves

Academy Aims and Objectives

- To raise the technical and footballing skills of youngsters to the highest standards by providing quality coaching.

- To provide the best facilities and equipment to enhance their footballing provision.

- To bring youngsters through to the reserve and first team squads.

- To develop motivation, self-discipline social skills and self-confidence.

- Promote and support good outcomes in terms of health, football development and educational achievement for its students.

- To enable parents and members of the player's family to be as involved as far as is practicable in a working partnership with the Academy.

- Recognise the significance of ethical and cultural diversity.

- To promote equal opportunities regardless of gender, age and ethnicity.

- Promote comprehensive Child Protection Policy.

Contact

BWFC Academy
Euxton Training Ground
Euxton Lane
Euxton
Lancashire PR7 6FA

Tel: 01257 226222
Fax: 01257 226220
email: kmatthews@bwfc.co.uk

Directory

Academy Manager
Chris Sulley

Assistant Academy Manager
Peter Farrell

Assistant Academy Manager
Peter Almond

Head of Education, Welfare & Childrens Officer
Fran Walsh

Recruitment Officer
Geoff McDougle

Performance Analyst
Gavin Fleig

Development Centre Recruitment Officer
Tom Critchley

Academy Physiotherapist
Stephen Foster

Administrative Secretary
Kath Matthews

Fitness Coach/Physiotherapist
Andrew Renshaw

Coach Education Officer
Jack Trainer

Transport Co-ordinator
Ian Connor

Assistant Transport Co-ordinator
Trevor Jackson

Lifestyle Coach
Martin Littlewood

Doctor
Phil Riley

Academy Physiotherapist
James Murphy

Barclays Premiership Reserve League North 2005/06

	P	W	D	L	F	A	GD	PTS
Man Utd Res	28	19	2	7	68	32	36	59
Aston Villa Res	28	16	8	4	59	26	33	56
Man City Res	28	15	8	5	47	37	10	53
Middlesbrough Res	28	15	7	6	50	27	23	52
Newcastle Res	28	12	8	8	45	40	5	44
Liverpool Res	28	13	5	10	31	31	0	44
Sunderland Res	28	11	7	10	40	41	-1	40
Everton Res	28	10	8	10	31	35	-4	38
Leeds Res	28	9	11	8	27	31	-4	38
Blackburn Res	28	8	7	13	38	46	-8	31
Birmingham Res	28	7	9	12	32	36	-4	30
Wolverhampton Res	28	6	8	14	28	37	-9	26
Bolton Res	**28**	**6**	**6**	**16**	**25**	**46**	**-21**	**24**
West Brom Res	28	6	6	16	26	55	-29	24
Wigan Res	28	5	4	19	24	51	-27	19

Results 2005/06

15 Aug 05	**Manchester United (H)**	**0-3**		**16 Jan 06**	**Newcastle United (H)**	**3-0**
5 Sep 05	**Everton (H)**	**0-1**		**23 Jan 06**	**Leeds United (H)**	**0-1**
14 Sep 05	Leeds United (A)	1-0		9 Feb 06	Liverpool (A)	0-0
19 Sep 05	**Liverpool (H)**	**2-3**		14 Feb 06	Aston Villa (A)	0-0
26 Sep 05	Wolves (A)	0-0		**20 Feb 06**	**Wolvers (H)**	**0-1**
3 Oct 05	**Aston Villa (H)**	**0-4**		**27 Feb 06**	**Manchester City (H)**	**0-2**
17 Oct 05	**West Brom (H)**	**0-2**		6 Mar 06	West Brom (A)	1-1
31 Oct 05	**Sunderland (H)**	**3-2**		**22 Mar 06**	**Birmingham City (H)**	**2-2**
14 Nov 05	**Blackburn Rovers (H)**	**2-3**		29 Mar 06	Sunderland (A)	0-2
22 Nov 05	Wigan Athletic (A)	0-1		**5 Apr 06**	**Wigan Athletic (H)**	**3-0**
29 Nov 05	Manchester City (A)	1-3		11 Apr 06	Middlesbrough (A)	3-1
5 Dec 05	**Middlesbrough (H)**	**1-3**		18 Apr 06	Birmingham City (A)	1-4
15 Dec 05	Manchester United (A)	0-5		24 Apr 06	Newcastle United (A)	0-1
10 Jan 06	Everton (A)	1-1		1 May 06	Blackburn Rovers (A)	1-0

FA Premier League U18 – 2005/06 Group C

	P	W	D	L	F	A	GD	PTS
Blackburn Yth	28	17	3	8	51	36	15	54
Man Utd Yth	28	16	4	8	56	30	26	52
Everton Yth	28	14	7	7	33	24	9	49
Man City Yth	28	14	7	7	50	37	13	49
Liverpool Yth	28	13	5	10	47	35	12	44
Stoke Yth	28	10	8	10	42	37	5	38
Bolton Yth	**28**	**9**	**11**	**8**	**31**	**35**	**-4**	**38**
Crewe Yth	28	9	8	11	38	42	-4	35
West Brom Yth	28	6	9	13	39	52	-13	27
Wolverhampton Yth	28	6	8	14	25	39	-14	26

Appearances & Goalscorers

Player	Apps (Subs)	Goals		Player	Apps (Subs)	Goals
Nathan Woolfe	26+4	4		Michael Roddy	18+11	1
Mark Charlesworth	25+3	2		Danny Stott	17+6	0
Leslie Thompson	24+4	3		Karl Luisi	15+6	4
Sean Mountford	24+2	0		Sam Ashton	10+11	0
Prezemyslaw Kazimierzak	21+6	0		Jaroslaw Fojut	9+3	0
Scott Jaimeson	20+3	1		Dale Whitehead	9+1	0
Mark Ellis	19+6	3		Johann Smith	8+9	3
James Sinclair	19+6	8		Bradley Hill	8+4	1
Robert Sissons	19+2	1		Blazej Augustyn	1+0	0
Matthew Cassidy	19+6	0				

Club Facts & Records

Bolton Wanderers Football Club

Year Formed 1874
Turned Pro 1880
Ltd Co 1895

Previous Names
1874 Christ Church FC;
1877 Bolton Wanderers

Club Nickname
Trotters, Superwhites

Previous Grounds
Park Recreation Ground, Cockle's Field, Pike's Lane
1881; Burnden Park 1895; Reebok Stadium 1997.

First FL Game
8th September 1888, v Derby County (h) L 3-6

Most League Points
61 (two for a win) FL3 1972-73
98 (three for a win) FL1, 1996-97

Highest League Scorer in a Season
Joe Smith, 38, FL1, 1920-21

Most League goals
In total   Nat Lofthouse, 255, 1946-61
In one match   5, Tony Caldwell v Walsall, FL3,
                10.09.1983

Most capped player
Mark Fish, 34, South Africa

Most League Appearances
Eddie Hopkinson, 519, 1956-70

Youngest League Player
Ray Parry,15 years 267 days
v Wolverhampton Wanderers, 13.10.1951

Honours

Football League Division One
Champions 1996-97
Promoted from Division One (play-offs) 2000-01

Football League Division Two
Champions 1908-09, 1977-78
Runners-Up 1899-00, 1904-05,1910-11, 1934-35,
1992-93

Football League Division Three
Champions 1972-73

FA Cup
Winners 1923, 1926, 1929, 1958
Runners-up 1894, 1904, 1953

Football League Cup
Runners-up 1995, 2004

Freight Rover Trophy
Runners-Up 1986

Sherpa Van Trophy
Winners 1989

FA Premier League Asia Trophy
Winners 2005

Top 20 Appearances
(As at 8 May 2006)

Eddie Hopkinson	578	(1956-1970)
Roy Greaves	567+8	(1965-1980)
Alex Finney	530	(1922-1937)
Warwick Rimmer	521+7	(1960-1975)
Brian Edwards	518	(1950-1965)
Ted Vizard	512	(1910-1931)
Nat Lofthouse	503	(1946-1961)
Paul Jones	502	(1970-1983)
Roy Hartle	498+1	(1952-1966)
Joe Smith	492	(1908-1927)
Doug Holden	463	(1951-1963)
Billy Butler	449	(1921-1933)
Stan Hanson	423	(1936-1956)
David Stokes	420	(1901-1920)
Steve Thompson	416+6	(1982-1992)
Fred Hill	410+2	(1957-1969)
Syd Farrimond	403+1	(1958-1971)
Jimmy Phillips	390+21	(1983-2001)
Bert Baverstock	388	(1905-1922)
J Seddon	375	(1913-1932)
John Ritson	375	(1967-1978)

Top 20 Goalscorers
The following rankings apply to first class fixtures only.
(As at 8 May 2006)

	Goals	Apps	
Nat Lofthouse	285	503	(1946-1961)
Joe Smith	277	492	(1908-1927)
David Jack	161	324	(1920-1929)
Jack Milsom	153	255	(1929-1938)
Ray Westwood	144	333	(1930-1948)
William Moir	134	358	(1946-1956)
John Byrom	130	340+11	(1996-1976)
Harold Blackmore	122	165	(1926-1932)
Neil Whatmore	121	322+16	(1972-1984)
John McGinlay	118	230+15	(1992-1998)
Francis Lee	106	210	(1960-1968)
James Cassidy	101	219	(1889-1898)
Dennis Stevens	101	310	(1953-1962)
Wattie White	93	217	(1902-1909)
Albert Shepherd	90	123	(1904-1909)
John Smith	87	174	(1922-1928)
Roy Greaves	85	567+8	(1965-1980)
George Gibson	81	255	(1926-1933)
Sam Marsh	81	201	(1902-1912)
Frank Roberts	80	168	(1914-1923)

Most Goals in a Single Game
(As at 8 May 2006)

5 Goals

B Struthers	04.11.1882	Bootle (H), FA Cup, 6-1
J Cassidy	01.02.1890	Sheff W (H), FA Cup,13-0
T Caldwell	10.09.1983	Walsall, FL3, 8-1
J Cassidy	30.11.1889	Derby C (H), FL1, 7-1

4 Goals

D Weir	18.01.1890	Belfast Dist (H), FA Cup,10-2
J Henderson	01.01.1895	Derby C (H), FL1, 6-0
A Shepherd	18.11.1905	Notts F (H), FL1, 6-0
D Jack	22.04.1925	Blackburn R (H), FL1, 6-0
H Blackmore	05.11.1927	Burnley, (H), FL1, 7-0
H Blackmore	28.12.1929	Everton (H), FL1, 5-0

J Milsom	30.12.1933	West Ham (H), FL2, 5-1
R Westwood	06.10.1934	Barnsley (H), FL2, 8-0
J Milsom	02.01.1935	Burnley (H), FL2, 7-0
J Hunt	11.01.1940	Oldham A (A), FLN, 5-3
J Hunt	16.01.1943	Oldham A (H), FLN, 5-0
J Currier	19.02.1944	Southport (H), FLN, 5-1
N Lofthouse	10.02.1945	Tranmere R (H), FLN, 6-1
N Lofthouse	07.04.1945	Blackpool (A), FLN, 4-1
W Moir	30.08.1948	Aston Villa (A), FL1, 4-2
M W Barrass	06.11.1948	Man City (H), FL1, 5-1
W Moir	27.12.1948	Sheff Utd (H), FL1, 6-1
N Lofthouse	10.12.1955	Birm C, (H), FL1, 6-0

Stats & Records

(As at 8 May 2006)

Scorelines

Wins		Defeats	
Overall	13-0 v Sheffield United (H), 01.02.1890, FA Cup Round Two, Pikes Lane	Overall	1-9 v Preston North End (A), 10.12.1887, FA Cup Round Two
League	8-0 v Barnsley (H), 06.10.1934, FL2, Burnden Park	League	0-7 v Burnley (A) 01.03.1890, FL1, Turf Moor
Premiership	5-0 v Leicester City (A), 18.08.2001, Filbert Street		0-7 v Sheffield Wednesday (A) 01.03.15, FL1, Hillsborough
			0-7 v Manchester City (A) 21.03.1936, FL1, Maine Road
		Premiership	0-6 v Manchester United (H) 25.02.96

Seasonal Records

	Overall		Premiership	
Most Wins	28	1996-97	16	2004-05
Most Home Wins	18	1924-25; 1972-73; 1992-93; 1996-97	11	2005-06
Most Away Wins	14	2000-01	8	2003-04
Most Defeats	25	1970-71; 1995-96	25	1995-96
Most Home Defeats	10	1909-10;1963-64;1970-71;1986-87;1995-96	10	1995-96
Most Away defeats	18	1984-85	15	1995-96
Most Draws	17	1991-92	14	2002-03
Most Home Draws	11	1979-80	8	1997-98; 2002-03; 2003-04
Most Away Draws	10	1986-87; 1996-97; 1998-99	6	2001-02; 2002-03; 2005-06
Fewest Wins	5	1979-80	8	1995-96
Fewest Home Wins	5	1979-80; 1995-96; 2001-02	5	1995-96; 2001-02
Fewest Away Wins	0	1949-50; 1970-71; 1979-80	2	1997-98
Fewest Defeats	4	1899-00; 1996-97	12	2004-05; 2005-06
Fewest Home Defeats	0	1910-11; 1920-21	3	2005-06
Fewest Away Defeats	3	1899-00; 1904-05; 1996-97	7	20004-5
Fewest Draws	1	1889-90; 1890-91	5	1995-96
Fewest Home Draws	0	1888-89; 1890-91; 1904-05	4	1995-96
Fewest Away Draws	0	1889-90; 1891-92	1	1995-96
Most Goals Scored	100	1996-97	49	20004-05; 2005-06
Most Home Goals Scored	63	1934-35	29	2005-06
Most Away Goals Scored	40	1996-97	24	2001-02; 2003-04; 2004-05
Most Goals Conceded	92	1932-33	71	1995-96
Most Home Goals Conceded	35	1952-53; 1957-58; 1963-64	31	1995-96; 2001-02
Most Away Goals Conceded	59	1932-33	40	1995-96
Fewest Goals Scored	28	1897-98	39	1995-96
Fewest Home Goals Scored	16	1995-96	16	1995-96
Fewest Away Goals Scored	10	1897-98	14	2002-03
Fewest Goals Conceded	25	1899-00	41	2005-06
Fewest Home Goals Conceded	7	1899-00	13	2005-06
Fewest Away Goals Conceded	16	1904-05	26	2004-05

Sequences

(As at 8 May 2006)

Scorelines

League Games Only		
Consecutive Wins	11	1904-05
Consecutive Defeats	11	07.04.1902-18.10.1902
Consecutive Draws	6	1912-13
Consecutive games unbeaten	23	1990-91
Consecutive games without a win	26	07.04.1902-10.01.1903
Consecutive home wins	13	1910-11
Consecutive home defeats	4	1902-03; 2004-05
Consecutive away wins	5	1904-05; 2000-01
Consecutive away defeats	11	1979-80; 1984-85
Consecutive home unbeaten	21	1920-21
Consecutive home without a win	10	1902-03; 1979-80; 2001-02
Consecutive away unbeaten	11	1904-05
Consecutive away without a win	21	1979-80
Consecutive without scoring	5	1897-98; 1989-90
Consecutive games scoring	24	1888-89; 1889-90; 1996-97
Consecutive games conceding	27	1901-02; 1902-03

Premiership Only		
Consecutive Wins	5	2003-04; 2004-05
Consecutive Defeats	6	2004-05
Consecutive Draws	3	2001-02
Consecutive games unbeaten	7	2004-05
Consecutive games without a win	12	1997-98; 2001-02
Consecutive home wins	4	2005-06
Consecutive home defeats	4	2004-05
Consecutive away wins	3	1995-96; 2003-04; 2004-05
Consecutive away defeats	4	1995-96; 2002-03
Consecutive home unbeaten	14	2005-06
Consecutive home without a win	10	2001-02
Consecutive away unbeaten	5	2001-02; 2005-06
Consecutive away without a win	17	1997-98
Consecutive clean sheets	4	2003-04
Consecutive without scoring	4	2005-06
Consecutive games scoring	15	2003-04
Consecutive games conceding	13	2004-05

Attendances

Highest	Lowest
Burnden Park Overall	**Burnden Park Overall**
69,912 v Manchester City FA Cup 5th Round 18 February 1933	1,507 v Rochdale (Autoglass Trophy) 10 December 1991
Burnden Park League	**Burnden Park League**
55,477 v Manchester United, FL1, 1 September 1951	2,017 v Sheffield United, FL1, 2 March 1901
Reebok Stadium Overall	**Reebok Stadium Overall**
28,353 v Leicester City, FAPL, 28 December 2003	3,673 v Gillingham, FLC2, 21 September 1999
Reebok Stadium Premiership	**Reebok Stadium League**
28,353 v Leicester City, FAPL, 28 December 2003	11,668 v Birmingham City, FL1, 5 September 1999

Bolton Wanderers Complete Record 1888/89–2005/06

Season	Lge	P	W	D	L	F	A	Pts	Posn
1888/89	D1	22	10	2	10	63	59	22	5th
1889/90	D1	22	9	1	12	54	65	19	9th
1890/91	D1	22	12	1	9	47	34	25	5th
1891/92	D1	26	17	2	7	51	37	36	3rd
1892/93	D1	30	13	6	11	56	55	32	5th
1893/94	D1	30	10	4	16	38	52	24	13th
1894/95	D1	30	9	7	14	61	62	25	10th
1895/96	D1	30	16	5	9	49	37	37	4th
1896/97	D1	30	12	6	12	40	36	30	8th
1897/98	D1	30	11	4	15	28	41	26	11th
1898/99	D1	34	9	7	18	37	51	25	17th
1899/00	D2	34	22	10	4	79	25	52	2nd
1900/01	D1	34	13	7	14	39	55	33	10th
1901/02	D1	34	12	8	14	51	56	32	12th
1902/03	D1	34	8	3	23	37	73	19	18th
1903/04	D2	34	12	10	12	59	41	34	7th
1904/05	D2	34	27	2	5	87	32	56	2nd
1905/06	D1	38	17	7	14	81	67	41	6th
1906/07	D1	38	18	8	12	59	47	44	6th
1907/08	D1	38	14	5	19	52	58	33	19th
1908/09	D2	38	24	4	10	59	28	52	1st
1909/10	D1	38	9	6	23	44	71	24	20th
1910/11	D2	38	21	9	8	69	40	51	2nd
1911/12	D1	38	20	3	15	54	43	43	4th
1912/13	D1	38	16	10	12	62	63	42	8th
1913/14	D1	38	16	10	12	65	52	42	6th
1914/15	D1	38	11	8	19	68	84	30	17th
1919/20	D1	42	19	9	14	72	65	47	6th
1920/21	D1	42	19	14	9	77	53	52	3rd
1921/22	D1	42	20	7	15	68	59	47	6th
1922/23	D1	42	14	12	16	50	58	40	13th
1923/24	D1	42	18	14	10	68	34	50	4th
1924/25	D1	42	22	11	9	76	34	55	3rd
1925/26	D1	42	17	10	15	75	76	44	8th
1926/27	D1	42	19	10	13	84	62	48	4th
1927/28	D1	42	16	11	15	81	66	43	7th
1928/29	D1	42	14	12	16	73	80	40	14th
1929/30	D1	42	15	9	18	74	74	39	15th
1930/31	D1	42	15	9	18	68	81	39	14th
1931/32	D1	42	17	4	21	72	80	38	17th
1932/33	D1	42	12	9	21	78	92	33	21st
1933/34	D1	42	21	9	12	79	55	51	3rd
1934/35	D2	42	26	4	12	96	48	56	2nd
1935/36	D1	42	14	13	15	67	76	41	13th
1936/37	D1	42	10	14	18	43	66	34	20th
1937/38	D1	42	15	15	12	64	60	45	7th
1938/39	D1	42	15	15	12	67	58	45	8th
1946/47	D1	42	13	8	21	57	69	34	18th
1947/48	D1	42	16	5	21	46	58	37	17th
1948/49	D1	42	14	10	18	59	68	38	14th

Season	Lge	P	W	D	L	F	A	Pts	Posn
1949/50	D1	42	10	14	18	45	59	34	16th
1950/51	D1	42	19	7	16	64	61	45	8th
1951/52	D1	42	19	10	13	65	61	48	5th
1952/53	D1	42	15	9	18	61	69	39	14th
1953/54	D1	42	18	12	12	75	60	48	5th
1954/55	D1	42	13	13	16	62	69	39	18th
1955/56	D1	42	18	7	17	71	58	43	8th
1956/57	D1	42	16	12	14	65	65	44	9th
1957/58	D1	42	14	10	18	65	87	38	15th
1958/59	D1	42	20	10	12	79	66	50	4th
1959/60	D1	42	20	8	14	59	51	48	6th
1960/61	D1	42	12	11	19	58	73	35	18th
1961/62	D1	42	16	10	16	62	66	42	11th
1962/63	D1	42	15	5	22	55	75	35	18th
1963/64	D1	42	10	8	24	48	80	28	21st
1964/65	D2	42	20	10	12	80	58	50	3rd
1965/66	D2	42	16	9	17	62	59	41	9th
1966/67	D2	42	14	14	14	64	58	42	9th
1967/68	D2	42	13	13	16	60	63	39	12th
1968/69	D2	42	12	14	16	55	67	38	17th
1969/70	D2	42	12	12	18	54	61	36	16th
1970/71	D2	42	7	10	25	35	74	24	22nd
1971/72	D3	46	17	16	13	51	41	50	7th
1972/73	D3	46	25	11	10	73	39	61	1st
1973/74	D2	42	15	12	15	44	40	42	11th
1974/75	D2	42	15	12	15	45	41	42	10th
1975/76	D2	42	20	12	10	64	38	52	4th
1976/77	D2	42	20	11	11	75	54	51	4th
1977/78	D2	42	24	10	8	63	33	58	1st
1978/79	D1	42	12	11	19	54	75	35	17th
1979/80	D1	42	5	15	22	38	73	25	22nd
1980/81	D2	42	14	10	18	61	66	38	18th
1981/82	D2	42	13	7	22	39	61	46	19th
1982/83	D2	42	11	11	20	42	61	44	22nd
1983/84	D3	46	18	10	18	56	60	64	10th
1984/85	D3	46	16	6	24	69	75	54	17th
1985/86	D3	46	15	8	23	54	68	53	18th
1986/87	D3	46	10	15	21	46	58	45	21st
1987/88	D4	46	22	12	12	66	42	78	3rd
1988/89	D3	46	16	16	14	58	54	64	10th
1989/90	D3	46	18	15	13	59	48	69	6th
1990/91	D3	46	24	11	11	64	50	83	4th
1991/92	D3	46	14	17	15	57	56	59	13th
1992/93	D2	46	27	9	10	80	41	90	2nd
1993/94	D1	46	15	14	17	63	64	59	14th
1994/95	D1	46	21	14	11	67	45	77	3rd
1995/96	PL	38	8	5	25	39	71	29	20th
1996/97	D1	46	28	14	4	100	53	98	1st
1997/98	PL	38	9	13	16	41	61	40	18th
1998/99	D1	46	20	16	10	78	59	76	6th
1999/00	D1	46	21	13	12	69	50	76	6th
2000/01	D1	46	24	15	7	76	45	87	3rd
2001/02	PL	38	9	13	16	44	62	40	16th
2002/03	PL	38	10	14	14	41	51	44	17th
2003/04	PL	38	14	11	13	48	56	53	8th
2004/05	PL	38	16	10	12	49	44	58	6th
2005/06	PL	38	15	11	12	49	41	56	8th

Arsenal °

Nickname:	The Gunners	Telephone:	020 7704 4000
Manager:	Arsène Wenger	Ticket Office:	020 7704 4040
Chairman:	Peter Hill-Wood	Club Shop:	020 7704 4120
Website:	www.arsenal.com		

Season Review 05/06

It was a season of mixed fortunes for an Arsenal side that grew up enormously over the course of the campaign.

Reaching the Champions League Final was a terrific achievement, with defeat to Barcelona tempered by Thierry Henry's decision to stay at the club. Prior to that, the Gunners said goodbye to Highbury by clinching fourth place at the expense of Tottenham.

Points / Position

▶ won ▶ drawn ▶ lost H home A away

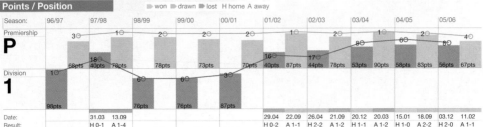

Season:	96/97	97/98	98/99	99/00	00/01	01/02	02/03	03/04	04/05	05/06
Premiership **P**	3	1	2	2	2	1	2	1	2	4
	68pts	40pts 78pts	78pts	73pts	70pts 40pts	87pts 44pts	78pts 53pts	90pts	58pts 83pts	56pts 67pts
Division **1**	1	18	6	6	3	16	17	8	6	8
	98pts		76pts	76pts	87pts					

Date:		31.03	13.09			29.04	22.09	26.04	21.09	20.12	20.03	15.01	18.09	03.12	11.02
Result:		H 0-1	A 1-4			H 0-2	A 1-1	H 2-2	A 1-2	H 1-1	A 1-2	H 1-0	A 2-2	H 2-0	A 1-1

Recent Meetings

18.09.04		15.01.05		03.12.05		11.02.06	
○○ **2-2**	Attendance: 37,010	○○ **1-0**	Attendance: 27,514	○○ **2-0**	Attendance: 26,792	○○ **1-1**	Attendance: 38,193
Referee: P.Dowd		Referee: M.Clattenburg		Referee: H.M.Webb		Referee: H.M.Webb	
○ 31 Henry	○ 63 Jaidi	○ 41 Giannakopoulos		○ 20 Diagne-Faye		○ 90 Gilberto Silva	○ 12 Nolan
○ 66 Pires	○ 85 Pedersen			○ 32 Giannakopoulos			

Prem. Head-to-Head

Facts	○ Bolton	Arsenal ○
Games		
Points	14	23
Won	3	6
Drawn	5	5
Goals		
For	15	20
Clean Sheets	3	2
Shots on Target	63	91
Disciplinary		
Fouls (5 years)	137	127
Yellow Cards	21	20
Red Cards	3	1

Goals by Area

○ Bolton   ○ Arsenal

3	3
10	12
2	5

Goals Scored by Period

2	1	4	1	2	5
0	15	30	45	60	75	90
0	5	4	4	2	5

Goals by Position

○ Bolton   ○ Arsenal

	Bolton		Arsenal
▶ forward:	5	▶ forward:	12
▶ midfield:	7	▶ midfield:	8
▶ defence:	2	▶ defence:	0
▶ own goals:	1		

Average Attendance

▶ **25,799**

▶ **37,927**

All-Time Records

Total Premiership Record	○ Bolton	Arsenal ○
Played	266	544
Points	320	1,013
Won	81	289
Drawn	77	146
Lost	108	109
For	311	911
Against	386	481
Players Used	109	113

All-Time Record vs Bolton						
Competition	Played	Won	Drawn	Lost	For	Against
League	106	42	31	33	184	146
FA Cup	12	5	3	4	16	11
League Cup	0	0	0	0	0	0
Other	0	0	0	0	0	0
Total	118	47	34	37	200	157

Aston Villa ○

Nickname: **The Villans**
Manager: **David OiLeary**
Chairman: **Doug Ellis**
Website: **www.avfc.co.uk**

Telephone: **0121 327 2299**
Ticket Office: **0121 327 5353**
Club Shop: **0121 326 1559**

Season Review 05/06

It was a season of frustration at Villa Park, with many disillusioned fans calling for the heads of Manager David O'Leary and Chairman Doug Ellis.

A 3-0 Carling Cup hammering at League One side Doncaster Rovers was the low point of a campaign in which Villa finished just eight points and two places away from relegation to the Championship.

Points / Position

■ won ■ drawn ■ lost H home A away

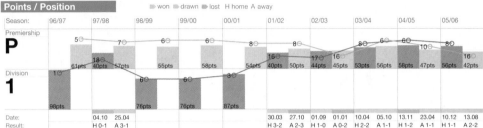

Season:	96/97	97/98	98/99	99/00	00/01	01/02	02/03	03/04	04/05	05/06
Premiership **P**	5○	7○	6○	6○	8○	8○	17○ 16○	8○ 6○	6○ 10○	8○ 16○
	61pts	40pts 57pts	55pts	58pts	54pts	40pts 50pts	44pts 45pts	53pts 56pts	58pts 47pts	56pts 42pts
Division **1**	1○		6○	6○	3○					
	98pts		76pts	76pts	87pts					
Date:		04.10 25.04				30.03 27.10	01.09 01.01	10.04 05.10	13.11 23.04	10.12 13.08
Result:		H 0-1 A 3-1				H 3-2 A 2-3	H 1-0 A 0-2	H 2-2 A 1-1	H 1-2 A 1-1	H 1-1 A 2-2

Recent Meetings

13.11.04	23.04.05	13.08.05	10.12.05
○○ **1-2** Attendance: 25,779	○○ **1-1** Attendance: 36,053	○○ **2-2** Attendance: 33,263	○○ **1-1** Attendance: 23,646
Referee: A.P.D'Urso	Referee: U.D.Rennie	Referee: M.A.Riley	Referee: P.Dowd
○ 21 Diouf ○ 41 McCann	○ 26 Hierro ○ 54 Speed	○ 4 Phillips ○ 6 Davies	○ 82 Diouf ○ 88 Angel
○ 89 Hitzlsperger		○ 9 Davis ○ 8 Campo	

Prem. Head-to-Head

Facts	○ Bolton	Aston Villa ○
Games		
Points	14	23
Won	3	6
Drawn	5	5
Goals		
For	17	21
Clean Sheets	1	4
Shots on Target	71	75
Disciplinary		
Fouls (5 years)	145	146
Yellow Cards	27	21
Red Cards	1	1

Goals by Area

○ Bolton   ○ Aston Villa

	Bolton	Villa
	3	5
	11	12
	3	4

Goals by Position

○ Bolton   ○ Aston Villa

■ forward: 11   ■ forward: 13
■ midfield: 4   ■ midfield: 6
■ defence: 1   ■ defence: 0
■ own goals: 1   ■ own goals: 2

Goals Scored by Period

4	2	2	4	1	4
0	15	30	45	60	75 90
6	3	3	5	1	3

Average Attendance

▶ **23,598**
▶ **33,592**

All-Time Records

Total Premiership Record	○ Bolton	Aston Villa ○
Played	266	544
Points	320	767
Won	81	203
Drawn	77	158
Lost	108	183
For	311	668
Against	386	632
Players Used	109	120

All-Time Record vs Bolton

Competition	Played	Won	Drawn	Lost	For	Against
League	140	55	33	52	222	224
FA Cup	6	1	3	2	3	5
League Cup	2	1	0	1	4	5
Other	0	0	0	0	0	0
Total	148	57	36	55	229	234

Blackburn Rovers

Nickname:	Rovers	Telephone:	08701 113 232
Manager:	Mark Hughes	Ticket Office:	08701 123 456
Chairman:	John Williams	Club Shop:	0870 042 3875
Website:	www.rovers.co.uk		

Season Review 05/06

Mark Hughes guided Blackburn to sixth place and UEFA Cup qualification in his first full season in charge. Despite operating with a relatively small squad, the Ewood Park outfit also reached the last four in the Carling Cup.

Craig Bellamy proved to be a shrewd acquisition, whilst the likes of Steven Reid and Morten Gamst Pedersen really shone.

Points / Position

▶ won ▶ drawn ▶ lost H home A away

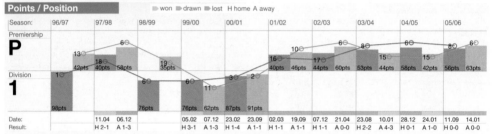

Season:	96/97	97/98	98/99	99/00	00/01	01/02	02/03	03/04	04/05	05/06
Premiership		13	6	19			16 10	17 6	8 6	15 6	8 6
P		42pts 18	40pts 58pts	35pts		40pts	46pts	44pts 60pts	53pts 44pts	58pts 42pts	56pts 63pts
Division 1	1			6	6 11	3 2				
	98pts		76pts	76pts 62pts	87pts 91pts					

Date:	11.04	06.12	05.02	07.12	23.02	23.09	02.03	19.09	07.12	21.04	23.08	10.01	28.12	24.01	11.09	14.01
Result:	H 2-1	A 1-3	H 3-1	A 1-3	H 1-4	A 1-1	H 1-1	A 1-1	H 1-1	A 0-0	H 2-2	A 4-3	H 0-1	A 1-0	H 0-0	A 0-0

Recent Meetings

28.12.04 ⚪⚪**0-1** Attendance: 27,038	**24.01.05** ⚪⚪**0-1** Attendance: 20,056	**11.09.05** ⚪⚪**0-0** Attendance: 24,405	**14.01.06** ⚪⚪**0-0** Attendance: 18,180
Referee: R.Styles	Referee: S.G.Bennett	Referee: G.Poll	Referee: M.A.Riley
⚪ 6 Dickov	⚪ 77 Diouf		

Prem. Head-to-Head

Facts	⚪ Bolton	Blackburn ⚪
Games		
Points	19	16
Won	4	3
Drawn	7	7
Goals		
For	16	17
Clean Sheets	4	4
Shots on Target	59	76
Disciplinary		
Fouls (5 years)	158	148
Yellow Cards	32	27
Red Cards	2	3

Goals by Area
⚪ Bolton   ⚪ Blackburn

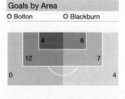

	4	6
12		7
0		4

Goals Scored by Period

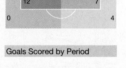

3	4	2	0	3	4	
0	15	30	45	60	75	90
4	2	1	2	2	6	

Goals by Position
⚪ Bolton   ⚪ Blackburn

	Bolton	Blackburn
▶ forward:	8	11
▶ midfield:	6	3
▶ defence:	2	3

Average Attendance

▶ **25,125**

▶ **24,644**

All-Time Records

Total Premiership Record	⚪ Bolton	Blackburn ⚪
Played	266	468
Points	320	695
Won	81	190
Drawn	77	125
Lost	108	153
For	311	650
Against	386	553
Players Used	109	124

All-Time Record vs Bolton

Competition	Played	Won	Drawn	Lost	For	Against
League	134	48	31	55	212	210
FA Cup	12	4	4	4	23	16
League Cup	2	1	0	1	5	2
Other	0	0	0	0	0	0
Total	**148**	**53**	**35**	**60**	**240**	**228**

Charlton Athletic

Nickname:	The Addicks
Manager:	Iain Dowie
Chairman:	Richard Murray
Website:	www.cafc.co.uk

Telephone:	020 8333 4000
Ticket Office:	020 8333 4010
Club Shop:	020 8333 4035

Season Review 05/06

The 2005/06 season will be remembered at Charlton as the last in Alan Curbishley's 15-year reign. A great start saw the Addicks win five of their first six league games, but they ultimately slipped to a respectable 13th place.

Darren Bent arrived from Ipswich with a bang, firing in 18 goals to finish as the leading English marksman in the Premiership.

Points / Position

▶ won ▶ drawn ▶ lost H home A away

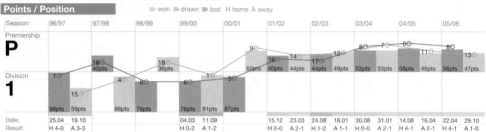

Season:	96/97	97/98	98/99	99/00	00/01	01/02	02/03	03/04	04/05	05/06
Premiership P						9○ 52pts	16○ 40pts 14○ 44pts 17○ 44pts	12○ 49pts 8○ 53pts 7○ 53pts	6○ 58pts 11○ 46pts	8○ 56pts 13○ 47pts
Division 1	1○ 98pts 15○ 59pts	4○ 88pts 6○ 76pts	18○ 40pts 18○ 36pts	6○ 76pts 1○ 91pts	3○ 87pts					

Date:	25.04	19.10			04.03	11.09	15.12	23.03	24.08	18.01	30.08	31.01	14.08	16.04	22.04	29.10
Result:	H 4-0	A 3-3			H 0-2	A 1-2	H 0-0	A 2-1	H 1-2	A 1-1	H 0-0	A 2-1	H 4-1	A 2-1	H 4-1	A 1-0

Recent Meetings

14.08.04
OO 4-1 Attendance: 24,100
Referee: P.Dowd
- O 11 Okocha
- O 30 Pedersen
- O 59 Okocha
- O 72 Pedersen
- O 67 Lisbie

16.04.05
OO 1-2 Attendance: 26,708
Referee: A.G.Wiley
- O 29 Jeffers
- O 7 Okocha
- O 58 Diouf

29.10.05
OO 0-1 Attendance: 26,175
Referee: M.Clattenburg
- O 72 Nolan

22.04.06
OO 4-1 Attendance: 24,713
Referee: U.D.Rennie
- O 14 Vaz Te
- O 21 Davies
- O 31 Borgetti
- O 89 Davies
- O 76 Bent D

Prem. Head-to-Head

Facts	O Bolton	Charlton O
Games		
Points	21	6
Won	6	1
Drawn	3	3
Goals		
For	17	8
Clean Sheets	3	2
Shots on Target	65	47
Disciplinary		
Fouls (5 years)	133	122
Yellow Cards	10	8
Red Cards	0	0

Goals by Area
O Bolton   O Charlton

4	2
9	6
4	0

Goals by Position
O Bolton   O Charlton

	Bolton		Charlton
▶ forward:	12	▶ forward:	6
▶ midfield:	5	▶ midfield:	1
▶ defence:	0	○ defence:	1

Goals Scored by Period

	0	15	30	45	60	75	90
	6	2	2	2	2		3
	1	2	0	2	2		1

Average Attendance

▶ **22,900**
▶ **26,309**

All-Time Records

Total Premiership Record	O Bolton	Charlton O
Played	266	266
Points	320	327
Won	81	85
Drawn	77	72
Lost	108	109
For	311	308
Against	386	382
Players Used	109	74

All-Time Record vs Bolton

Competition	Played	Won	Drawn	Lost	For	Against
League	72	23	12	37	88	126
FA Cup	6	1	1	4	4	12
League Cup	0	0	0	0	0	0
Other	0	0	0	0	0	0
Total	78	24	13	41	92	138

Chelsea °

Season Review 05/06

Chelsea dominated the league season from start to finish, though they were less successful in cup competitions. Barcelona, Liverpool and Charlton ensured that José Mourinho had to be content with the Premiership and Community Shield.

John Terry and Frank Lampard were once again star performers, whilst Joe Cole found the consistency to match his abundance of skill.

Points / Position

● won ● drawn ● lost H home A away

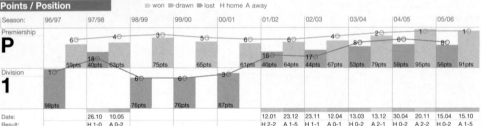

Season:	96/97	97/98	98/99	99/00	00/01	01/02	02/03	03/04	04/05	05/06
Premiership	6	4	3	5	6	6	4	2	1	1
		18				16	17	8	6	8
	59pts	40pts 63pts	75pts	65pts	61pts	40pts 64pts	44pts 67pts	53pts 79pts	58pts 95pts	56pts 91pts
Division 1	1	6	6	3						
	98pts	76pts	76pts	87pts						

| Date: | | 26.10 10.05 | | | | 12.01 23.12 | 23.11 12.04 | 13.03 13.12 | 30.04 20.11 | 15.04 15.10 |
| Result: | | H 1-0 A 0-2 | | | | H 2-2 A 1-5 | H 1-1 A 0-1 | H 0-2 A 2-1 | H 0-2 A 2-2 | H 0-2 A 1-5 |

Recent Meetings

	20.11.04			30.04.05			15.10.05			15.04.06
○○ **2-2**	Attendance: 42,203		○○ **0-2**	Attendance: 27,653		○○ **5-1**	Attendance: 41,775		○○ **0-2**	Attendance: 27,266

Referee: D.J.Gallagher
- ○ 1 Duff
- ○ 48 Tiago
- ○ 52 Davies
- ○ 87 Jaidi

Referee: S.W.Dunn
- ○ 60 Lampard
- ○ 76 Lampard

Referee: R.Styles
- ○ 52 Drogba
- ○ 55 Lampard
- ○ 59 Lampard
- ○ 61 Drogba
- ○ 74 Gudjohnsen
- ○ 4 Giannakopoulos

Referee: P.Dowd
- ○ 44 Terry
- ○ 59 Lampard

Prem. Head-to-Head

Facts	○ Bolton	Chelsea ○
Games		
Points	12	27
Won	3	8
Drawn	3	3
Goals		
For	14	29
Clean Sheets	1	5
Shots on Target	62	81
Disciplinary		
Fouls (5 years)	134	119
Yellow Cards	24	23
Red Cards	2	1

Goals by Area
○ Bolton ○ Chelsea

	1	7
12		16
1		6

Goals Scored by Period

3	0	3	2	3	3
0	15	30	45	60	75	90
2	2	3	10	7	5

Goals by Position
○ Bolton ○ Chelsea

	Bolton	Chelsea
● forward:	5	13
● midfield:	5	11
● defence:	3	4
● own goals:	1	1

Average Attendance

▶ **24,729**

▶ **35,818**

All-Time Records

Total Premiership Record	○ Bolton	Chelsea ○
Played	266	544
Points	320	930
Won	81	261
Drawn	77	147
Lost	108	136
For	311	848
Against	386	556
Players Used	109	135

All-Time Record vs Bolton

Competition	Played	Won	Drawn	Lost	For	Against
League	96	37	25	34	152	148
FA Cup	2	2	0	0	4	0
League Cup	4	1	1	2	9	5
Other	0	0	0	0	0	0
Total	**102**	**40**	**26**	**36**	**165**	**153**

Everton °

Everton

Nickname:	The Toffees
Manager:	David Moyes
Chairman:	Bill Kenwright
Website:	www.evertonfc.com

Telephone:	0870 442 1878
Ticket Office:	0870 442 1878
Club Shop:	0870 442 1878

Season Review 05/06

Everton followed up the amazing form of their previous campaign with a mid-table finish. A return to European football brought only heartbreak, as the Toffees fell early in both the Champions League and UEFA Cup.

Nigel Martyn continued to defy his advancing years in goal, whilst James Beattie began to show what he could do at the other end.

Points / Position

won drawn lost H home A away

Season:	96/97	97/98	98/99	99/00	00/01	01/02	02/03	03/04	04/05	05/06
Premiership		15 / 42pts	18 / 40pts · 17 / 40pts	14 / 43pts	13 / 50pts	16 / 42pts	16 / 40pts · 15 / 43pts	7 / 44pts · 8 / 59pts · 17 / 53pts	6 / 39pts · 4 / 58pts	8 / 61pts · 11 / 56pts	50pts
Division 1	1 / 98pts		6 / 76pts	6 / 76pts	3 / 87pts					

Date:	01.09	28.12				03.11	01.04	28.01	28.12	29.11	08.05	15.05	04.12	21.08	17.12
Result:	H 0-0	A 2-3				H 2-2	A 1-3	H 1-2	A 0-0	H 2-0	A 2-1	H 3-2	A 2-3	H 0-1	A 4-0

Recent Meetings

04.12.04	15.05.05	21.08.05	17.12.05
3-2 Attendance: 35,929	**3-2** Attendance: 27,701	**0-1** Attendance: 25,608	**0-4** Attendance: 34,500
Referee: H.M.Webb	Referee: N.S.Barry	Referee: A.G.Wiley	Referee: A.G.Wiley
O 45 Ferguson O 16 Davies	O 53 Jaidi O 9 Cahill	O 52 Bent M	O 32 Davies
O 75 Gravesen O 59 Davies	O 61 Davies O 63 Carsley		O 75 Giannakopoul
O 85 Jaidi	O 66 Giannakopoulos		O 79 Speed
			O 80 Giannakopoul

Prem. Head-to-Head

Facts	O Bolton	Everton O
Games		
Points	16	22
Won	4	6
Drawn	4	4
Goals		
For	20	21
Clean Sheets	4	4
Shots on Target	70	70
Disciplinary		
Fouls (5 years)	114	129
Yellow Cards	23	15
Red Cards	3	2

Goals by Area

O Bolton   O Everton

	5	6	
13			12
2			3

Goals Scored by Period

3	2	3	3	4	5
0	15	30	45	60	75	90
1	2	6	3	4	5

Goals by Position

O Bolton   O Everton

forward: 9 midfield: 7 defence: 4

forward: 10 midfield: 5 defence: 5 own goals: 1

Average Attendance

▶ **25,240**

▶ **37,858**

All-Time Records

Total Premiership Record	O Bolton	Everton O
Played	266	544
Points	320	677
Won	81	177
Drawn	77	146
Lost	108	221
For	311	651
Against	386	739
Players Used	109	132

All-Time Record vs Bolton

Competition	Played	Won	Drawn	Lost	For	Against
League	126	63	29	34	211	171
FA Cup	11	3	5	3	21	18
League Cup	2	1	1	0	2	1
Other	0	0	0	0	0	0
Total	**139**	**67**	**35**	**37**	**234**	**190**

Fulham ○

Nickname:	The Cottagers	Telephone:	0870 442 1222
Manager:	Chris Coleman	Ticket Office:	0870 442 1234
Chairman:	Mohamed Al Fayed	Club Shop:	0870 442 1223
Website:	www.fulhamfc.com		

Season Review 05/06

Fulham experienced a real Jekyll and Hyde campaign, with an abysmal away record undoing much of their good work at Craven Cottage. It took Chris Coleman's team until April to win on the road, whilst they claimed 13 Premiership victories on home soil.

Luis Boa Morte excelled in his role as captain, notably scoring the only goal in a memorable win against local rivals Chelsea.

Points / Position

● won ● drawn ● lost H home A away

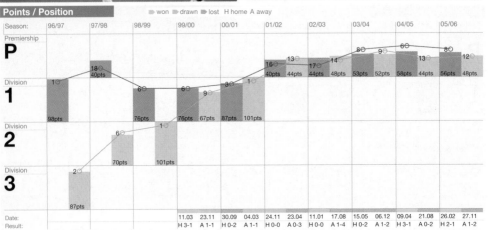

Season:	96/97	97/98	98/99	99/00	00/01	01/02	02/03	03/04	04/05	05/06

Premiership: P — 16○ 40pts, 13○ 44pts, 17○ 44pts, 14○ 48pts, 8○ 53pts, 9○ 52pts, 6○ 58pts, 13○ 44pts, 8○ 56pts, 12○ 48pts

Division 1 — 1○ 98pts, 18○ 40pts, 6○ 76pts, 6○ 76pts, 9○ 67pts, 3○ 87pts, 1○ 101pts

Division 2 — 6○ 70pts, 1○ 101pts

Division 3 — 2○ 87pts

Date:	11.03	23.11	30.09	04.03	24.11	23.04	11.01	17.08	15.05	06.12	09.04	21.08	26.02	27.11
Result:	H 3-1	A 1-1	H 0-2	A 1-1	H 0-0	A 0-3	H 0-0	A 1-4	H 0-2	A 1-2	H 3-1	A 0-2	H 2-1	A 1-2

Prem. Head-to-Head

Facts	○ Bolton	Fulham ○
Games		
Points	8	20
Won	2	6
Drawn	2	2
Goals		
For	8	17
Clean Sheets	2	5
Shots on Target	45	54
Disciplinary		
Fouls (5 years)	125	136
Yellow Cards	14	10
Red Cards	1	1

Goals by Area

○ Bolton   ○ Fulham

	2	3	
6			11
0			3

Goals Scored by Period

2	0	2	2	1	1
0	15	30	45	60	75	90
3	2	4	1	2	5

Goals by Position

○ Bolton   ○ Fulham

	Bolton		Fulham
● forward:	2	● forward:	12
● midfield:	4	● midfield:	5
● defence:	0	● defence:	0
● own goals:	2		

Average Attendance

▶ **24,997**

▶ **17,229**

All-Time Records

Total Premiership Record	○ Bolton	Fulham ○
Played	266	190
Points	320	236
Won	81	63
Drawn	77	47
Lost	108	80
For	311	229
Against	386	258
Players Used	109	60

All-Time Record vs Bolton

Competition	Played	Won	Drawn	Lost	For	Against
League	64	22	16	26	86	84
FA Cup	2	0	0	2	1	4
League Cup	3	0	2	1	5	6
Other	0	0	0	0	0	0
Total	69	22	18	29	92	94

Liverpool

Nickname:	The Reds	Telephone:	0151 263 2361
Manager:	Rafael Benitez	Ticket Office:	0870 444 4949
Chairman:	David Moores	Club Shop:	0870 066 7036
Website:	www.liverpoolfc.tv		

Season Review 05/06

Liverpool added both the UEFA Super Cup and FA Cup to their trophy collection, with captain Steven Gerrard winning the PFA Player of the Year award.

A clear improvement was also evident in the league, as Rafael Benitez's team finished 24 points better off than 12 months previously. In fact, only Champions Chelsea could boast a better defensive record than the Merseysiders.

Points / Position

won drawn lost H home A away

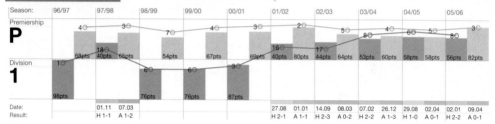

Season:	96/97	97/98	98/99	99/00	00/01	01/02	02/03	03/04	04/05	05/06
Premiership	4	3	7	4	3	2	5	4	5	3
	68pts	40pts 65pts	54pts	67pts	69pts	40pts 80pts	44pts 64pts	53pts 60pts	58pts 58pts	56pts 82pts
Division 1	1	18	6	6	3	16	17			
	98pts	76pts	76pts	87pts						

Date:		01.11	07.03				27.08	01.01	14.09	08.03	07.02	26.12	29.08	02.04	02.01	09.04
Result:		H 1-1	A 1-2				H 2-1	A 1-1	H 2-3	A 0-2	H 2-2	A 1-3	H 1-0	A 0-1	H 2-2	A 0-1

Recent Meetings

29.08.04	**02.04.05**	**02.01.06**	**09.04.06**
OO 1-0 Attendance: 27,880	OO 1-0 Attendance: 43,755	OO 2-2 Attendance: 27,604	OO 1-0 Attendance: 44,194
Referee: U.D.Rennie	Referee: S.G.Bennett	Referee: M.Clattenburg	Referee: R.Styles
O 38 Davies	O 86 Biscan	O 10 Jaidi O 67 Gerrard	O 45 Fowler
		O 71 Diouf O 82 Garcia	

Prem. Head-to-Head

Facts	O Bolton	Liverpool O
Games		
Points	10	28
Won	2	8
Drawn	4	4
Goals		
For	15	25
Clean Sheets	1	4
Shots on Target	65	91
Disciplinary		
Fouls (5 years)	133	109
Yellow Cards	28	17
Red Cards	0	1

Goals by Area

O Bolton   O Liverpool

7	5
6	19
2	1

Goals Scored by Period

3	1	1	2	1	7	
0	15	30	45	60	75	90
2	2	3	6	8	4	

Goals by Position

O Bolton   O Liverpool

	Bolton	Liverpool
forward:	8	15
midfield:	3	7
defence:	4	3

Average Attendance

▶ **26,230**

▶ **42,963**

All-Time Records

Total Premiership Record	O Bolton	Liverpool O
Played	266	544
Points	320	931
Won	81	265
Drawn	77	136
Lost	108	143
For	311	868
Against	386	552
Players Used	109	108

All-Time Record vs Bolton

Competition	Played	Won	Drawn	Lost	For	Against
League	106	43	29	34	164	132
FA Cup	11	3	2	6	11	22
League Cup	4	1	1	2	7	8
Other	0	0	0	0	0	0
Total	121	47	32	42	182	162

Manchester City

★ ★ ★

Nickname:	The Citizens	Telephone:	0870 062 1894
Manager:	Stuart Pearce	Ticket Office:	0870 062 1894
Chairman:	John Wardle	Club Shop:	0870 062 1894
Website:	www.mcfc.co.uk		

Season Review 05/06

It was largely a season of disappointment for the blue half of Manchester. Stuart Pearce's team made an encouraging start to the campaign, but lost nine of their final 10 games to slide down the table.

There was still reason for optimism, however, with the continued emergence of talented youngsters such as Micah Richards and Stephen Ireland.

Points / Position

■ won ■ drawn ■ lost H home A away

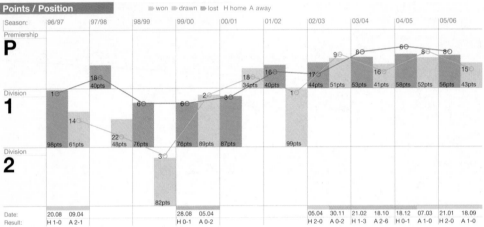

Season:	96/97	97/98	98/99	99/00	00/01	01/02	02/03	03/04	04/05	05/06
Date:	20.08 09.04			28.08 05.04			05.04 30.11	21.02 18.10	18.12 07.03	21.01 18.09
Result:	H 1-0 A 2-1			H 0-1 A 0-2			H 2-0 A 0-2	H 1-3 A 2-6	H 0-1 A 1-0	H 2-0 A 1-0

Prem. Head-to-Head

Facts	○ Bolton	Man City ○
Games		
Points	13	16
Won	4	5
Drawn	1	1
Goals		
For	10	14
Clean Sheets	4	3
Shots on Target	49	48
Disciplinary		
Fouls (5 years)	96	98
Yellow Cards	13	16
Red Cards	0	2

Goals by Area

○ Bolton   ○ Man City

4	2
5	12
1	0

Goals Scored by Period

0	2	4	2	1	1
0	15	30	45	60	75	90
2	3	1	6	1	1

Goals by Position

○ Bolton   ○ Man City

■ forward:	4	■ forward:	5
■ midfield:	6	■ midfield:	6
■ defence:	0	■ defence:	2
		■ own goals:	1

Average Attendance

▶ **25,808**

▶ **39,309**

All-Time Records

Total Premiership Record	○ Bolton	Man City
Played	266	354
Points	320	410
Won	81	103
Drawn	77	101
Lost	108	150
For	311	413
Against	386	482
Players Used	109	126

All-Time Record vs Bolton

Competition	Played	Won	Drawn	Lost	For	Against
League	100	39	22	39	153	157
FA Cup	9	5	1	3	18	10
League Cup	2	1	0	1	3	4
Other	0	0	0	0	0	0
Total	**111**	**45**	**23**	**43**	**174**	**171**

Manchester United

Nickname:	The Red Devils	Telephone:	0870 442 1994
Manager:	Sir Alex Ferguson	Ticket Office:	0870 442 1994
Owner:	Malcolm Glazer	Club Shop:	0870 111 8107
Website:	www.manutd.com		

Season Review 05/06

A Carling Cup triumph and second place in the Premiership would be seen as success at most clubs, but not at Manchester United. In fact, Sir Alex Ferguson's charges never genuinely threatened Chelsea's grip on the title.

The performances of Wayne Rooney continued to win him admirers across the globe, with Edwin van der Sar providing calm assurance in goal.

Points / Position

won drawn lost H home A away

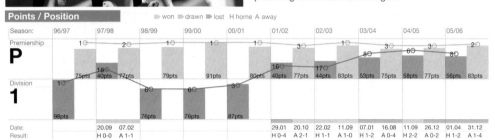

Season:	96/97	97/98	98/99	99/00	00/01	01/02	02/03	03/04	04/05	05/06
Premiership P	1	2	1	1	1	3	1	3	3	2
	75pts	40pts 77pts	79pts	91pts	80pts	16 40pts 77pts	17 44pts 83pts	8 53pts 75pts	6 58pts 77pts	56pts 83pts
Division 1	1	18	6	6	3					
	98pts		76pts	76pts	87pts					
Date:		20.09 07.02				29.01 20.10	22.02 11.09	07.01 16.08	11.09 26.12	01.04 31.12
Result:		H 0-0 A 1-1				H 0-4 A 2-1	H 1-1 A 1-0	H 1-2 A 0-4	H 2-2 A 0-2	H 1-2 A 1-4

Recent Meetings

11.09.04	26.12.04	31.12.05	01.04.06
◯◯ **2-2** Attendance: 27,766	◯◯ **2-0** Attendance: 67,867	◯◯ **4-1** Attendance: 67,858	◯◯ **1-2** Attendance: 27,718
Referee: M.D.Messias	Referee: D.J.Gallagher	Referee: S.G.Bennett	Referee: A.G.Wiley
O 52 Nolan O 44 Heinze	O 10 Giggs	O 8 N'Gotty O 33 Speed	O 26 Davies O 33 Saha
O 90 Ferdinand O 90 Hunt	O 89 Scholes	O 44 Saha	O 79 van Nistelrooy
		O 68 Ronaldo	
		O 90 Ronaldo	

Prem. Head-to-Head

Facts	O Bolton	Man Utd O
Games		
Points	10	28
Won	2	8
Drawn	4	4
Goals		
For	10	32
Clean Sheets	2	6
Shots on Target	63	116
Disciplinary		
Fouls (5 years)	136	112
Yellow Cards	23	16
Red Cards	1	0

Goals by Area

O Bolton   O Man Utd

	5	15
4		14
1		3

Goals by Position

O Bolton   O Man Utd

	Bolton	Man Utd
forward:	5	12
midfield:	4	16
defence:	1	2
own goals:		2

Goals Scored by Period

0	1	2	2	1	4
0	15	30	45	60	75	90
5	3	7	0	4	13

Average Attendance

▶ **26,327**

▶ **60,932**

All-Time Records

Total Premiership Record	O Bolton	Man Utd O
Played	266	544
Points	320	1,143
Won	81	339
Drawn	77	126
Lost	108	79
For	311	1,057
Against	386	489
Players Used	109	99

All-Time Record vs Bolton

Competition	Played	Won	Drawn	Lost	For	Against
League	106	42	24	40	162	151
FA Cup	3	2	0	1	3	3
League Cup	0	0	0	0	0	0
Other	0	0	0	0	0	0
Total	**109**	**44**	**24**	**41**	**165**	**154**

Middlesbrough

Nickname:	Boro		Telephone:	0870 421 1986
Manager:	Gareth Southgate		Ticket Office:	0870 421 1986
Chairman:	Steve Gibson		Club Shop:	0870 421 1986
Website:	www.mfc.co.uk			

Season Review 05/06

An unforgettable season at the Riverside saw Boro struggle in the league but thrive in cup competitions. Victories against FC Basle and Steaua Bucharest resulted in a UEFA Cup Final appearance, whilst an FA Cup Semi-Final was also reached.

Following weeks of intense speculation, manager Steve McClaren was finally unveiled as the successor to Sven-Goran Eriksson as England boss in May.

Points / Position

won drawn lost H home A away

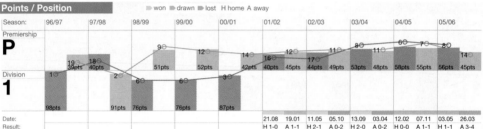

Season:	96/97	97/98	98/99	99/00	00/01	01/02	02/03	03/04	04/05	05/06
Premiership	P		9	12	14	16 12	17 11	8 11	6 7	8 14
		19 18	51pts	52pts	42pts	40pts 45pts	44pts 49pts	53pts 48pts	58pts 55pts	56pts 45pts
Division 1	1	39pts 40pts	2 6	6	3					
	98pts	91pts 76pts	76pts	87pts						

Date:						21.08	19.01	11.05	05.10	13.09	03.04	12.02	07.11	03.05	26.03
Result:						H 1-0	A 1-1	H 2-1	A 0-2	H 2-0	A 0-2	H 0-0	A 1-1	H 1-1	A 3-4

Recent Meetings

07.11.04
OO **1-1** Attendance: 29,656
Referee: P.Walton
O 90 Boateng   O 72 Pedersen

12.02.05
OO **0-0** Attendance: 24,322
Referee: A.G.Wiley

26.03.06
OO **4-3** Attendance: 25,971
Referee: H.M.Webb
O 8 Hasselbaink   O 3 Giannakopoulos
O 30 Viduka   O 58 Okocha
O 47 Hasselbaink   O 81 Jaidi
O 90 Parnaby

03.05.06
OO **1-1** Attendance: 22,733
Referee: H.M.Webb
O 51 Vaz Te   O 47 Johnson

Prem. Head-to-Head

Facts	O Bolton	Boro O
Games		
Points	17	14
Won	4	3
Drawn	5	5
Goals		
For	16	14
Clean Sheets	3	3
Shots on Target	69	63
Disciplinary		
Fouls (5 years)	145	139
Yellow Cards	25	23
Red Cards	1	1

Goals by Area
O Bolton   O Middlesbrough

	5	2	
7			12
4			0

Goals by Position
O Bolton   O Middlesbrough

	Bolton	Middlesbrough
forward:	7	5
midfield:	6	6
defence:	3	2
own goals:		1

Goals Scored by Period

3	3	2	2	4	2
0	15	30	45	60	75	90
2	2	2	3	2	3

Average Attendance

▶ **23,306**
▶ **28,700**

All-Time Records

Total Premiership Record	O Bolton	Boro O
Played	266	422
Points	320	516
Won	81	131
Drawn	77	123
Lost	108	168
For	311	506
Against	386	582
Players Used	109	132

All-Time Record vs Bolton

Competition	Played	Won	Drawn	Lost	For	Against
League	102	31	25	46	150	171
FA Cup	7	3	3	1	7	2
League Cup	2	2	0	0	4	2
Other	0	0	0	0	0	0
Total	111	36	28	47	161	175

Newcastle United °

Nickname:	The Magpies	Telephone:	0191 201 8400
Manager:	Glenn Roeder	Ticket Office:	0191 261 1571
Chairman:	Freddy Shepherd	Club Shop:	0191 201 8426
Website:	www.nufc.co.uk		

Season Review 05/06

Glenn Roeder was the toast of Tyneside as he led Newcastle from a position of adversity to InterToto Cup qualification. The team collected 32 points from 15 games under the former West Ham boss, thus earning him the job on a permanent basis.

Alan Shearer finally hung up his boots, bowing out of competitive action with a goal in the 4-1 triumph at arch-rivals Sunderland.

Points / Position

won ■ drawn ■ lost H home A away

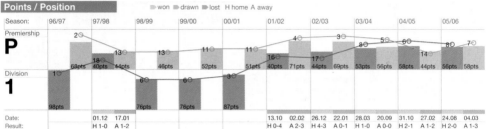

Season:	96/97	97/98	98/99	99/00	00/01	01/02	02/03	03/04	04/05	05/06
Premiership **P**	2	18 / 13	13	11	11	16 / 4	17 / 3	8	5 / 6 / 14	8 / 7
	68pts	40pts / 44pts	46pts	52pts	51pts	40pts / 71pts	44pts / 69pts	53pts / 56pts	58pts / 44pts	56pts / 58pts
Division **1**	1		6	6	3					
	98pts		76pts	76pts	87pts					
Date:		01.12 17.01				13.10 02.02	26.12 22.01	28.03 20.09	31.10 27.02	24.08 04.03
Result:		H 1-0 A 1-2				H 0-4 A 2-3	H 4-3 A 0-1	H 1-0 A 0-0	H 2-1 A 1-2	H 2-0 A 1-3

Recent Meetings

	31.10.04		27.02.05		24.08.05		04.03.06
○○ **2-1**	Attendance: 27,196	○○ **2-1**	Attendance: 50,430	○○ **2-0**	Attendance: 25,904	○○ **3-1**	Attendance: 52,012
Referee: G.Poll		Referee: S.W.Dunn		Referee: R.Styles		Referee: A.G.Wiley	
○ 52 Diouf	○ 55 Ambrose	○ 35 Bowyer	○ 41 Giannakopoulos	○ 37 Diouf		○ 34 Solano	○ 72 Davies
○ 70 Davies		○ 69 Dyer		○ 50 Giannakopoulos		○ 45 Shearer	
						○ 70 Ameobi	

Prem. Head-to-Head

Facts	○ Bolton	Newcastle ○
Games		
Points	16	25
Won	5	8
Drawn	1	1
Goals		
For	17	24
Clean Sheets	4	3
Shots on Target	74	90
Disciplinary		
Fouls (5 years)	117	130
Yellow Cards	17	18
Red Cards	1	0

Goals by Area
○ Bolton   ○ Newcastle

	5	6	
8			14
4			4

Goals by Position
○ Bolton   ○ Newcastle

	Bolton	Newcastle
■ forward:	9	15
■ midfield:	4	9
■ defence:	4	0

Goals Scored by Period

3	3	4	3	4	0
0	15	30	45	60	75 90
3	3	6	2	4	6

Average Attendance

▶ **25,449**

▶ **47,409**

All-Time Records

Total Premiership Record	○ Bolton	Newcastle ○
Played	266	502
Points	320	786
Won	81	218
Drawn	77	132
Lost	108	152
For	311	761
Against	386	606
Players Used	109	125

All-Time Record vs Bolton

Competition	Played	Won	Drawn	Lost	For	Against
League	102	48	17	37	183	133
FA Cup	6	3	2	1	11	8
League Cup	0	0	0	0	0	0
Other	0	0	0	0	0	0
Total	108	51	19	38	194	141

Portsmouth

Nickname:	Pompey	Telephone:	02392 731 204
Manager:	Harry Redknapp	Ticket Office:	0871 230 1898
Chairman:	Milan Mandaric	Club Shop:	02392 778 552
Website:	www.pompeyfc.co.uk		

Season Review 05/06

Portsmouth seemed destined to be relegated for much of the season, but were saved by a combination of Alexandre Gaydamak's millions and the nous of returning manager Harry Redknapp.

Having picked up just 18 points from their first 28 games, an astonishing turnaround in form saw the South Coast club collect a further 20 to beat the drop with a match to spare.

Points / Position

won   drawn   lost   H home   A away

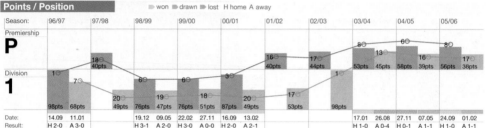

Season:	96/97	97/98	98/99	99/00	00/01	01/02	02/03	03/04	04/05	05/06
Premiership								8	6	8
P			18 40pts			16 40pts	17 44pts	13 45pts	16 39pts	17 38pts
Division	1	7	6	6	9			53pts	58pts	56pts
1			20	19	18	20	17	1		
	98pts	68pts	49pts	76pts 47pts	76pts 51pts	87pts 49pts	53pts	98pts		
Date:	14.09	11.01	19.12	09.05	22.02	27.11	16.09	13.02	17.01	26.08	27.11	07.05	24.09	01.02
Result:	H 2-0	A 3-0	H 3-1	A 2-0	H 3-0	A 0-0	H 2-0	A 2-1	H 1-0	A 0-4	H 0-1	A 1-1	H 1-0	A 1-1

Recent Meetings

	27.11.04		07.05.05		24.09.05		01.02.06
0-1	Attendance: 25,008	1-1	Attendance: 20,188	1-0	Attendance: 23,134	1-1	Attendance: 19,128
Referee: S.W.Dunn		Referee: M.D.Messias		Referee: M.Clattenburg		Referee: D.J.Gallagher	
	45 De Zeeuw	72 Yakubu	11 Diouf	25 Nolan		85 Karadas	69 Fadiga

Prem. Head-to-Head

Facts	Bolton	Portsmouth
Games		
Points	8	8
Won	2	2
Drawn	2	2
Goals		
For	4	7
Clean Sheets	2	2
Shots on Target	27	28
Disciplinary		
Fouls (5 years)	78	71
Yellow Cards	9	6
Red Cards	0	1

Goals by Area

Bolton   Portsmouth

	0	2	
3			5
1			0

Goals Scored by Period

1	1	0	1	1	0
0	15	30	45	60	75	90
0	0	1	2	1	3

Goals by Position

Bolton   Portsmouth

	Bolton		Portsmouth
forward:	2	forward:	5
midfield:	2	midfield:	1
defence:	0	defence:	1

Average Attendance

24,900

19,810

All-Time Records

Total Premiership Record	Bolton	Portsmouth
Played	266	114
Points	320	122
Won	81	32
Drawn	77	26
Lost	108	56
For	311	127
Against	386	175
Players Used	109	64

All-Time Record vs Bolton

Competition	Played	Won	Drawn	Lost	For	Against
League	84	28	20	36	103	132
FA Cup	5	2	1	2	7	5
League Cup	0	0	0	0	0	0
Other	0	0	0	0	0	0
Total	89	30	21	38	110	137

Reading

Nickname:	**The Royals**	Telephone:	**0118 968 1100**
Manager:	**Steve Coppell**	Ticket Office:	**0870 999 1871**
Chairman:	**John Madejski**	Club Shop:	**0118 968 1234**
Website:	**www.readingfc.co.uk**		

Season Review 05/06

Reading were an unstoppable force as they blazed a trail towards promotion to the top-flight. The 106 points amassed by the Royals were a record for the second-tier of English football, whilst 99 goals were also scored along the way.

Manager Steve Coppell engendered a real spirit of togetherness amongst his troops, with no one player more important than the team.

Points / Position

won drawn lost H home A away

Season:	96/97	97/98	98/99	99/00	00/01	01/02	02/03	03/04	04/05	05/06

Premiership **P**

	18 40pts				16 40pts	17 44pts	8 53pts	6 58pts	8 56pts

Division **1**

1 / 6 / 6 / 3 / 4 / 9 / 7 / 1

98pts 57pts — 18 — 24 42pts 76pts 76pts 87pts 79pts 70pts 70pts 106pts

Division **2**

11 / 10 / 3 / 2

61pts 62pts 86pts 84pts

Date:	29.10	08.02
Result:	H 2-1	A 2-3

Prem. Head-to-Head

Facts	O Bolton	Reading O
Games		
Points	0	0
Won	0	0
Drawn	0	0
Goals		
For	0	0
Clean Sheets	0	0
Shots on Target	0	0
Disciplinary		
Fouls (5 years)	0	0
Yellow Cards	0	0
Red Cards	0	0

Goals by Area

O Bolton   O Reading

	0	0
0		0
0		0

Goals by Position

O Bolton   O Reading

- forward: 0   forward: 0
- midfield: 0   midfield: 0
- defence: 0   defence: 0

Goals Scored by Period

0	0	0	0	0	0
0	15	30	45	60	75	90
0	0	0	0	0	0

Average Attendance

All-Time Records

Total Premiership Record	O Bolton	Reading O
Played	266	0
Points	320	0
Won	81	0
Drawn	77	0
Lost	108	0
For	311	0
Against	386	0
Players Used	109	0

All-Time Record vs Bolton

Competition	Played	Won	Drawn	Lost	For	Against
League	18	7	3	8	21	24
FA Cup	4	1	1	2	4	6
League Cup	0	0	0	0	0	0
Other	1	0	0	1	3	4
Total	**23**	**8**	**4**	**11**	**28**	**34**

Sheffield United

Nickname:	The Blades	Telephone:	0870 787 1960
Manager:	Neil Warnock	Ticket Office:	0870 787 1799
Chairman:	Derek Dooley	Club Shop:	0870 442 8705
Website:	www.sufc.co.uk		

Season Review 05/06

Having been in the top-two for most of the season, few could argue that Sheffield United deserved to win promotion. Ten wins from the opening 11 games of the campaign laid the foundations for success.

Manager Neil Warnock continued to court controversy on the touchline, getting into a war of words with Norwich's Nigel Worthington and being sent to the stands against Leeds.

Points / Position

▶ won ▶ drawn ▶ lost H home A away

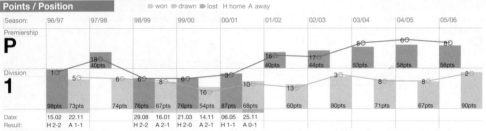

Season:	96/97	97/98	98/99	99/00	00/01	01/02	02/03	03/04	04/05	05/06
Premiership P						16○ 40pts	17○ 44pts	8○ 53pts	6○ 68pts	8○ 56pts
Division 1	1○ 98pts	18○ 40pts 5○ 73pts	6○ 74pts	6○ 8○ 76pts 67pts	6○ 76pts 3○ 54pts	10○ 87pts	13○ 68pts 60pts	3○ 80pts	8○ 8○ 71pts 67pts	2○ 90pts
Date:	15.02	22.11		29.08	16.01	21.03	14.11	06.05	25.11	
Result:	H 2-2	A 1-1		H 2-2	A 2-1	H 2-0	A 2-1	H 1-1	A 0-1	

Recent Meetings

14.11.99	21.03.00	25.11.00	06.05.01
○○ **1-2** Attendance: 10,013	○○ **2-0** Attendance: 11,891	○○ **1-0** Attendance: 14,962	○○ **1-1** Attendance: 14,836
Referee: M.R.Warren	Referee: W.M.Jordan	Referee: C.R.Wilkes	Referee: R.Pearson
○ 34 Bent M ○ 2 Farrelly ○ 36 Hansen	○ 32 Johnston ○ 45 O'Kane	○ 81 Sandford	○ 90 Holden ○ 53 Asaba

Prem. Head-to-Head

Facts	○ Bolton	Sheff Utd ○
Games		
Points	0	0
Won	0	0
Drawn	0	0
Goals		
For	0	0
Clean Sheets	0	0
Shots on Target	0	0
Disciplinary		
Fouls (5 years)	0	0
Yellow Cards	0	0
Red Cards	0	0

Goals by Area

○ Bolton   ○ Sheff Utd

0	0
0	0
0	0

Goals by Position

○ Bolton   ○ Sheff Utd

▶ forward:	0	▶ forward:	0
▶ midfield:	0	▶ midfield:	0
▶ defence:	0	▶ defence:	0

Goals Scored by Period

0	0	0	0	0	0
0	15	30	45	60	75 90
0	0	0	0	0	0

Average Attendance

▶ —
▶ —

All-Time Records

Total Premiership Record	○ Bolton	Sheff Utd ○
Played	266	84
Points	320	94
Won	81	22
Drawn	77	28
Lost	108	34
For	311	96
Against	386	113
Players Used	109	34

All-Time Record vs Bolton

Competition	Played	Won	Drawn	Lost	For	Against
League	106	41	21	44	183	182
FA Cup	7	4	0	3	9	20
League Cup	2	0	0	2	2	4
Other	0	0	0	0	0	0
Total	115	45	21	49	194	206

Tottenham Hotspur

Nickname:	Spurs	Telephone:	0870 420 5000
Manager:	Martin Jol	Ticket Office:	0870 420 5000
Chairman:	Daniel Levy	Club Shop:	020 8365 5042
Website:	www.tottenhamhotspur.com		

Equipment LTD

Season Review 05/06

Despite being pipped to Champions League qualification by their great rivals Arsenal on the final day of the season, Spurs could still look back on a campaign in which they made tremendous progress.

Manager Martin Jol was unafraid to put his faith in youth, allowing the likes of Aaron Lennon and Michael Dawson to shine.

Points / Position

■ won ■ drawn ■ lost H home A away

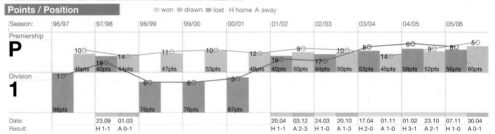

Season:	96/97	97/98	98/99	99/00	00/01	01/02	02/03	03/04	04/05	05/06
Premiership **P**		10 / 46pts	14 / 18 / 44pts	11 / 47pts	10 / 53pts	12 / 16 / 49pts	9 / 17 / 40pts 50pts	10 / 44pts 50pts	8 / 14 / 53pts 45pts	6 / 9 / 58pts 52pts	8 / 56pts	5 / 65pts
Division **1**	1 / 98pts		6 / 76pts	6 / 76pts	3 / 87pts					
Date:		23.09 01.03				20.04 03.12	24.03 20.10	17.04 01.11	01.02 23.10	07.11 30.04
Result:		H 1-1 A 0-1				H 1-1 A 2-3	H 1-0 A 1-3	H 2-0 A 1-0	H 3-1 A 2-1	H 1-0 A 0-1

Recent Meetings

23.10.04	01.02.05	07.11.05	30.04.06
○○ **1-2** Attendance: 36,025	○○ **3-1** Attendance: 24,780	○○ **1-0** Attendance: 26,634	○○ **1-0** Attendance: 36,179
Referee: C.J.Foy	Referee: M.L.Dean	Referee: H.M.Webb	Referee: A.G.Wiley
○ 41 Keane ○ 11 Jaidi	○ 49 Diouf ○ 66 Defoe	○ 32 Nolan	○ 60 Lennon
○ 75 Pedersen	○ 86 Ben Haim		
	○ 87 Davies		

Prem. Head-to-Head

Facts	○ Bolton	Tottenham ○
Games		
Points	21	18
Won	6	5
Drawn	3	3
Goals		
For	19	17
Clean Sheets	4	2
Shots on Target	90	69
Disciplinary		
Fouls (5 years)	123	132
Yellow Cards	19	20
Red Cards	0	1

Goals by Area

○ Bolton   ○ Tottenham

	Bolton	Tottenham
	3	5
	12	11
	4	1

Goals by Position

○ Bolton   ○ Tottenham

■ forward: 8   ■ forward: 11
■ midfield: 6   ■ midfield: 6
■ defence: 5   ■ defence: 0

Goals Scored by Period

3	1	1	2	6	6	
0	15	30	45	60	75	90
1	1	2	7	4	2	

Average Attendance

▶ **24,002**

▶ **33,716**

All-Time Records

Total Premiership Record	○ Bolton	Tottenham ○
Played	266	544
Points	320	728
Won	81	195
Drawn	77	143
Lost	108	206
For	311	716
Against	386	732
Players Used	109	139

All-Time Record vs Bolton

Competition	Played	Won	Drawn	Lost	For	Against
League	76	34	11	31	116	104
FA Cup	9	3	4	2	13	9
League Cup	3	2	0	1	11	9
Other	0	0	0	0	0	0
Total	88	39	15	34	140	122

Watford

Nickname:	The Hornets	Telephone:	0870 111 1881
Manager:	Adrian Boothroyd	Ticket Office:	0870 111 1881
Chairman:	Graham Simpson	Club Shop:	01923 496 005
Website:	www.watfordfc.co.uk		

Season Review 05/06

Watford were the surprise package of the Championship, finishing third and going on to gain promotion through the Play-Offs.

Success was built around a belief instilled in his players by ultra-confident young boss Aidy Boothroyd. The likes of Marlon King and Matthew Spring were given a new lease of life, whilst Ashley Young and Jay DeMerit blossomed into stars.

Points / Position

> won   drawn   lost   H home   A away

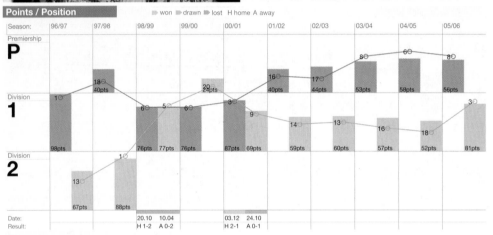

Season:	96/97	97/98	98/99	99/00	00/01	01/02	02/03	03/04	04/05	05/06

Date: 20.10 10.04 03.12 24.10
Result: H 1-2 A 0-2 H 2-1 A 0-1

Prem. Head-to-Head

Facts	O Bolton	Watford O
Games		
Points	0	0
Won	0	0
Drawn	0	0
Goals		
For	0	0
Clean Sheets	0	0
Shots on Target	0	0
Disciplinary		
Fouls (5 years)	0	0
Yellow Cards	0	0
Red Cards	0	0

Goals by Area
O Bolton   O Watford

Goals by Position
O Bolton   O Watford

	forward:	0		forward:	0
	midfield:	0		midfield:	0
	defence:	0		defence:	0

Goals Scored by Period

0	0	0	0	0	0
0	15	30	45	60	75	90
0	0	0	0	0	0

Average Attendance

All-Time Records

Total Premiership Record	O Bolton	Watford O
Played	266	38
Points	320	24
Won	81	6
Drawn	77	6
Lost	108	26
For	311	35
Against	386	77
Players Used	109	32

All-Time Record vs Bolton

Competition	Played	Won	Drawn	Lost	For	Against
League	18	9	4	5	26	22
FA Cup	2	1	0	1	2	4
League Cup	4	2	1	1	6	5
Other	1	1	0	0	2	0
Total	25	13	5	7	36	31

West Ham United

Nickname:	The Hammers	Telephone:	020 8548 2748
Manager:	Alan Pardew	Ticket Office:	0870 112 2700
Chairman:	Terence Brown	Club Shop:	020 8548 2730
Website:	www.whufc.com		

Season Review 05/06

West Ham enjoyed a memorable return to the top-flight, finishing ninth and reaching the FA Cup Final. The Hammers came within four minutes of lifting the trophy, but were ultimately undone by some magic from Liverpool's Steven Gerrard.

Manager Alan Pardew won over his many critics with a stylish brand of attacking football firmly in keeping with the traditions of the club.

Points / Position

■ won ■ drawn ■ lost H home A away

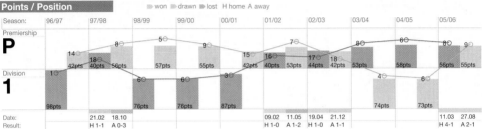

Season:	96/97	97/98	98/99	99/00	00/01	01/02	02/03	03/04	04/05	05/06
Premiership P		14 / 18 / 42pts 40pts	8 / 56pts	5 / 57pts	9 / 55pts	15 / 42pts	16 / 40pts 53pts	7 / 17 / 18 44pts 42pts	8 / 53pts	6 / 58pts	8 / 9 56pts 55pts
Division 1	1 / 98pts		6 / 76pts	6 / 76pts	3 / 87pts				4 / 74pts	6 / 73pts	
Date:		21.02 18.10				09.02 11.05	19.04 21.12			11.03 27.08	
Result:		H 1-1 A 0-3				H 1-0 A 1-2	H 1-0 A 1-1			H 4-1 A 2-1	

Recent Meetings

21.12.02	19.04.03	27.08.05	11.03.06
○○ 1-1 Attendance: 34,892	○○ 1-0 Attendance: 27,160	○○ 1-2 Attendance: 31,629	○○ 4-1 Attendance: 24,461
Referee: S.G.Bennett	Referee: U.D.Rennie	Referee: P.Dowd	Referee: M.L.Dean
○ 17 Pearce ○ 65 Ricketts	○ 38 Okocha	○ 90 Sheringham ○ 59 Nolan ○ 85 Campo	○ 12 Giannakopoulos ○ 79 Sheringham ○ 33 Giannakopoulos ○ 45 Speed ○ 81 Pedersen

Prem. Head-to-Head

Facts	○ Bolton	West Ham ○
Games		
Points	14	14
Won	4	4
Drawn	2	2
Goals		
For	11	13
Clean Sheets	2	3
Shots on Target	54	62
Disciplinary		
Fouls (5 years)	82	70
Yellow Cards	19	22
Red Cards	2	2

Goals by Area

○ Bolton   ○ West Ham

3	2
4	10
4	1

Goals Scored by Period

1	0	4	1	2	3
0	15	30	45	60	75	90
0	2	1	1	3	6

Goals by Position

○ Bolton   ○ West Ham

■ forward: 4   ■ forward: 6
■ midfield: 6   ■ midfield: 5
■ defence: 1   ■ defence: 2

Average Attendance

► 24,002
► 30,003

All-Time Records

Total Premiership Record	○ Bolton	West Ham ○
Played	266	426
Points	320	555
Won	81	148
Drawn	77	111
Lost	108	167
For	311	514
Against	386	590
Players Used	109	142

All-Time Record vs Bolton

Competition	Played	Won	Drawn	Lost	For	Against
League	46	17	7	22	73	87
FA Cup	6	2	2	2	4	5
League Cup	4	2	0	2	12	7
Other	0	0	0	0	0	0
Total	56	21	9	26	89	99

Wigan Athletic

Nickname:	**The Latics**	Telephone:	**01942 774 000**
Manager:	**Paul Jewell**	Ticket Office:	**0870 112 2552**
Chairman:	**Dave Whelan**	Club Shop:	**01942 216 945**
Website:	**www.wiganlatics.co.uk**		

Season Review 05/06

Wigan surprised pundits and supporters alike by finishing in the top half of the table. A trip to Cardiff in the Carling Cup Final also served to highlight just how far the club had come in such a short space of time.

The platform for success was built early in the season, with Paul Jewell's men amassing 25 points from their first 11 Premiership matches.

Points / Position

▶ won ▶ drawn ▶ lost H home A away

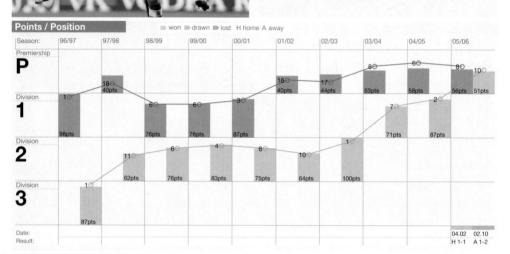

Season:	96/97	97/98	98/99	99/00	00/01	01/02	02/03	03/04	04/05	05/06

Premiership

P: 16⊖ 40pts (01/02), 17⊖ 44pts (02/03), 8⊖ 53pts (03/04), 6⊖ 58pts (04/05), 8⊖ 56pts / 10⊖ 51pts (05/06)

Division 1: 1⊖ 98pts (96/97), 18⊖ 40pts (97/98), 6⊖ 76pts (98/99), 6⊖ 76pts (99/00), 8⊖ 87pts (00/01), 7⊖ 71pts (03/04), 2⊖ 87pts (04/05)

Division 2: 11⊖ 62pts, 6⊖ 76pts, 4⊖ 83pts, 6⊖ 75pts, 10⊖ 64pts, 1⊖ 100pts

Division 3: 1⊖ 87pts

Date:		04.02	02.10
Result:		H 1-1	A 1-2

Prem. Head-to-Head

Facts	○ Bolton	Wigan ○
Games		
Points	1	4
Won	0	1
Drawn	1	1
Goals		
For	2	3
Clean Sheets	0	0
Shots on Target	13	13
Disciplinary		
Fouls (5 years)	26	23
Yellow Cards	2	4
Red Cards	0	0

Goals by Area

○ Bolton   ○ Wigan

	1	1
1		2
0		0

Goals by Position

○ Bolton   ○ Wigan

	Bolton	Wigan
▶ forward:	0	1
▶ midfield:	1	2
▶ defence:	1	0

Goals Scored by Period

0	0	0	0	2	0
0	15	30	45	60	75	90
0	0	0	1	1	1

Average Attendance

▶ **25,854**

▶ **20,553**

All-Time Records

Total Premiership Record	○ Bolton	Wigan ○
Played	266	38
Points	320	51
Won	81	15
Drawn	77	6
Lost	108	17
For	311	45
Against	386	52
Players Used	109	25

All-Time Record vs Bolton

Competition	Played	Won	Drawn	Lost	For	Against
League	20	8	5	7	24	24
FA Cup	0	0	0	0	0	0
League Cup	3	2	0	1	7	4
Other	0	0	0	0	0	0
Total	**23**	**10**	**5**	**8**	**31**	**28**

Bolton Wanderers EFL

Date	Team	Home/Away 05-06		Played	96-97	97-98	98-99	99-00	00-01	01-02	02-03	03-04	04-05	05-06	Goals for	Goals against	Scored first	Best result	Worst
19.08.06	Tottenham	H	1-0	7											11	6	5	3-1	2-3
23.08.06	Fulham	A	1-2	5											3	13	2	1-4	1-4
26.08.06	Charlton	A	1-0	5											8	4	4	2-1	1-1
09.09.06	Watford	H	N/A	0											0	0	0	N/A	N/A
16.09.06	Middlesbrough	H	1-1	6											7	3	4	2-0	1-1
25.09.06	Portsmouth	A	1-1	3											2	6	2	1-1	0-4
30.09.06	Liverpool	H	2-2	7											10	10	4	2-1	2-3
15.10.06	Newcastle	A	1-3	7											6	13	1	0-0	1-3
21.10.06	Blackburn	A	0-0	7											8	10	3	4-3	1-3
28.10.06	Man Utd	H	1-2	7											5	17	2	2-2	0-6
04.11.06	Wigan	H	1-1	1											1	1	1	1-1	1-1
11.11.06	Sheff Utd	A	N/A	0											0	0	0	N/A	N/A
18.11.06	Everton	A	4-0	7											11	13	3	4-0	0-3
25.11.06	Arsenal	H	2-0	7											7	6	3	2-0	0-2
28.11.06	Chelsea	H	0-2	7											6	10	2	2-1	0-2
02.12.06	Reading	A	N/A	0											0	0	0	N/A	N/A
09.12.06	West Ham	H	4-1	5											7	5	3	4-1	0-3
16.12.06	Aston Villa	A	2-2	7											9	11	3	3-1	0-2
23.12.06	Man City	A	1-0	5											4	9	3	1-0	2-6
26.12.06	Newcastle	H	2-0	7											11	11	5	2-0	0-4
30.12.06	Portsmouth	H	1-0	3											2	1	2	1-0	0-1
01.01.07	Liverpool	A	0-1	7											5	15	1	1-1	2-5
13.01.07	Man City	H	2-0	5											6	5	3	2-0	1-3
20.01.07	Middlesbrough	A	3-4	6											9	11	3	4-1	0-2
30.01.07	Charlton	H	4-1	5											9	4	3	4-1	1-2
03.02.07	Watford	A	N/A	0											0	0	0	N/A	N/A
10.02.07	Fulham	H	2-1	5											5	4	1	3-1	0-2
24.02.07	Tottenham	A	0-1	7											8	11	3	2-1	1-3
03.03.07	Blackburn	H	0-0	7											8	7	5	2-1	0-1
17.03.07	Man Utd	A	1-4	7											5	15	2	2-1	0-4
31.03.07	Sheff Utd	H	N/A	0											0	0	0	N/A	N/A
07.04.07	Wigan	A	1-2	1											1	2	0	1-2	1-2
09.04.07	Everton	H	0-1	7											9	8	3	2-0	1-2
14.04.07	Arsenal	A	1-1	7											8	14	3	2-2	1-4
21.04.07	Reading	H	N/A	0											0	0	0	N/A	N/A
28.04.07	Chelsea	A	1-5	7											8	19	3	2-1	1-5
05.05.07	West Ham	A	2-1	5											4	8	1	2-1	0-3
13.05.07	Aston Villa	H	1-1	7											8	10	4	3-2	0-2

Barclays Premiership 2006/07

Premiership history

won drawn lost not played